Asia Bible Commentary Series

1 & 2 KINGS

GLOBAL LIBRARY

Asia Bible Commentary Series

1 & 2 KINGS

Jesudason Baskar Jeyaraj

General Editor
Andrew B. Spurgeon

Old Testament Consulting Editors
**Yohanna Katanacho, Joseph Shao,
Havilah Dharamraj, Koowon Kim**

New Testament Consulting Editors
Steve Chang, Brian Wintle

© 2022 Jesudason Baskar Jeyaraj

Published 2022 by Langham Global Library
An imprint of Langham Publishing
www.langhampublishing.org

Langham Publishing and its imprints are a ministry of Langham Partnership

Langham Partnership
PO Box 296, Carlisle, Cumbria, CA3 9WZ, UK
www.langham.org

Published in partnership with Asia Theological Association

ATA
QCC PO Box 1454–1154, Manila, Philippines
www.ataasia.com

ISBNs:
978-1-83973-069-6 Print
978-1-83973-642-1 ePub
978-1-83973-644-5 PDF

Jesudason Baskar Jeyaraj has asserted his right under the Copyright, Designs and Patents Act, 1988 to be identified as the Author of this work.

All rights reserved. No part of this publication may be reproduced, stored in a retrieval system or transmitted, in any form or by any means, electronic, mechanical, photocopying, recording or otherwise, without the prior written permission of the publisher or the Copyright Licensing Agency.

Requests to reuse content from Langham Publishing are processed through PLSclear. Please visit www.plsclear.com to complete your request.

All Scripture quotations, unless otherwise indicated, are taken from the Holy Bible, New International Version®, NIV®. Copyright ©1973, 1978, 1984, 2011 by Biblica, Inc.™ Used by permission of Zondervan.

British Library Cataloguing-in-Publication Data
A catalogue record for this book is available from the British Library

ISBN: 978-1-83973-069-6

Cover & Book Design: projectluz.com

Langham Partnership actively supports theological dialogue and an author's right to publish but does not necessarily endorse the views and opinions set forth here or in works referenced within this publication, nor can we guarantee technical and grammatical correctness. Langham Partnership does not accept any responsibility or liability to persons or property as a consequence of the reading, use or interpretation of its published content.

To my beloved wife,
Dr. Nirmala Jeyaraj,
who encouraged me to accept this commentary project
and to contribute to Christian ministry

CONTENTS

Commentary

Author's Preface ix
Series Preface xi
List of Abbreviations xiii
Introduction 1
Outline 17
1 Kings 19
2 Kings 175
Selected Bibliography 307

Topics

The Significance of *Yhwh* 57
The Hebrew Calendar and the Temple 65
The Priesthood 113
A Comparison of the Miracles in 1 & 2 Kings 196
Secret Christians 206

AUTHOR'S PREFACE

The books of 1 and 2 Kings have valuable principles for leadership and governance, even today in our modern context. The nation of Israel needed healthy cooperation between the kings – who represented the political institution of power and authority – and the priests and prophets – who represented the religious institution. But the frequent tension between these two institutions disturbed the peace and progress of the nation. Many of the stories in 1 and 2 Kings gave me insights into the socio-political and religious context of Asia today, particularly India.

I am thankful to the Asia Theological Association (ATA) for asking me to write this commentary on 1 and 2 Kings, which is designed for pastors, evangelists, and theological students. I offer detailed explanation on some verses because many pastors and lay preachers do not have access to other commentaries on these books. Those who serve God in rural areas or the hill stations of India, Nepal, Sri Lanka, Bangladesh, and Myanmar have limited resources in the English language as well as limited access to any library.

Knowing the limitations, I have used only a few Hebrew terms, giving the English transliteration without accent marks in parenthesis.

I spent more than three years writing this commentary. I am grateful to ATA and Langham Partnership for encouraging me to spend three months at the Asbury Theological Seminary in Kentucky, USA, to make use of the library resources. I thank the Union Biblical Seminary in Pune, India, where I stayed for two months to use the library and incorporate the comments of the editorial committee of ABCS and complete this final draft. I am grateful for the valuable comments of Drs. Federico Villanueva and Kelvin Friebel, the consulting editors, to guide me as I revised my initial draft. I also appreciate ATA for giving me extra time to revise the draft and to expand the introduction.

I am thankful for the support of Nirmala, my wife, Tephillah, my daughter, and Paul, my son, for encouraging me to write books, publish papers, and make theological contributions through literature for the future generations. I thank the Lord for giving me health and inspiration to write this commentary. Glory to God.

Jesudason Baskar Jeyaraj
Madurai, India

SERIES PREFACE

What's unique about the Asia Bible Commentary Series? It is a commentary series written especially for Asian Christians, which incorporates and addresses Asian concerns, cultures, and practices. As Asian scholars – either by nationality, passion, or calling – the authors identify with the biblical text, understand it culturally, and apply its principles in Asian contexts to strengthen the churches in Asia. Missiologists tell us that Christianity has shifted from being a Western majority religion to a South, South-Eastern, and Eastern majority religion and that the church is growing at an unprecedented rate in these regions. This series meets the need for evangelical commentaries written specifically for an Asian audience.

This is not to say that Asian churches and Asian Christians don't want to partner with Western Christians and churches or that they spurn Western influences. A house divided cannot stand. The books in this series complement the existing Western commentaries by taking into consideration the cultural nuances familiar to the Eastern world so that the Eastern readership is not inundated with Western clichés and illustrations that they are unable to relate to and which may not be applicable to them.

The mission of this series is "to produce resources that are biblical, pastoral, contextual, missional, and prophetic for pastors, Christian leaders, cross-cultural workers, and students in Asia." While using approved exegetical principles, the writers strive to be culturally relevant, offer practical applications, and provide clear explanations of the texts so that readers can grow in understanding and maturity in Christ, and so that Christian leaders can guide their congregations into maturity. May we be found faithful to this endeavor and may God be glorified!

Andrew B. Spurgeon
General Editor

LIST OF ABBREVIATIONS

BOOKS OF THE BIBLE

Old Testament

Gen, Exod, Lev, Num, Deut, Josh, Judg, Ruth, 1–2 Sam, 1–2 Kgs, 1–2 Chr, Ezra, Neh, Esth, Job, Ps/Pss, Prov, Eccl, Song, Isa, Jer, Lam, Ezek, Dan, Hos, Joel, Amos, Obad, Jonah, Mic, Nah, Hab, Zeph, Hag, Zech, Mal

New Testament

Matt, Mark, Luke, John, Acts, Rom, 1–2 Cor, Gal, Eph, Phil, Col, 1–2 Thess, 1–2 Tim, Titus, Phlm, Heb, Jas, 1–2 Pet, 1–2–3 John, Jude, Rev

BIBLE TEXTS AND VERSIONS

Divisions of the canon

NT	New Testament
OT	Old Testament

Ancient texts and versions

LXX	Septuagint
MT	Masoretic Text

Modern versions

NIV	New International Version

Journals, reference works, and series

ABC	*Africa Bible Commentary*
ABCS	Asia Bible Commentary Series
ANET	Ancient Near Eastern Texts
AOTC	Abingdon Old Testament Commentary
COTOT	Commentary on the Old Testament
HALOT	*Hebrew and Aramaic Lexicon of the Old Testament*
NAC	The New American Commentary

NBD	*New Bible Dictionary*
NIBC	New International Biblical Commentary
NIEE	The New Illustrated Everyman's Encyclopedia
OTL	Old Testament Library
TOTC	Tyndale Old Testament Commentary
SABC	South Asia Bible Commentary
WBC	Word Biblical Commentary

INTRODUCTION

PURPOSE AND RELEVANCE OF THE BOOKS OF KINGS

Telling the stories of the achievements and failures of kings and queens is common in every society. In India, people from generation to generation read and recite the stories of Akbar (AD 1542–1605), Shah Jahan (AD 1592–1666), Chhatrapati Shivaji (AD 1630–1680), and Veerapandiya Kattabomman (AD 1760–1799).[1] Similarly, Jews and Christians repeat stories of the Jewish kings, which are outlined in the books of 1 and 2 Kings.

Following the exodus and settlement of the people of Israel in the land of Canaan, they entered a monarchical period (ca 1050–586 BC), when kings and queens governed the people. The books of 1 and 2 Kings provide valuable information about the political, social, economic, and religious contexts of this period. The main focus of these books is theological: how God delivered the people from their enemies by the works of the kings.

Title and Placement in the Old Testament

Although the Hebrew title *melakim* ("kings") is appropriate since these books speak of the life and activities of the kings, it also speaks of the prophets who ministered during the monarchical period: Nathan, Ahijah of Shiloh, Elijah, Elisha, and Micaiah. These books reflect the expectations, values, and principles of the God of Israel for his rulers and the people. These books follow 1 and 2 Samuel, which depict the story of the earlier monarchs. Scholars categorize these books as narrative, historical, and teaching literature.[2]

Purpose and Structure

Although we do not know the author's name, 1 and 2 Kings reveal the author's purpose in telling these stories, which is to answer: Why was the Jewish kingdom destroyed? Since the kings are mandated to live by the laws of Deuteronomy, 1 and 2 Kings are part of the Deuteronomistic history, including Joshua, Judges, and 1 and 2 Samuel.[3]

---

1. See The New Illustrated Everyman's Encyclopaedia, vol. 1 (London: Octopus Books, 1985).
2. Iain W. Provan, *1 and 2 Kings*, NIBC (Boston: Hendrickson Publishers, 2008), 1–15.
3. Gina Hens-Piazza, *1–2 Kings*, AOTC (Nashville: Abingdon Press, 2006), 3.

1 and 2 Kings speak of three major periods: the united monarchy (1 Kings 1–11), the divided kingdoms of Israel (northern kingdom) and Judah (southern kingdom) through the fall of Israel (1 Kings 12–2 Kings 17), and the kingdom of Judah through the fall of Jerusalem and the release of King Jehoiachin from prison in Babylon (2 Kings 18–25). A total of forty-three kings ruled during the monarchical period, starting with Saul, David, and Solomon. Leaving out these three kings of united monarchy, the narrator tells the stories of twenty kings who ruled the northern kingdom of Israel, and another twenty kings who ruled Judah. Of these, Jeroboam II ruled northern Israel for forty-one years, and Manasseh ruled Judah for fifty-five years.

Style of Communication

The writer uses storytelling as the main narrative style for recounting the history of the kings. Within this category, the author uses metaphors (2 Kgs 19:26), proverbs (1 Kgs 12:10), fables (2 Kgs 14:8–10), numbers (1 Kgs 20:15–16), lists (1 Kgs 4:1–19), signs (1 Kgs 13:3–5), miracles (1 Kgs 18:38), sagas (1 Kgs 17–19), parallelisms (1 Kgs 12:16), and rhetorical questions (2 Kgs 4:28). Each king is introduced by stating his name, parents, year of ascension, age at ascension, number of years reigned, place of reign, an evaluation of the king's performance, and the way he was buried. Each king is evaluated on the basis of his faithfulness to the law rather than his achievements and failures. In addition, the kings are always measured against David and/or Jeroboam I.

South Asia: Parallels and Implications

These books are valuable for people in Asia, as the stories speak of faith, worship, prayer, understanding God, leadership and governance, power and authority, and relating to people of other faiths. The sacred history of Israel is the story of a living community of Jews who worship and have a sober understanding of their politics.

Some of the features of the monarchy in ancient Israel are similar to ancient eastern monarchies. Following are some that share commonality with Indian history.

First, the kings came to the throne by lineage or by a military coup. Many kings misused their powers to suppress the dissenting voices of the prophets (1 Kgs 22:26–27) and elders (1 Kgs 12:6–8). They also accumulated wealth and led a luxurious life. Mogul rulers in India came to power and behaved in similar ways. During the Mogul period, Aurangzeb (AD 1618–1707) murdered

Introduction

his own brother to become king and imprisoned his own father, Shah Jahan, in the citadel of Agra.[4]

Second, the kings of Judah and Israel often engaged in war against Syria (1 Kgs 20:1–12), Assyria (2 Kgs 17:3–17), and Babylon (2 Kgs 25:1–4). Similarly, British colonial expansion caused infighting between Pakistan, India, Sri Lanka, and Myanmar. The persistent wars in Israel and Judah resulted in people becoming slaves (2 Kgs 24:15–16) and migrating to nations (2 Kgs 17:24–27), something that continues to happen in south Asia today.

Third, religion and religious institutions grew as the kingdom of Israel expanded. Solomon built the temple in Jerusalem (1 Kgs 8:17–21). Babylonians captured Judah, destroyed the temple, and carried away the wealth (2 Kgs 24:13). A parallel incident happened when Gajini Mohammad invaded India, attacked the temple in Somnath, and plundered its gold and silver. Even in modern days, extreme religious groups attack and destroy temples, mosques, Buddhist shrines, and churches.

Fourth, just as the kings of Israel were subject to the law of Moses, in India, King Akbar developed a judicial system, a military with 12,000 horsemen, and a large empire.[5] Also, kings contributed to building projects, like Solomon building the temple in Jerusalem. King Wadiyar built a huge palace in Mysore and furnished it with fine wood, silk, glasses, and ivory. Shah Jagan built Taj Mahal, a mausoleum for his wife, Mumtaz. Just as the queen of Sheba went to see Solomon's temple in Jerusalem, people still flock to see Taj Mahal and the palace in Mysore.

GUIDELINES FOR STUDYING 1 & 2 KINGS

1 and 2 Kings offers practical lessons for Christians. First, these books offer positive and negative portrayals of the kings. For example, Solomon is appreciated for asking for wisdom rather than wealth and fame (1 Kgs 3:4–15), but he is criticized for initiating idol worship in Israel (1 Kgs 11:1–13). Josiah is appreciated for reforming religion in Judah (2 Kgs 22:18–20), yet his reformation was temporary (2 Kgs 23:26–27). The man of God went to Bethel in obedience to Yahweh's instruction and prophesied to Jeroboam, but he disobeyed God's instruction on his return (1 Kgs 13:1–22). These examples show even the greatest people can do good and bad actions.

---

4. NIEE, Vol. 1, 108.
5. Percival Spear, *A History of India*, vol. 2 (London: Penguin Books, 1970), 42–45.

Second, the prophets who prophesied believed that they received the words from the Lord and they would be fulfilled. The courage of the prophets to interact with powerful kings and risk their lives can continue to challenge us. Do we have a similar faith in our preaching of God's word to people? Are we willing to raise a prophetic voice against the disobedience of people and the injustice of oppressive rulers?

Third, these books show that prophets and the narrator used different methods of communication. How can we apply some of these methods to our communication today?

Fourth, these books testify that Yahweh prohibits the Israelites from marrying people of other religious communities in the land of Canaan. Just as Solomon's marriage to unbelievers led the nation to worship other gods (1 Kgs 11:1–6), Christians marrying non-Christians can have adverse consequences.

SOURCES, AUTHORSHIP, AND DATE

What sources did the writer of 1 and 2 Kings use? Who wrote these books? When were they written?

Sources

The narrator uses a number of sources. First, the author uses the Torah. The author refers to the Exodus (2 Kgs 17:36) and making a covenant (2 Kgs 17:35).

Second, the author refers to the annals of Solomon (1 Kgs 11:41), the kings in Israel (1 Kgs 15:31), and the kings in Judah (2 Kgs 8:23). The secretaries or chroniclers in the royal court would have kept these records in their libraries or archives.[6]

Third, the writer refers to peace treaties or terms and conditions outlining the payment of tributes between Israel and their conquerors, which were written or carved on stones and kept in public places in the defeated nation.

Fourth, within the stories, the author refers to messages that the prophets sent to the kings (1 Kgs 22:9–11) and written negotiations between the kings (2 Kgs 5:7). The prophetic oracle of Isaiah to Hezekiah is recorded in 2 Kings (19:21–34) and Isaiah (37:22–32).

---

6. NIEE mentions Akbar Namah (the history of Akbar's reign) as the annals used to write the history of Akbar. NIEE, 27.

Introduction

Fifth, the writer may have used outside archaeological sources.[7] Archaeologists have found that Omri built the city of Samaria (1 Kgs 16:23–24) and made it his capital.[8]

Sixth, the author may have collected information about the families of kings that were circulating in the oral tradition. He himself may have been from a royal family and may have been familiar with oral traditions.

Authorship

1 and 2 Kings do not mention the name of the author, but scholars have suggested possibilities.[9] One possibility is that a single author, perhaps Jeremiah, collected and compiled the history of the kings from sources. Jeremiah lived during the later period of the kings, and he mentions the fall of Jerusalem and the captivity and exile of the Israelites in Babylon in his prophetic book. He sent a letter to the captives encouraging them not to rebel against the king of Babylon but to trust the Lord until he brought them back to the Promised Land (Jeremiah 27–30).

Other scholars have identified Isaiah of Jerusalem as the author. He prophesied to Ahaz, the king of Judah, during the threat of the Syro-Ephraimite war (2 Kgs 16:5–9; Isa 7:1–17). He also spoke to Hezekiah, the king of Judah, during the attack of Assyria (2 Kgs 19:20–34; Isa 37:30–35).

Some scholars suggest that 1 and 2 Kings were written by an unknown author, perhaps a prophet of the post-exilic period, who had been exiled in Babylon but knew about Jehoiachin's release (2 Kgs 25:27–30).[10]

Finally, some consider the books of Joshua, Judges, 1 and 2 Samuel, and 1 and 2 Kings as a collective narrative of the Deuteronomistic history, and a single author – known as the Deuteronomist – compiled and composed them.[11] The writer of this commentary holds to this view – a single Deuteronomist finalized the compilation and editing of the final draft of 1 and 2 Kings.

---

7. Donald J. Wiseman, *1 and 2 Kings: An Introduction and Commentary*. TOTC (Nottingham: IVP, 2008), 37–38.
8. Bright quotes archaeological evidences from the writings of G. E. Wright and P. R. Ackroyd on Samaria. John Bright, *A History of Israel* (London: SCM Press, 1976), 240.
9. Wiseman discusses the various views on authorship. Wiseman, *1 and 2 Kings*, 56–62.
10. Georg Fohrer, *Introduction to the Old Testament* (SPCK: London, 1974), 228–231.
11. Hens-Piazza, *1–2 Kings*, 6–9.

Date

The narrative mentions the fall of Jerusalem, which took place in 586 BC (2 Kgs 25:27–30; Jer 52:31–34), and it ends with King Jehoiachin's release, which happened during the period of Awel-Marduk (2 Kgs 25:27). Awel-Marduk (also known as "Evil-Merodach") became the king in Babylon around 560 BC. This information suggests that these books were composed between 586–560 BC.[12]

MESSAGE AND MISSION

1 and 2 Kings have a total of forty-seven chapters, which trace the stories of the kings who reigned over Israel for a period of four hundred years.[13] The author of these books evaluates how well did these kings rule over their kingdoms in obedience to Yahweh. Because Israel is a special community who is covenanted with Yahweh, the kings are evaluated based on their faithfulness to the covenantal relationship with God. All the activities of the kings, including their personal lives, are evaluated on the basis of Deuteronomy 17:14–20.

The author also communicates God's views based on the law of Moses, using formulas such as, "the sins of Jeroboam," (2 Kgs 3:3; 13:2; 14:24; 15:9, 18, 24), "his heart had turned away from the LORD" (1 Kgs 11:9), "Jeroboam did not change his evil ways" (1 Kgs 13:33), "Judah did evil in the eyes of the LORD . . . stirred up his jealous anger" (1 Kgs 14:22), and "he did evil in the eyes of the LORD, following the ways of his father" (1 Kgs 15:26). Furthermore, the author uses statements that convey theological critique, such as, "they aroused the anger of the LORD" (1 Kgs 16:13); "he did evil in the eyes of the LORD" (1 Kgs 22:52; 2 Kgs 8:18, 27); "he . . . sacrificed his son in the fire, engaging in the detestable practices of the nations the LORD had driven out" (2 Kgs 16:3); "following the ways of Jeroboam" (1 Kgs 15:34); "he followed the ways of the kings of Israel, as the house of Ahab had done" (2 Kgs 8:18); "but not as his father David had done" (2 Kgs 14:3); and "because of all that Manasseh had done to arouse his anger" (2 Kgs 23:26).

The narrator's appreciation of some kings follows a formula: He "did what was right in the eyes of the LORD" (1 Kgs 22:43; 2 Kgs 12:2). None of the kings who ruled the northern kingdom were given this positive evaluation. God's

---

12. Musa Gotom, "1 and 2 Kings," in *Africa Bible Commentary*, ed. Tokunboh Adeyemo (Nairobi: Word Alive Publishers, 2006), 409.
13. For the chronological year of the kings in Judah and Israel see the chart in SABC. Brian Wintle, ed. *South Asia Bible Commentary: A One-Volume Commentary on the Whole Bible* (Udaipur, Rajasthan: Open Door Publication, 2015), 475–476.

blessing and punishment of kings, royal families, and the nation depended upon their obedience or disobedience to the Lord.

RELATIONSHIP TO THE CHRONICLES AND PROPHETIC BOOKS

This section explores the relationship between 1 and 2 Kings and 1 and 2 Chronicles as well as many of the prophetic books: Hosea, Amos, Micah, and Zephaniah.

Relationship with Chronicles

Some of the stories in 1 and 2 Kings are repeated in 1 and 2 Chronicles, but both these sets of books were written during different times in the history of Israel. While 1 and 2 Kings were written by a single author between 589 to 560 BC, the Chronicles were written around 400 BC. The books of 1 and 2 Kings focus on the failure of the kings to keep God's law that resulted in the failure of the monarchy, but the books of 1 and 2 Chronicles cover the entire history of Israel, outlining the story of the creation, the exodus, the people's settlement in Canaan, the period of monarchy, exile, return, and the restoration of the Israelites to the land. The author of 1 and 2 Kings wants people to realize their mistakes, repent, and return to the Lord. The author of 1 and 2 Chronicles does not want the people to dwell on the destruction of the monarchy and the period of exile; instead, he wants them to focus on what the Lord will do for the people to whom he gave his promises, made a covenant, and communicated his prophecies through the prophets.

In addition, the author of 1 and 2 Chronicles used different sources than the author of 1 and 2 Kings. The Chronicler used the annals of the kings of Israel and Judah, the books of 1 and 2 Kings, and the prophecies and memoirs of Ezra and Nehemiah. Because the authors used different sources, their accounts have variations. For example, in 1 Chronicles 29:21–25, the narrator presents the story of Solomon succeeding to the throne briefly, without any reference to the involvement of Nathan and Bathsheba (see 1 Kgs 1:11–31). In 2 Kings 15:5, the narrator does not state the reason for Azariah's leprosy, but 2 Chronicles 26:16–21 mentions his rebellion as the cause of his leprosy. 2 Kings 21:1–18 presents Manasseh as a wicked king who arouses the anger of the Lord, but 2 Chronicles 33:10–13 portrays him as praying, repenting, and humbling himself before the Lord. The collapse of Jerusalem mentioned in 2 Kings 25:1–30 ends with Jehoiachin's release, but 2 Chronicles 36:15–23 includes the fulfillment of the prophecies of Jeremiah about Cyrus, the king of Persia, who issued a decree that allowed the exiles to return to Jerusalem and rebuild the temple.

Relationship with Prophetic Books

During the time of monarchy, God raised several prophets and prophetesses to represent him. They interacted with the kings and the people. Isaiah, for example, proclaimed his prophecies to King Ahaz (Isa 7:11–14) and King Hezekiah (2 Kgs 19:20–34). Jeremiah prophesied about the fall of Jerusalem to the people and encouraged them not to flee to Egypt but to stay in Judah (Jer 27:1–22).

Many of the prophetic interactions recorded in the books of 1 and 2 Kings reflect the theme of prophecy and fulfillment. For example, the prophecy of the man of God from Bethel about the altar splitting (1 Kgs 13:3) fulfills as soon as Jeroboam touches the altar (1 Kgs 13:5). Similarly, Ahijah's prophecy to Jeroboam about the death of his son (1 Kgs 14:1–12) fulfills as soon as Jeroboam's wife crosses the threshold into her home (1 Kgs 14:17–18). Micaiah's prophecies to Ahab about the king's death and the outcome of the battle between Israel and Aram (1 Kgs 22:17–28) fulfill when Ahab dies and Israel loses the battle at Ramoth Gilead (1 Kgs 22:37–38). Elisha's prediction about the end of Samaria's siege (2 Kgs 7:1–2) fulfills on the following day when the people realize that the Aramean army has fled, and so they plunder its camp (2 Kgs 7:3–19).

Israel is a special community that is bound by their covenant with Yahweh, and so their unique history happened within the context of that covenantal relationship. Those who live in Asia should study 1 and 2 Kings along with Deuteronomy and 1 and 2 Chronicles to see aspects of the "culture movement," which upholds the oppressive policies of the rulers and fails to follow the divine principles of Yahweh. The prophets spoke against wrong policies of the rulers of their day, who were oppressing peasants and denying justice to orphans, widows, and the needy (Amos 5:21–27; Mic 3:1–12; Isa 3:11–15). Studying these prophets challenging the kings and the people can prepare us to fight against injustices in our own societies and cultures.

Introduction

PROPHETS AND PROPHECIES

Our study of 1 and 2 Kings cannot ignore the role of prophets, for their prophecies are intertwined with the stories of the kings.[14] In their prophecies, certain patterns are evident.

First, the prophets are only channels through whom God communicates to the kings, which is indicated by the phrase, "the Word of the LORD." Second, the content of the prophet's message is from Yahweh alone and not the prophet. Third, the prophets do not have power to fulfill the prophecies. Only Yahweh has the power to fulfill them. Fourth, the prophecies often include a reason for God's actions. Following are some of the prophets who play a role in 1 and 2 Kings.

Nathan

Nathan's prophetic ministry began during the kingship of David. When David wanted to build a temple for the Lord, he spoke with Nathan the prophet who, in turn, communicated God's word to David (2 Sam 7:1–29). When David took Uriah's wife, Nathan rebuked him and interceded on his behalf (2 Sam 12:1–14). After David's death, when Adonijah wanted to usurp the throne, Nathan reminded Bathsheba about the prophecy that Yahweh had given to David to ensure that Solomon, her son, would be appointed as his successor (1 Kgs 1:11–14).

Shemaiah

Shemaiah appeared in the context of the division of the kingdom (1 Kgs 12:22–24). When Rehoboam wanted to fight against the northern tribe of Israel, the prophet Shemaiah delivered God's message and asked Rehoboam not to fight the Israelites, since they were brothers. Rehoboam obeyed the prophecy of Shemaiah.

Man of God

The text does not reveal the identity of this prophet, but he came to Bethel from Judah (1 Kgs 13:1–10). When Jeroboam placed golden calves in Bethel and asked the people of Israel to worship them (1 Kgs 12:31–33), this prophet prophesied about the birth of Josiah (13:2) and gave the sign of the altar

---

14. Gray discusses the fulfillment of the word of God in prophecy as one of the guiding principles of the Deuteronomist in writing the stories of the kings. John Gray, *I and II Kings: A Commentary*, OTL (SCM Press, London, 1980), 11–13.

splitting (13:3). Jeroboam went against the man of God, his hand withered. Then the man of God interceded for him and restored his hand.

Old Prophet

The name of this old prophet is not mentioned, but he lived in Bethel and prophesied against "the man of God" mentioned above (1 Kgs 13:11–32). God had told the man of God not to return to Judah and eat bread or drink water. The old prophet lied to the man of God saying that God asked him to return. When the man of God did that, the old prophet prophesied that he would receive the punishment of death by a lion attack. This punishment served as a warning to Jeroboam, for if judgment came against God's own prophet for his disobedience, how would a king escape God's judgment?

Ahijah of Shiloh

Ahijah of Shiloh prophesied to Jeroboam, with a visual aid of a garment torn in twelve pieces, that the Lord God of Israel would tear the kingdom of Solomon (1 Kgs 11:29–39). He also prophesied that all the males in Jeroboam's family would be killed because they had made idols and abandoned Yahweh (14:10). Dogs would eat those who were killed in the city, and birds would prey on their bodies in the countryside (14:11). These prophecies were fulfilled when Baasha took over the throne of Israel (15:29–30).

Jehu, Son of Hanani

Jehu delivered prophecies against Baasha, who followed the same evil practices of Jeroboam (1 Kgs 16:1–4). Baasha aroused the anger of Yahweh, and so dogs and birds ate the dead bodies of his family, just as it had happened to Jeroboam's family. Jehu's prophecy was fulfilled when Zimri killed Baasha's entire family (16:11–13).

Elijah

Elijah prophesied during the time of Ahab. The phrase, "the word of the Lord came" to Elijah, appears several times, indicating the source of these prophecies (1 Kgs 17:2; 18:1). Elijah also used the oath formulas, "As the Lord, the God of Israel lives, whom I serve," (17:1) or "As the Lord Almighty lives, whom I serve" (18:15). Elijah prophesied that God would stop the rain as a warning to Ahab and the people (17:1). While the land suffered from drought, God provided for Elijah miraculously (17:15–16). After the contest with the prophets of Baal on Mount Carmel, Elijah prayed again, and it rained (18:45). Jezebel joined Ahab's sin, and so Elijah prophesied against her that dogs would eat her dead body (21:23). This prophecy was later fulfilled (22:37–38). Elijah also prophesied against Ahaziah, the king of Israel, for seeking the help of Baal-Zebub, a god of Ekron (2 Kgs 1:3–4). Ahaziah died according to this prophecy (1:16–17).

Micaiah

Micaiah prophesied during the time of Jehoshaphat, the king of Judah, for going against the king of Aram (Syria) to recover Ramoth Gilead from Aram's control (1 Kgs 22:9–28). The king and the people persecuted Micaiah for proclaiming this prophecy of defeat and God's judgment (22:26–27).

Elisha

Elijah called Elisha to the ministry (1 Kgs 19:19–21). After Elijah died, Elisha inherited the spirit of his mentor and started his prophetic ministry. When the armies of Israel, Judah, and Edom were lacking water in the battlefield, Elisha proclaimed the prophecy to Joram that Yahweh would provide water and deliver Moab into the hands of Joram's army (2 Kgs 3:14–19). This prophecy was fulfilled on the next day (3:20–25). He later prophesied that Israel would be delivered from the hands of Ben-Hadad, and the siege of Samaria would come to an end, and people would get food (6:32–7:1). This prophecy was also fulfilled just as Elisha predicted (7:15–19). Elisha prophesied that Hazael would become the king of Aram, which was also fulfilled (8:10–13). Before dying, Elisha prophesied to Jehoash, using a symbolic action of having the king striking the ground three times to predict that he would defeat the king of Aram three times (13:15–19). This prophecy was fulfilled as predicted by Elisha (13:25).

Isaiah

Isaiah, one of the writing prophets, ministered during the reign of Hezekiah in Judah. His prophecy is recorded in 2 Kings (19:5–20:19) and the Book of Isaiah (37:1–35). When Sennacherib, the king of Assyria, came to attack Jerusalem, his commander delivered a humiliating speech about Hezekiah's trust in Yahweh and ordered him to surrender (2 Kgs 18:19–24). At this critical moment, Yahweh sent Isaiah to Hezekiah to deliver a message of hope and deliverance as an answer to his trust and prayer (19:6–7). As predicted by Isaiah, deliverance came to Jerusalem. Isaiah also prophesied about Hezekiah being healed from his illness and having his life extended for another fifteen years (20:4–6). This prophecy was confirmed by a sign (20:9–11). Isaiah also prophesied that the Babylonians would attack Judah and take away all its wealth and deport its people to Babylon (25:1–21), but this prophesy was not fulfilled until 587 BC, centuries after his death.

Servants the Prophets

Nameless prophets of Yahweh are called "servants the prophets" (2 Kgs 9:7; 17:23; 21:10; 24:2). Manasseh, the king of Judah, was warned by such prophets of Yahweh for worshiping idols and practicing the detestable customs of the Amorites (21:10–15), but Manasseh did not listen. As such, Babylon, Aram, Moab, and Ammon attacked Jerusalem, leading to its destruction during the period of Zedekiah (24:1–25:21).

Huldah

1 and 2 Kings narrates the stories of several brave women, including Bathsheba (1 Kgs 1:28–40), Jezebel (1 Kgs 18– 21), Athaliah and Jehosheba (2 Kgs 11:1–3), and the prophetess, Huldah (2 Kgs 22:14–20). Huldah prophesied before Hilkiah, the high priest, who had been sent to her by Josiah during the temple restoration, after they had found the Law. Huldah prophesied about the coming punishment on Judah for the sins they had committed against Yahweh (22:15–17), and if they repented, God would show mercy on Josiah (22:18–20).

In summary, these books about the stories of the kings of Israel and Judah also include stories about the lives and ministries of the prophets and priests. The main message that is often repeated in these books is the failure of the kings to obey the law and to honor God. Idolatry is shunned, and the people of Israel and Judah are punished when they are delivered into the hands of their enemies. By reading 1 and 2 Kings, a reader can get a bird's-eye view of how God used the prophets to act in the history of Israel throughout the monarchical period.

THEOLOGICAL THEMES IN 1 AND 2 KINGS

1 and 2 Kings do not merely present the political or secular history of the kings of Israel, but also the way God of the Bible acts in the history of his people. As such, history and theology are integrated, and so the characters, stories, events,

and festivals in these books always have a theological perspective. Several of these theological themes are discussed below.[15]

Yahweh and Monotheism

Yahweh (the Lord) is the main player in the history of kings. The names "Yahweh" (translated as "Lord") and "Elohim" (God) occur over 700 times in these books. Both these names refer to the Lord God of the people of Israel.

There are several descriptions or titles for God, including "the Sovereign Lord" (1 Kgs 2:26), "the Lord Almighty" (1 Kgs 18:15), "he is God" (1 Kgs 18:24), "no God like you in heaven above or on earth below" (1 Kgs 8:23), "You have made heaven and earth" (2 Kgs 19:15), "God of Abraham, Isaac, and Israel" (1 Kgs 18:36), and "the God of your father David" (2 Kgs 20:5).

Some of God's actions include raising up kings (1 Kgs 11:23), driving out nations (2 Kgs 16:3; 17:8), removing enemies from his presence (2 Kgs 17:20), striking Israel (1 Kgs 14:15), and preserving a remnant (2 Kgs 19:30–31).

When the kings disobeyed the law, the Lord God sent prophets to warn them of the impending danger, as the above section on prophets illustrated. Although kings ruled the people, God was ultimately in control of the nation, both northern Israel and the southern Judah.

Temple and Central Worship

A second theological theme in 1 and 2 Kings is the centralization of worship in the temple of the Lord. Nathan prophesied that David's kingdom would continue through his descendants, and one of them would build a temple for his name in Jerusalem (2 Sam 7:11–14). The people were to worship him alone in his temple in Jerusalem. Solomon fulfilled this prophecy by building the temple and dedicating it to the Lord. Then he centralized the worship and festivals so that they would take place in the temple. With the temple firmly established as the center of worship in Jerusalem, the Israelites would no longer have to worship in the high places and shrines that were scattered throughout the land.

Any violation of this law was regarded as disobedience and a sin against Yahweh. Various kings ignored this law and built different altars for offering sacrifices to the gods of the nations, and then they worshiped the idols of those gods. As a punishment for these collective sins of the people, the temple

---

15. Wiseman lists various themes in the books of 1 and 2 Kings. Wiseman, *1 and 2 Kings*, 18–27; Hens-Piazza, *1–2 Kings*, 6–9.

itself was eventually destroyed, and the people could no longer worship God in Jerusalem.

Miracles of Yahweh through the Prophets

Miracles were common during the reign of the kings. As God's servants, prophets performed these miracles. Elijah and Elisha were prominent miracle workers.[16]

Miracles reveal the power of God. Since God created the world and controls and sustains it, he can perform miracles whenever it is necessary for the people's welfare. He used ravens to feed Elijah (1 Kgs 17:1–6), made flour and oil to last through the famine to feed the widow in Zarephath, her son, and Elijah (1 Kgs 17:8–16), turned bitter water in a spring in Jericho into drinkable water (2 Kgs 2:19–22), multiplied a loaf of bread for feeding a hundred men (2 Kgs 4:42–44), used the river Jordan to heal the leprosy of Naaman (2 Kgs 5:13–14), temporarily blinded the enemies of Israel (2 Kgs 6:18–20), and stopped or started the rain (1 Kgs 17–18). Miracles prove that the Lord alone is the true God.

God's Prophecies and Fulfillment

Every prophecy that is fulfilled in 1 and 2 Kings attests to God's power. Prophecies usually came as a punishment for the people's or king's sins. When prophecies were fulfilled, they brought fear into the hearts of the people, which led them to repentance and holiness. Prophecies warned the people not to worship other gods and thus violate God's laws and break their covenantal relationship.

Sovereignty of Yahweh over the Kings

A key message in the books of 1 and 2 Kings is the sovereignty of Yahweh (LORD) over the kings, whom he appointed over Israel and Judah. Yahweh was also sovereign over the kings of Aram, Assyria, and Babylon, which led him to punish them when they came against Israel or Judah. Because Yahweh was sovereign over his people and their kings, he deported some to Assyria (2 Kgs 17:22–23) and others to Babylon (2 Kgs 25:1–21). The theological implication is that Yahweh could use any nation as his instrument, because Yahweh was sovereign over all the kings of the earth.

---

16. Paul R. House, *1, 2 Kings: An Exegetical and Theological Exposition of Holy Scripture NIV Text*, NAC, vol. 8 (Nashville: Broadman & Holman Publishers, 1995), 53.

Introduction

His sovereignty extended even when the kings of Israel or Judah sinned. Solomon initiated the worship of other gods by marrying women from other nations (1 Kgs 11:1–6). He built high places for Chemosh, the god of Moab, and Molek, the god of the Ammonites, and he burned incense and offered sacrifices to foreign gods (11:7–8). Jeroboam created another religion by placing golden calves at shrines in Bethel and Dan and instructing the people of Israel to worship them as Yahweh (12:28–30). He also built other shrines on high places and appointed non-Levitical priests (12:31). Ahab and Jezebel promoted the worship of Baal and killed the prophets of Yahweh (16:29–33). Ahaziah and Manasseh worshiped other gods, offered sacrifices to them, and practiced detestable customs, including sacrificing children (2 Kgs 3:26–27). Yahweh sent prophets to warn the kings against their impending punishments because he hated the inhuman practices of the foreign gods.

Leadership and Governance

The kings had great power and were responsible for governing the nation. They were not to behave like the kings of other nations because they represented God to the people. They were meant to serve as the guardians of Yahweh's religion and the protectors of his people. The kings did not function in isolation from the community but were part of the society and had a responsibility to lead the community to follow Yahweh and practice Yahweh's law. The kings were supposed to administer justice and develop the country with security and peace, and so they were warned and punished when they misused their power and authority. As such, 1 and 2 Kings reveal how leadership and governance go hand in hand. Their stories also tell us of conflict between religion and politics during the leadership of some kings.

Unfortunately, the kings of Judah and Israel often disobeyed Yahweh by insulting his prophets and oppressing his people. Jeroboam, for example, tried to seize the prophet who spoke against him (1 Kgs 13:4). Ahab and Jezebel killed Naboth and took his vineyard (2 Kgs 21:1–16). The false prophet Zedekiah slapped Micaiah for not pronouncing a prophecy that was in favor of Ahab, the king of Israel (1 Kgs 22:24–28). Moreover, kings often used their power and authority to promote idol worship.

However, not all the actions of the kings were evil. Solomon built the temple and centralized worship in Jerusalem. He also developed an administrative structure and earned gold and silver by trading with the surrounding nations. Ahab and Joram fought wars to protect their country from the attacks of Aram (1 Kgs 22:29–37) and Moab (2 Kgs 3:24–25). Hezekiah and Josiah engaged in religious reform in Judah. The Tamil proverb, "The ways of a nation are as the ways of its king" (*Mannan eppadiyo, naddum appadiye*), reflects the basic message of 1 and 2 Kings: when the kings obeyed God, the people obeyed God; when the kings disobeyed God, the people disobeyed God.

OUTLINE

FIRST BOOK OF KINGS

1:1–53	Power Struggle for the Throne
2:1–46	Solomon Establishes the Kingdom
3:1–28	God's Gift of Wisdom for Solomon
4:1–34	Solomon's Administration and Fame
5:1–18	Preparation for Building the Temple
6:1–38	Magnificence of the Temple
7:1–51	Building Palaces and Furnishing the Temple
8:1–66	Dedication of the Temple
9:1–28	God's Appearance and Solomon's Activities
10:1–29	Solomon's Wisdom and Wealth
11:1–43	Solomon's Decline
12:1–33	Rehoboam and Jeroboam: A Divided Monarchy
13:1–34	The Consequences of Jeroboam's Sin
14:1–31	End of Jeroboam and Rehoboam
15:1–16:34	Judah and Israel: Two Kingdoms
17:1–24	The Prophets of Israel
18:1–46	Elijah's Challenge: Choose Yahweh
19:1–21	Elijah's Setback and Rebound
20:1–43	Ahab's Victories and Accountability
21:1–29	Ahab's Injustice to Naboth
22:1–53	Defeat and Death of Ahab

SECOND BOOK OF KINGS

1:1–18	Elijah Condemns Ahaziah
2:1–25	Transition from Elijah to Elisha
3:1–27	Alliance to Defeat Moab
4:1–44	Elisha's Ministries
5:1–27	Healing of Naaman

6:1–7:20	Rescuing Israel from War and Famine
8:1–29	Elisha and the Kings of Aram and Judah
9:1–10:36	Jehu's Kingship in Israel
11:1–21	Jehoiada, Priest and Kingmaker
12:1–21	Joash Over Judah
13:1–25	Reign of Jehoahaz and Jehoash
14:1–29	Amaziah's Rule
15:1–38	Seven Kings of Israel and Judah
16:1–20	Ahaz, King of Judah
17:1–41	Collapse of Israel
18:1–37	Hezekiah's Trust in Yahweh
19:1–37	Hezekiah's Prayer and Isaiah's Prophecy
20:1–21	Hezekiah's Healing and Mistake
21:1–26	Disintegration of Judah
22:1–23:30	Josiah King of Judah
23:31–25:7	Final Four Kings
25:8–30	The Fall of Jerusalem

1 KINGS

1 KINGS 1:1–53
POWER STRUGGLE FOR THE THRONE

1 Kings continues the stories of the kings narrated in 1 and 2 Samuel. Those books narrated the origin of the monarchy and explained the reigns of Saul and David. 1 Kings 1 begins with the last days of David, Adonijah's attempt to become the successor to the throne after David, and Solomon's appointment as the next king. The strife between Adonijah and Solomon, two sons of David who are contending for the throne, is resolved by Nathan, the court prophet, and Bathsheba, Solomon's mother. The story of the power struggle is narrated in a simple style that describes the declining health of David (1 Kgs 1:1–4), Adonijah's attempt to become king (1:5–10), and Solomon's appointment as the next king (1:11–53).

The narrative employs various literary styles, such as speeches to convince the ruling King David to anoint Solomon, a report by Jonathan, royal court language of a son of Abiathar to Adonijah, and a command to implement the will of David to make Solomon his successor. The writer uses these various literary styles so that readers can enjoy the stories.

1:1–4 DAVID'S OLD AGE

David is old and advanced in years. Though the text does not identify David's age, the terms "very old" indicates that he is bedridden and unable to do any administrative work beyond listening to people. He is unable to remain warm even with thick covers (1:1). The servants search for a virgin girl (1:2) and find Abishag to sleep beside him to provide warmth (1:3). Her name means "my father is a wanderer." She is a "Shunammite," from Shunem, a town in the territory of Issachar near Jezreel (Josh 19:18; 1 Sam 28:4). Providing a girl for warmth in old age was a common practice in countries in the ancient Near East. Abishag is a very beautiful girl with a heart of servitude (1:4a). David had no sexual relationship with her (1:4b).

David has not made any arrangement about who will succeed him in leadership. Developing the next line of leadership for a nation is an important duty of a ruling king so that there will be a smooth transition of power to the next generation, without any strife or bloodshed. Although David had appointed

Solomon as his successor (2 Sam 7:11–17), the narrator of 1 Kings describes a struggle in the story of succession.

Providing a virgin girl for warming an ailing father would be disgraceful in India. Instead, the family members are responsible for caring for old people, or else they provide a male servant to care for an elderly man or a female servant to care for an elderly woman.

1:5-10 ADONIJAH'S ATTEMPT TO BECOME KING

The name "Adonijah" literally means "my Lord is Yahweh." We do not know why David named his son "Adonijah," perhaps in the hope that his son would keep Yahweh as his Lord and follow his God. The text also identifies Adonijah's mother's name as "Haggith" (1 Kgs 1:5). Adonijah is the fourth eldest and surviving son of David after the deaths of Kaleb, Ammon, and Absalom (2 Sam 3:2–4; 13:28; 18:15). The narrator says that David has never rebuked Adonijah by asking, "Why do you behave as you do?" (1:6), implying that David has failed to discipline and guide his son. The possible reason for this failure is connected with the next statement in the text: Adonijah is handsome, a detail that connects him with Absalom, who was also handsome (2 Sam 14:25–26). Absalom planned conspiracy to declare himself as king, and David had to flee from him (2 Sam 15:10–13), suggesting that David was an ineffective father in dealing with Absalom[1] because Absalom was not disciplined, and yet David loved Absalom – perhaps because he was handsome. By setting Adonijah parallel to Absalom, the narrator implies that Adonijah has not been guided by David and is heading for disaster just like Absalom. Negligence in parenting or showing favoritism to one child allows the favored child to grow and live as he likes, as we also see with the story of Isaac and Rebekah (Gen 26:34; 27:1–13). Whatever the reason was, Adonijah wants to capture the power and become the king of the nation. This intention leads him to exalt himself and declare, "I will be king" (1:5).

With this idea in his mind, Adonijah starts working to become the king. His first strategy is to send chariots, horsemen, and fifty men to go before him to the place where he will declare himself as the king to prevent anyone from attacking him. In the Indian tradition, anyone who is a king must have chariots and horses.[2] Without a small army of men and chariots, the king will not be recognized. However a king in Israel should not accumulate too

---

1. House, *1, 2 Kings: An Exegetical and Theological Exposition of Holy Scripture*, 88.
2. This comes from oral traditions such as Tamil songs.

many horses (Deut 17:16). Moreover, in the religious culture of Israel, no one could be accepted as king unless priests and prophets were part of the consecration ceremony. The priests and prophets represented God's approval of the king. Without the participation of priests, prophets, and an army, a king would not be accepted by the public. Adonijah knows these formalities and procedures, and so he "confers" with Joab, the commander of the army, and Abiathar, the priest, and mobilizes them to support him and be present during the enthronement ceremony (1:7).

Adonijah's second strategy is to sacrifice sheep, oxen, and fatted cattle to provide a good feast after the enthronement ceremony. Since there is no mention of a priest offering prayers of thanksgiving or sacrifices for the forgiveness of sins before declaring Adonijah king, the feast is clearly given to please his supporters. Adonijah carefully selects the place where he will claim himself as king, choosing to hold the ceremony and the feast by the side of the "stone of Zoheleth" (serpent's stone or well), which is located near En-rogel (1:9). Scholars locate En-rogel ("spring of the fuller") in the southeast of Jerusalem, where the tribes of Benjamin and Judah would have had easy access, as it is situated close to their borders (Josh 15:7; 18:16). This placement is significant because most of Adonijah's supporters are from Judah.

Adonijah's third strategy is to invite all his brothers and royal officials to the feast while excluding Solomon or any of the faithful warriors of David whom Adonijah cannot convince to support him (1:9). Thus Adonijah deliberately does not invite Zadok, an important priest during David's reign, Benaiah, the trustworthy captain of David's bodyguard, Nathan, the court prophet, or Shimei and Rei, officers of the royal guard and supporters of Solomon (1:8, 10). These individuals would want to follow David's instruction and might cause problems for Adonijah, which suggests that there might have been some sort of division about the successor for David among the royal court officials and priests as David grew old. Absalom also created division between the officials when he drew supporters to his side, but he failed (2 Sam 15:1–6).

But a new trend developed regarding the succession to the throne. It was not by the status of being the eldest surviving son but by the approval of the existing king. This trend provided opportunity to appoint a better candidate to the throne. Jonathan could be the natural successor to Saul but David was chosen by God to be the successor of Saul.

Even now, it's not the natural but divine order that determines God's leadership. This principle is implied in the qualifications required for leadership which can be noticed in the NT (1 Tim 3:1–10).

1:11–53 SOLOMON'S APPOINTMENT AS THE KING

Adonijah's attempt to take the throne of David is spoiled by Nathan, Bathsheba, and David. This section narrates Nathan's conversation with Bathsheba (1:11–14), Bathsheba's reminder to David of his promise (1:15–21), Nathan's speech with David (1:22–27), and David's appointment of Solomon to the throne (1:28–40). The chapter concludes with the appointment of Solomon as the king (1:41–48) and Solomon's forgiveness of Adonijah (1:49–53).

1:11–14 Nathan's Conversation with Bathsheba

Nathan the prophet worked closely with the king and royal family. The stories of his ministry and contribution during the period of David help us to understand how much he loved the nation, the king, and the king's family. Previously, Nathan courageously pointed out David's adultery with Bathsheba, whose name means "seventh child in her family" (just as the tenth girl child is called as *Padma* in some Indian families). Later, Nathan accepts David and Bathsheba's marriage but pronounces the death of the first child born to Bathsheba as God's judgment on David for killing Uriah (2 Sam 11–12). These details reveal that Nathan knows David and Bathsheba well and feels free to communicate his prophecies and views to them.

Nathan alerts Bathsheba and stands against Adonijah's plot to become king because he is so loyal to the king and Bathsheba (1 Kgs 1:11–12). He is concerned about the risk that she and her son, Solomon, will face when Adonijah takes over the government. He is also more concerned about the way David is ignored by Adonijah and his followers and is kept in darkness without any attempt to seek his approval for the king. Nathan considers Adonijah's declaration as a political coup. Because Adonijah does not become king through the proper channel or by divine approval, Nathan cannot accept Adonijah's secret actions against the ruling king. Nathan is not consulted, and so God's will is ignored. If Adonijah had consulted Nathan, the prophet would have given him a negative reply, because a prophet can only say what God tells him. Adonijah knew that Nathan would not have supported him as the king, and so Adonijah made his plot without consulting Nathan.

Nathan knows the promise David gave to Bathsheba to make Solomon the king after him. So he asks her to go and tell David, "My lord the king, did you not swear to me your servant: 'Surely Solomon your son shall be king after me, and he will sit on my throne'? Why then has Adonijah become king?" (1 Kgs 1:13). The words, "your servant," refers to Bathsheba, but an explicit reference to David giving this promise to her is difficult to find (2 Sam 11–12). The story in Chronicles mentions God's promise to David, but it does not say that David repeated it to Bathsheba (1 Chr 28:1–10). Nor does the text mention David swearing to Bathsheba to name her son Solomon as his successor. This raises a question about why Nathan urges Bathsheba to go and speak these words to David (1 Kgs 1:13). Perhaps Nathan tells her about God's promise to David so that she will claim it, even if David never made an oath to her. God's prophecy is more valid than David's oath to his wife, and so it seems that Nathan's words were meant to urge Bathsheba to motivate David to act as early as possible.[3] This suggests that a prophet can use his knowledge of the prevailing situation of a country to intervene in order to select the right king for the nation. Nathan wanted the dynasty of David to continue in Israel through Solomon because he knew the promise that God had communicated to David (2 Sam 7:11–17). So he promises to follow her visit to the king and to support her (1 Kgs 1:14).

1:15–21 Bathsheba Reminds David of His Promise

After listening to Nathan, Bathsheba goes to David, bows down, and pays respect to the king according to the custom (1:15–16a). David asks the reason for her visit and tribute (1:16b). In her reply, she uses the royal court language of respect, calling the king "my lord" and addressing herself as his "servant" rather than "wife" or "queen." Her speech includes a reminder, information, and a request for action. First, she reminds David about God's promise to make Solomon rule the country as his successor. She does not begin with the controversial information about Adonijah. Instead, by reminding David of God's promise, she alerts him that he should do something before his death. Second, she informs David that Adonijah has declared himself king without David's consent. She tells David about the sacrifice and feast given by Adonijah and how he invited other officials and priests while leaving out Solomon (1:18–19). Third, she asks David to tell all the people of Israel that his choice is for Solomon to succeed him on the throne (1:20). She wants the king to declare this choice publicly so that the people will not believe the words of Adonijah, as the king's words carry authority and demand the people's obedience. If David fulfills this promise, she and Solomon will be safe. If he does not, they will be treated as offenders and possibly be put to death (1:21). Her request is both for the nation and for her and Solomon's lives.

---

3. Simon J. DeVries, *1 Kings*, WBC, vol. 12 (Waco, Texas: Word Books, 1985), 15.

1:22–27 Nathan Confirms the Words of Bathsheba

After Bathsheba makes her request, the prophet Nathan enters David's room to pay respect to the king and confirm that Bathsheba is telling the truth (1:22–23). In Nathan's speech to the king, he asks if David is planning to make Adonijah the next king (1:24). Nathan informs the king that Adonijah has provided a celebratory feast for a group of followers and declared himself king, adding that the people accept his kingship and greet him by saying, "Long live King Adonijah" (1:25). This phrase is used to greet the king with a wish that he will live longer and be a channel of blessing to his people. Furthermore, Nathan launches a complaint that he and Solomon were not invited to the feast in order to reveal that Adonijah's action was illegal and secret (1:26). Finally, Nathan asks the king to tell Nathan who should sit on the throne after David dies (1:27). In this request, Nathan makes it clear that he is not accepting Adonijah as king and is looking to David to pronounce Solomon as his successor.

1:28–40 David Appoints Solomon as His Successor

After hearing Bathsheba's and Nathan's speeches, King David responds. This unit has three sections: David calls Bathsheba and conveys his wish (1:28–31); David calls his officials to anoint Solomon as king (1:32–37); and Zadok, the priest, anoints Solomon and declares him as king (1:38–40).

First, the king says, "Call in Bathsheba," which is an official term used to communicate a message (1:28). Bathsheba is brought to the king to listen to his order. The king swears to Bathsheba, using the formulaic phrase, "As surely as the LORD lives" (1:29). This phrase affirms that David worships the Lord, the God of Israel. David says that he believes in this eternal and living God because David has experienced God's deliverances in his life (1:29–30). Swearing in the name of a living God has validity because the living God is a witness, who alone can help people fulfill their oath. David's oath is very specific, promising that Bathsheba's son, Solomon, will succeed David as king and sit on the throne in David's place. David swears in front of the bodyguards, Nathan, and Bathsheba, assuring her that he will implement what he has sworn to her in the name of the Lord by saying, "I will surely carry out this very day" (1:30). When someone swears in the name of the Lord in Israel, the person is responsible to fulfill his or her promise. Bathsheba thanks the king and wishes him to live forever (1:31). Bathsheba leaves with confidence that she can bring about political change with Nathan's help because of David's personal oath.

Next the king summons Zadok, the priest, Nathan, and Benaiah and orders them to anoint Solomon and make him king over Israel (1:32). The king gives clear instructions about how they should make Solomon a king. First, they should go with David's servants, which might include his bodyguards in order to protect Solomon. Second, Solomon should ride on David's mule to Gihon (1:33). This symbolic procession announces that Solomon is the king. Jesus also rode on a mule, and all his followers hailed him as the king of the Jews (Matt 21:1–9). Third, Solomon should be anointed by a priest in the presence of a prophet (1 Kgs 1:34–35). The prophet represents God's will that Solomon is the divine choice; the priest fulfills God's will by anointing the chosen person.

David's officials agree with David (1:36–37) and carry out his command (1:38). Zadok brings the horn of anointing oil from the "sacred tent" (1:39), which refers to the tabernacle, the place where the people came to worship and offer sacrifices. They blow the trumpet. All the people watch Solomon's anointing and shout, "Long live King Solomon!" (1:39). Having symbolically accepted Solomon as king, they rejoice by playing the pipes and following the king in a procession (1:40).

Adonijah's self-proclamation as king (1:5) contrasts with Solomon's rightful appointment through David's declaration and the support of the prophet and priest. If leaders are going to lead God's people according to the will and promises of the everlasting and living God, then they need to be chosen and selected according to divine principles. The Apostles emphasized these principles as well (Acts 6; 1 Tim 3:1–12; 2 Pet 1:5–19).

1:41–48 Solomon Becomes King

The sound of trumpets, pipes, and flutes reverberate so loudly in the city that, in the distance, Adonijah and his followers hear the sound just as they are finishing the feast (1 Kgs 1:41). Joab senses that something is going against Adonijah's plan, and his suspicion is confirmed by Jonathan, son of Abiathar. But Adonijah expects good news from Jonathan, calling him a worthy or reliable man (1:42).

Jonathan arrives with details about the events going on in the city (1:43). David has made Solomon the king of Israel. David sent Zadok, Nathan, Benaiah, and other Kerethites and Pelethites to put Solomon on David's mule, a symbolic action that signals David's desire for Solomon to succeed him (1:44). The priest and prophet together anointed Solomon at Gihon (1:45). The people accepted Solomon as king with sounds of cheer, joy, and rejoicing.

Solomon has taken the seat of the royal throne in the city (1:46), and all the court officials have accepted David's decision. Their greeting, "May your God make Solomon's name more famous than yours and his throne greater than yours!" (1:47), conveys their conviction that David has obeyed God's will, and therefore Solomon's fame and rule will be greater than David's, which is their wish and expectation. Jonathan also informs them that David responded to the court officials by thanking the God of Israel for enabling him to select a successor and see his wish fulfilled (1:48).

The responsibility of any leader is to find a suitable successor who is worthy of leadership and train him or her in accordance with the divine approval and plan. Many leaders try to promote their sons and daughters or kith and kin to the top positions, whether or not they are suitable or chosen by God.

1:49–53 Solomon Forgives Adonijah

After hearing the full story from Jonathan, Adonijah's guests are afraid, and so they desert Adonijah and run away from that place (1:49). Adonijah panics and runs to hold the horns of the altar of the tent of the meeting to seek asylum (1:50). In ancient Israel, a provision was made for those seeking asylum from vengeance. They could flee to the cities and stay there until justice is served (Num 35:9–15). Why Adonijah ran to hold the horns of the altar is uncertain. Adonijah knows that Solomon can kill him for conspiracy by declaring himself the king. Holding onto the horns, he pleads for assurance that Solomon will not put him to death with the sword (1 Kgs 1:51). Solomon swears to show mercy on Adonijah, but he makes certain conditions. Adonijah must prove himself as worthy by not rebelling against Solomon. He must be honest to the king. He should not do anything evil to the king or the nation of Israel. If he remains faithful to Solomon, he will not be punished. If he does not remain faithful, he will be put to death (1:52). After hearing Adonijah's reply to these conditions, Solomon sends his men to bring Adonijah from the altar. Adonijah bows down to Solomon to save his own life. Solomon spares Adonijah's life and lets him go free (1:53).

The story of this royal power struggle challenges us to study the theology of leadership. Whether leading a family, church, or nation, godly leaders must follow God's divine plan and value biblical principles for leadership. Not everyone who is ambitious for position and power can be a leader, for leaders must be chosen by God, called by the church, the community, or an institution and also be publicly accepted by those who will follow them.

1 KINGS 2:1–46

SOLOMON ESTABLISHES THE KINGDOM

The next step for Solomon is to establish his rule. The first part of 1 Kings 2 recounts David's instructions to Solomon about how to establish the kingdom cumulating with David's death (2:1–12). The second part describes how Solomon follows his father's work and takes the necessary steps to consolidate his position (2:13–46). Two phrases govern this chapter: "His rule was firmly established" (2:12) and "The kingdom was now established in Solomon's hands" (2:46). This chapter reveals how politics and religion are interrelated when establishing a monarchical kingdom.

2:1–12 DAVID'S FINAL INSTRUCTIONS TO SOLOMON

This section has three parts: David's instructions to Solomon to follow the Lord (2:1–4), to punish those who worked against the king and to reward those who worked for him (2:5–9), and an account of the death of David, years of reign, and the beginning of Solomon's reign (2:10–12).

2:1–4 Obedience to the Lord

"When the time drew near for David to die" (2:1), David realizes that he should pass on the leadership to Solomon with final instructions, just as other leaders had done right before stepping down from their leadership. Moses, for example, gave final instructions to Joshua and the people of Israel at the banks of the Jordan before he died (Deut 5:1–33).

The phrase, "I am about to go the way of all the earth," is a cultural expression for death (2:2). In many cultures, the words "death" or "dying" are avoided when referring to an old person in favor of a more polite expression of respect that affirms how the aging person has lived a full life and is not dying prematurely. For example, Tamil culture uses the phrase *iyarkkai eithal'* that means, "joining with the nature," acknowledging that death is part of life. David describes his death as a natural part of life, since all people on this earth have to die one day. His words do not express sorrow but rather a sense of completion and satisfaction.

David begins his instruction by encouraging Solomon to be strong physically, spiritually, and mentally. Moses exhorts Joshua in a similar fashion

(Josh 1:1–7). To lead Israel, a king needs to be physically and mentally strong to understand the political situation, analyze problems, and draw conclusions while also controlling his emotions. He should also have an unshakeable faith in God and maintain relationships of trust with others. In addition to being strong, David tells Solomon to "act like a man." This Hebrew word (*ish*) not only refers to the masculine gender but also expresses the nature and qualities of adulthood or humanity in leadership. To "act like a man" means to be human. In Asian culture, men are expected to be bold and courageous, and women are expected to be gentle and soft. Indian culture even states that men should not cry about problems or hardships, but women should. In biblical narratives, however, a number of women act boldly (e.g., Rahab, Josh 2:2–16; Deborah, Judges 4–5). David is not contrasting manly and womanly behavior here but is exhorting Solomon to remember himself as a human king and to act accordingly, that is, with humility and dependence in God.

David's exhortation emphasizes the spiritual qualities of observing God's commandments, obeying the Lord, and practicing God's instructions written in the law of Moses (1 Kgs 2:3). The phrases "walk in obedience," "keep his decrees," "watch how they live," and "walk faithfully" (2:3–4) reflect Deuteronomic language (compare Deut 4:29; 6:2; 8:6; 11:1) that emphasizes following the law of Moses and being faithful to the covenantal relationship. When Solomon does these, God will bless Solomon and fulfill his promise.

According to the Deuteronomic law, God's blessing on a king is conditional (Deut 17:18–20). Though God promises to bless David's kingship without laying down any conditions (2 Sam 7:11–16), David makes the conditions of the Deuteronomic law mandatory for Solomon because David knows that the people of Israel – as a covenanted community – are required to follow Yahweh and obey the law (Deut 6:1–3). David is aware of the cause and effect of disobedience as it was laid down by Yahweh (Deut 28:1–68). The phrase, "The LORD may keep his promise to me" (1 Kgs 2:4), refers to Nathan's prophecy to David (2 Sam 7:11–16), which will continue through the descendants of the family of David. Having established the monarchy and ruled Israel for forty years, David is concerned about continuing his dynasty and ensuring that his descendants will lead the nation for many years to come.

2:5–9 Retribution and Reward

David is concerned about the adversaries who might hinder Solomon's rule. So he advises his son to take appropriate action against Joab (2:5–6) and Shimei

(2:8–9). He also wants Solomon to show kindness to the sons of Barzillai who were gracious to him (2:7).

2:5–6 Action against Joab

David brings charges against Joab, the chief commander of his army, for killing Abner and Amasa during peacetime (1 Kgs 2:5). Joab is identified as the son of Zeruiah, who is Abigail's sister (2 Sam 17:25). His name "Joab" means "Yahweh is father."

Abner had planned to segregate some of the northern tribes and to appoint Ish-Bosheth, the son of Saul, to rule them. Joab considered Abner and his plan to be a threat to David's rule in Hebron over the tribe of Judah, and so he went to fight against Abner. In that fight, Abner killed Asahel, Joab's brother. Joab was waiting for a chance to kill Abner. But David and Abner made a peace treaty when Abner promised to bring the northern tribes to accept David as their king and to reject Ish-Bosheth (2 Sam 3:17–21). Joab did not like David's compromise and killed Abner (1 Kgs 2:5). David lamented Abner's brutal death and gave him a state funeral, saying that a "commander and a great man has fallen in Israel this day" (2 Sam 3:38). During Abner's funeral, David said he was not responsible for Abner's death (2 Sam 3:31–39). But, he could not punish Joab for killing Abner because Joab had been loyal to David's rule.

Amasa was the son of Jether and Abigail (2 Sam 17:25). He joined Absalom as the commander of his rebel army and fought against David. David forgave Amasa, saying, "Are you not my own flesh and blood?" (2 Sam 19:13). But Joab killed Amasa (1 Kgs 2:5). So, David regards Joab as dangerous and tells Solomon, "Do not let his grey head go down to the grave in peace" (1 Kgs 2:6). Joab deserves punishment because he violated human rights in spite of his loyalty to the king.

2:7 Favor to the Sons of Barzillai

David then asks Solomon to remember the sons of Barzillai with kindness (1 Kgs 2:7). Barzillai and his family helped David when Absalom was trying to kill him in Mahanaim (2 Sam 17:27–29). At that critical moment, they protected David and his men and provided them with food, water, milk, and assistance. David wants Solomon to repay them with kindness (1 Kgs 2:7). The Hebrew word for "kindness" here (*hesed*) connotes continuous love and favor. The idiomatic expression, "eating at the table," includes more than the literal sense of dining with Solomon every day; it includes benefits such as a royal allowance of food, clothing, housing, and land that will support them

(2 Sam 9:7; 2 Kgs 25:30). While David received temporary help from this family, he wants Solomon to repay it continually. This gesture reveals David's generosity along with his gratitude to those who have helped him.

2:8–9 Action against Shimei

David finally instructs Solomon to punish Shimei (1 Kgs 2:8–9). When David was fleeing for his life and came to the town of Bahurim in the territory of Benjamin, Shimei, the son of Gera, cursed David and threw stones at him to drive him out because Shimei belonged to Saul's clan and wanted Saul's dynasty to rule the Israelites (2 Sam 16:5–8). Shimei accused David of being a "murderer" who was trying to rule in the place of Saul (16:7).

In spite of Shimei's actions, David remained calm. David did not know if the curse from Shimei was from the Lord (16:10). Wanting to avoid another painful clash, David said, "Leave him alone; let him curse" (16:11). Later, Shimei confessed his mistake and asked David for pardon (19:19–23). David accepted this confession and made an oath that he himself would not kill Shimei by the sword (1 Kgs 2:8). Keeping his word, he reminds Solomon that Shimei is not an innocent man and Solomon is to use his wisdom in punishing Shimei: "you will know what to do to him" (1 Kgs 2:9). David's oath to Shimei will no longer be valid after David dies.

2:10–12 David's Death and Solomon's Reign

After giving these instructions, David "rested with his ancestors," a phrase that means that David has passed away from this world and joined his ancestors. The Israelites believed that the dead go to Sheol, the name for the world under the earth where all the dead are gathered. David is buried in Jerusalem, which is also known as the City of David (2:10).

The narrator concludes the story of David with a statement about the number of years he ruled in Hebron, seven years, and Jerusalem, thirty-three years (2:11). His forty-year reign covers a long period. David was a good king with powerful leadership and efficient administration. He will be the standard by which all subsequent kings will be evaluated.

With David's death, Solomon "sat on the throne of his father David" (2:12). From the outset, the narrator informs the readers "his rule was firmly established" (2:12b).

1 KINGS 2:1–46

2:13–46 SOLOMON ESTABLISHES HIS THRONE

The second section of 1 Kings 2 narrates how Solomon carried out David's instructions to deal with Joab and Shimei. In addition, he deals with two others who oppose him: Adonijah and Abiathar the priest. This section thus covers punishments against Adonijah (2:13–25), Abiathar the priest (2:26–27), Joab (2:28–35), and Shimei (2:36–46).

The monarchy, initiated with Saul as the first king, continued through David, who established it by consolidating the throne. Though he faced external and internal rivalry, he ruled for forty years, and yet the problem of internal rivalry continued. Those who supported Absalom and Adonijah would not have wanted the descendants of their family to accept Solomon as the king for the entire Israelite community. The second section ends with a note that the kingdom has now been established in Solomon's hand (2:46). Any leader who inherits a large kingdom riddled with internal rivalry and then seeks to establish it firmly will need courage, faith, and wisdom.

2:13–25 Adonijah's Request and Punishment

After facing defeat, Adonijah accepts the kingship of Solomon and then comes to Bathsheba with a request. This unit has three inner sections: the dialogue between Adonijah and Bathsheba (2:13–18), the dialogue between Bathsheba and Solomon (2:19–22), and Solomon's pronouncement of the death penalty for Adonijah (2:23–25).

In the first unit, Adonijah approaches peacefully Bathsheba, the queen mother, without any political motive against Solomon. He acknowledges that the kingship has been given to Solomon by the divine will and plan of the Lord (2:15). He wants her to speak to Solomon on his behalf; he wants Abishag, the young Shunammite who warmed David, as his wife (2:17; compare 1:1–4). Bathsheba says she will speak to Solomon (2:18). She doesn't see the immensity of Adonijah's request or she tells it to provoke Solomon. Either way, when Solomon hears Adonijah's request, he regards it as a serious threat to his kingship. He says, "Why do you request Abishag the Shunammite for Adonijah? You might as well request the kingdom for him" (2:22).

Solomon connects Adonijah's request for Abishag as equivalent to a request for the kingdom, for if Abishag becomes Adonijah's wife, then Adonijah could legally claim a share of the kingdom for Abishag. The kingdom would then have to be divided between Bathsheba and Abishag, and Solomon and Adonijah would have to share the throne by dividing the territory. In this plot, Adonijah could become a king parallel to Solomon and plan to defeat

Solomon at a later stage, thereby inheriting the entire kingdom. Previously, Absalom attempted a similar strategy by taking David's concubines to inherit the kingdom (2 Sam 16:21). Solomon concludes that Adonijah is using a similar strategy, and so he regards his request as treason. Similar attempts to divide the kingdom between the sons of the ruling wife and the concubines of the ruling king can be noticed throughout the monarchical history of India and other countries in Asia. This kind of strife continues today amongst polygamous families of Hindus and Muslims in India, who have to divide and share businesses or properties among many sons and daughters.

Solomon also connects Adonijah's request to the betrayals of Abiathar and Joab. They had wanted to make Adonijah king. In Solomon's mind, if Adonijah gets the kingdom through this kind of scheming and support, it is equivalent to getting the kingdom for Abiathar and Joab as well. So, Solomon pronounces death penalty for Adonijah (1 Kgs 2:23–25).

Solomon swears in the name of the Lord. If one swears by the name of the Lord, that person should fulfill his oath, or it will be regarded as misusing the name of the Lord (Deut 23:21). Solomon believes that he has come to power because God is fulfilling the promise made to David, for God is a living God who is still acting in history. As such, if Solomon does not foil Adonijah's attempts to become king, he is refusing to fulfill God's will for the dynasty of David (2:23–24). Solomon orders Benaniah, son of Jehoiada, to kill Adonijah, and he obeys (2:25). Although Solomon forgave him earlier (1:50–53), now he sees Adonijah as a continuous threat and ends his life. Solomon's swearings, "May God deal with me" and "As surely as the LORD lives," proclaim his strong faith in God (2:23). He is acting as God's viceroy.

Politicians in democratic countries today often seek to "religionize" politics and politicize religion to gain their agendas.[1] They are not acting with pure motives; they are promoting their personal agendas in the name of religion.

2:26–27 Abiathar's Punishment

Solomon then deals with Abiathar who had sided with Adonijah to make him the king in the place of Solomon (1:7; 2:22). Instead of killing Abiathar for joining Adonijah's group, Solomon removes Abiathar from his priestly position at Jerusalem and asks him to return to his hometown of Anathoth. Solomon

---

1. J. B. Jeyaraj, "Religion and Politics in Ancient Israel: Interactions and Issues," in *Integral Mission: The Way Forward*, ed. C. V. Mathew (Tiruvalla, India: Christava Sahitya Samithi, 2006), 113–128.

spares Abiathar's life for two reasons. First, Abiathar carried the ark of the Lord when David brought it to Jerusalem (2:26a). Second, Abiathar shared David's hardships during the time he was fleeing Saul (2:26b). Abiathar's punishment (2:27) is a fulfillment of the punishment of the Lord that was spoken at Shiloh about Eli's family for failing to minister honestly (1 Sam 3:11–14). Abiathar was a descendant of Eli's son, Ahimelech (1 Sam 22:17–20).[2] This event reveals the biblical pattern of prophecy and fulfillment.

2:28–35 Joab's Punishment

Solomon then punishes Joab, just as David had requested (2:5–6). When Joab hears about the punishment of Abiathar, he runs to the tent of the meeting (the worshiping center) and hides behind the altar (2:28), like Adonijah did earlier (1:50). Knowing this, Solomon orders Benaiah to strike Joab even in the tent of the Lord (2:29). Benaiah does not want to kill Joab in the vicinity of the altar, and so he asks him to come out of that place (2:30). Joab replies fearfully, "No, I will die here." Joab is struggling to save his life. Perhaps, Joab wants a trial. Solomon interprets his words literally and orders Benaiah to kill him by the altar in the tent of the Lord.

He sees killing Joab by the altar would clear him and his family "of the guilt of the innocent blood that Joab shed" (2:31). He is referring to how Joab killed Abner and Amasa during peacetime (2:32; compare 2:5–6). In this way, the guilt for shedding the blood of Abner and Amasa will remain with Joab and his descendants forever rather than David's family. Killing innocent people, as Joab did, carries the guilt of that bloodshed. By executing punishment on those who killed the innocent people, thereby bringing them to accountability, clears Solomon of the guilt (2:33). Leaders who fail to punish culprits will lose the blessing of God. Solomon believes this idea firmly, and so he punishes those who are guilty and claims God's blessing for the family and throne of David in the name of the Lord. Solomon is acting justly and not brutally, according to the instruction of his father, and so he deserves God's blessing; God will strengthen his throne. Benaiah obeys Solomon and kills Joab by the altar and buries him in his hometown, in the country (2:34). When he returns, Solomon promotes Benaiah to become the commander of Solomon's army, a position Joab once held (2:35a). Similarly, he appoints Zadok as the

---

2. C. F. Keil and F. Delitzsch, *Joshua, Judges, Ruth, 1 and 2 Samuel*, COTOT, vol. 2 (Peabody, MA: Hendrickson, 2006), 517–518.

high priest in Jerusalem, a position held by Abiathar (2:35b) because Zadok sided with him (1:32–35).

2:36–46 Shimei's Punishment

Solomon finally punishes Shimei son of Gera, a Benjaminite, as David instructed him (2:8–9). Shimei had cursed David, but David had sworn not to kill him (2:8). But at his deathbed, he warned Solomon not to treat him as an innocent man but deal with him prudently (2:9). According to David's instructions, Solomon does not kill Shimei but punishes him by keeping him under house arrest. Shimei is confined to his house in Jerusalem and instructed not to cross the Kidron valley (2:36–37a). If he violates this condition, he will be put to death (2:37b). Shimei agrees to this condition, but after three years, he goes beyond the boundary in search of two of his slaves, who ran away to Achish at Gath, and he brings them back to Jerusalem (2:38–40).

When Solomon hears about Shimei's violation, he informs him how he has broken the agreement and falsely sworn by the Lord (3:42). He has neither kept the oath to the Lord nor kept Solomon's command (3:43). He has always been wrong and the Lord was repaying his wrongdoing (2:44). Shimei is responsible for his own death (2:44–45). With those reminders, he pronounces the death penalty, and Benaiah carries it out and kills Shimei (2:46).

By inflicting these punishments, Solomon was securing David's throne "before the LORD forever" (2:45). The narrator concludes by saying, "The kingdom was now established in Solomon's hands" (2:46). As ruthless as these acts may seem, each individual was given mercy and kindness until he failed to accept it. Adonijah was first given a warning; then, the death penalty. Abiathar was not killed but dismissed from his role as the high priest in Jerusalem. Joab killed innocent people, and as David requested, Solomon inflicted punishment on him for shedding innocent blood. Shimei was given grace to live in his own home in Jerusalem. But when he violated, Solomon punished him. Biblical punishment is not blind, as in terrorism. Instead, people are given grace and when they disobey God and violate grace, they are punished. This remains a warning to us all.

1 KINGS 3:1–28
GOD'S GIFT OF WISDOM FOR SOLOMON

1 Kings 3 is well-known to many Christians because it speaks of the wisdom of Solomon, which helped him to discern and render justice, strengthen his administration, and achieve the construction of the temple and palace – the key marks of his reign that raised him to fame. Seminars on leadership highlight the way that Solomon received wisdom from God and then practiced it. In Sunday schools, children are encouraged to seek the gift of wisdom and excel in their studies and competitive exams to reach a high position in their future careers. This chapter has three sections: Solomon's marriage, his stay in the City of David, and commitment to God (3:3); the dream at Gibeon and Solomon's request for wisdom (3:4–15); and a test case of Solomon's wise judgment (3:16–28).

3:1–3 SOLOMON'S MARRIAGE AND COMMITMENT TO GOD

The narrative does not mention how many years have passed since Solomon punished his adversaries and established the throne, but scholars think that at least three years could have passed (2:39). Because there are no longer any internal threats, Solomon is free to marry and settle down (3:1). At the same time, he has the task of building the temple (3:2) as he was walking according to the instructions David had given him (3:3).

3:1 Solomon's Marriage and Stay in the City of David

Solomon marries the daughter of Pharaoh, the king of Egypt, for political alliance (3:1a). Alliances between nations by a covenant or treaty often included giving and taking sons and daughters in marriage. This custom kept peace between kingdoms, avoided war or territorial occupation, and promoted trade and commerce. The Israelites had been warned not to marry people from other regions (Deut 7:1–4); Egypt was not included in that list. As such, Solomon was not committing sin against the Lord. His marriage was unlike Ahab marrying Jezebel, the daughter of Ethbaal, the king of Sidonians that begins the worship of Baal in Israel (16:31–33).

Solomon's marriage is not inter-religious marriage but a political alliance. Both the OT and NT advise against inter-religious marriage because the spouses of other religions can bring their gods and intermingle their worship with the worship of the Lord God (Deut 7:1–4; 2 Cor 6:14–17). However, the Bible does not forbid inter-racial, inter-cultural, inter-denominational, and inter-national marriages between Christians or Israelites. Boaz married Ruth, a Moabite (Ruth 4:9–10). Solomon marrying an Egyptian princess for political alliance is not wrong. However, he needs to be cautious not to intermingle with the religion of Egypt. His marriage for political alliance places trust in the king of another nation, which questions his strong faith in the God of Israel.

After marriage, he and his wife settle in the City of David "until he finished building his palace and the temple of the LORD, and the wall around Jerusalem" (3:1b). The kingdom needs a palace for him and his new bride to live, a temple in the capital where the people can come to worship and offer sacrifices, and a wall around Jerusalem to protect the city from external enemies. Although David brought the ark of the covenant to Jerusalem, making the city acceptable as both a political and religious capital, the temple had not yet been constructed.[1] So, Solomon stays in the City of David and focuses on building the palace, temple, and wall.

3:2 The Absence of the Temple

The people continue to worship the Lord in high places (3:2a). Even the royal king and his family still worship and offer sacrifices in high places (3:4). The term "high places" in Hebrew (*bamah*) refers to a simple stone altar erected under a tree on a hilltop or in a valley without a proper building or shed over it (Deut 12:2). People go and offer sacrifices with the help of a Levi priest who works in such places.

The Canaanites used such high places to worship their gods and offer sacrifices to pray for the fertility of the land and for children for the family. Some even offered their sons and daughters on such altar to the god of Molek, which the Lord God forbid (Lev 18:21). During the time of the judges, the Israelites joined with the Canaanites and Midianites to worship Baal and Asherah on such high places, believing that the fertility of their land came from these agricultural deities (Judg 6:1–6).

Solomon and the people, however, weren't worshiping in such foreign-gods' high places. They were worshiping at Israel's own high places, for example, the

---

1. Bright appreciates David's wise action of placing the ark in Jerusalem, which had been a neutral territory belonging to Jebusites. This action binds all the tribes to the new capital and protects the sacred traditions of the past. Bright, *History of Israel*, 196.

one in Gibeon (1 Kgs 3:4a) because "a temple had not yet been built for the Name of the LORD" (3:2b). The Law speaks of a centralized worshiping center where God will place his name and there alone should the people worship him (Deut 12:1–14). When they do, they should destroy all other high places of worship. Since Solomon hasn't yet built that temple in Jerusalem, the people and he are worshiping in high places, such as the one in Gibeon (1 Kgs 3:4).

3:3 Solomon's Commitment to God

Even without the temple built, Solomon's commitment to God is clear: "Solomon showed his love for the LORD by walking according to the instructions given him by his father David" (3:3a). Right before his death, David said to Solomon, "Be strong, act like a man, and observe what the LORD your God requires: Walk in obedience to him, and keep his decrees and commands, his laws and regulations, as written in the Law of Moses" (2:2b–3a). Just as David instructed, Solomon expressed his love for God by obeying his laws.

Since he hasn't yet built the temple, he offers sacrifices and burned incense on the high places (3:3b). One such place was at Gibeon (3:4). As mentioned earlier, this was not the high places of Canaanites or Midianites; it was where the Israelites worshiped until the temple was built.

As the subsequent chapters show, Solomon's rule will reveal the tension between Solomon's love for God and his love for worldly pleasure and fame (4:1–11:42). At the same time, he began his rule just as his father David did, by loving God with all his heart.

3:4–15 THE DREAM AND SOLOMON'S REQUEST FOR WISDOM

Individuals often encounter divine revelation in worshiping centers. Abraham, for example, received the divine revelation of God's promises while worshiping the Lord and offering sacrifices, either before or after the divine revelation (Gen 15:10; 22:15–16). The places where God appeared to individuals in the biblical narrative have become important worship centers. Gibeon in the northwest of Jerusalem is such an example. Originally, it was a Canaanite city. The Gibeonites tricked Joshua and made a peace treaty to save their lives from the invasion of the Israelites (Josh 9:3–27). Soon thereafter, Gibeon became a prominent center of worship for Israel because the tabernacle was kept there. David left Zadok, the priest, along with his fellow priests, to offer burnt offerings before the tabernacle in Gibeon, and the tabernacle remained in Gibeon even after the ark of the covenant was moved to Jerusalem (1 Chr 16:39–40). Gibeon was allotted to the tribe of Benjamin (Josh 21:17).

Although of the tribe of Judah, Solomon goes to Gibeon to offer sacrifices (1 Kgs 3:4a) perhaps because it is near to Jerusalem. Solomon offers a thousand burnt offerings on that altar (3:4b). In light of the history recounted above, this verse suggests that Solomon is worshiping in the tabernacle. Solomon is offering numerous sacrifices to express his love and thanksgiving to God for helping him in establishing the kingdom. A king can make so many offerings because he has ample resources.

At Gibeon, God appears to Solomon during the night in a dream (3:5a). He does not appear because of these numerous offerings. Divine revelation is based on God's initiative – not our merits, offerings of huge sums of money, sacrifices, or building projects. God communicated with people through dreams and visions throughout the biblical narrative (Gen 17:1–22; Exod 3:1–4:17; Judg 13:2–5). Similarly, he appears to Solomon and asks Solomon to make a request for anything and he will grant it to him (1 Kgs 3:5b). This invitation is not meant to test Solomon to see if he will ask for the right gift but to reveal that the Lord is with Solomon and is concerned with his rule. When the living and eternal God wants to bless people, he will make them promises and grant them gifts. God wants Solomon to rule the nation properly, and so any gift from God should be used to benefit the Israelites. Today, prosperity sermons emphasize individual prosperity, but the biblical message makes it clear that all the gifts of God are meant to benefit people. God asks all leaders who receive gifts to be channels of blessing to their communities. A gift from God is not meant to be kept and enjoyed for personal prosperity but to share with others.

In responding to God's invitation, Solomon acknowledges God's kindness to his family, particularly to David, his father, whom he describes as God's servant (3:6). Kings in Israel are not masters but servants of God. They are servants of God and people. Kings represent God to his people and vice versa. Kings are political leaders and guardians of Israel's faith and promoters of Yahweh's worship. They take care of the community of Yahweh by providing welfare, justice, and security. Solomon affirms that his father, David, was faithful to the Lord, righteous, and upright in heart. Thus, he fulfilled his role as a servant of both God and people.

While Solomon recognizes God's kindness to David, he connects it with David's faithfulness. Because David was obedient to the Lord, he enjoyed the kindness and blessings of God. Even Solomon's ability to continue David's line on the throne is due to the kindness of God. In remembering this, Solomon echoes David's instructions during the transfer of power (2:2–4), recognizing that he needs the same kindness and blessings because the Lord made him king (3:7). Solomon claims that the God of David is his God, and he addresses himself as the servant of the Lord and "a little child." The phrase "little child" does not refer to his age. Some commentators think that Solomon was already married and had fathered Rehoboam before becoming king.[2] Instead, it refers to his youthfulness and inexperience in administration. Solomon is using this cultural expression about his unworthiness to humble himself before the Lord. Solomon's sense of his inadequacy to be able to lead the chosen people of Israel, who are numerous, prompts him to ask God for a discerning heart so that he can govern the nation and be able to distinguish between right and wrong (3:8–9). The phrase "discerning heart" is "hearing heart" in Hebrew. In the Israelite society, "hearing" means "listening carefully and obeying" or implementing the message that one has heard. In ancient days, people believed that the heart was the seat of our emotions and wills. Solomon is asking for the gift of being able to listen to the people and advise them properly to govern them well. Listening is a basic requirement for all of us, and a listening heart is one that can exercise discernment. The gift of discernment helps a leader distinguish between right and wrong to render fair justice.

The Lord's response to Solomon is positive. First, the Lord is pleased with Solomon for choosing the gift of listening rather than asking for wealth, long life, or the death of his enemies (3:10–12). Often, people in power ask God for wealth, fame, long life, and protection from those who might be a threat to them. These are all worldly values that Solomon does not prioritize. God is pleased by Solomon's request for a discerning (hearing) heart and offers him a "wise" and "understanding" heart (3:12). God grants Solomon wisdom and understanding, which is more important for a king than wealth and fame. Wisdom (*hokmah*) is not academic knowledge but the practical knowledge of knowing right from wrong. Godly wisdom comes from God alone and can be gained only by knowing God and daily listening to his voice, attending to the guidance of the Spirit, meditating on his words, praying, and evaluating our heart and actions. Proverbs instructs us to seek wisdom if we want to be wise in conducting our lives on this earth (Prov 1:7). God knows that Solomon needs discernment and adds wisdom to discernment.

God also blesses Solomon with wealth and honor, although he did not ask for them (1 Kgs 3:13). They are consequences of the way he administers, with wisdom and discernment. A leader gains respect and honor by the way

---

2. Hens-Piazza, *1–2 Kings*, 38.

s/he administers people wisely, upholding justice and protecting human rights. While the leader may not seek honor, it will come to him/her automatically as people watch his/her life and administration and enjoy welfare and justice. Solomon is endowed with so much of God's blessing that no one will equal him during his lifetime.

God knows that Solomon needs protection from enemy attacks to provide security for the people of Israel. God assures Solomon that he will have a long life, which includes protection from enemies, diseases, or starvation (3:14b). However, Solomon's long life is conditional; he has to obey the laws and commandments of the Lord, just as his father kept them during his lifetime (3:14a). The phrase, "as David your father did" to describe obeying God and following his laws, will echo throughout the narratives in 1–2 Kings, highlighting David as a prototype for evaluating kings. While the blessings of wealth and fame can be earned by a person's own efforts, only God can grant the blessing of a long life because all life comes from God, and so God alone can protect us. To receive the blessing of a long life, the Israelites must keep God's values and principles, as described in the list of blessings and curses in Deuteronomy (chs. 26–29).

After Solomon wakes up from this revelatory dream, he returns to Jerusalem and stands before the ark of the covenant, where he sacrifices burnt offerings and peace offerings, indicating that he accepts both the blessings and condition of the Lord (1 Kgs 3:15a). Then Solomon celebrates his joy with his court officials by giving them a grand feast (3:15b).

3:16–28 A TEST CASE OF SOLOMON'S WISE JUDGMENT

In rural India, problems between people or villages are brought to the *panchayat*, a grassroot governing group of elders, who meet at the town gate. In ancient Israel, people brought their cases before the elders of the town who assembled at the city gate (e.g., Ruth 4:1). After the development of the monarchy in Israel, cases that could not be solved locally were brought to the royal court.

In this particular story, two sex workers bring their dispute to Solomon to demonstrate his wisdom and discernment in deciding the verdict. This unit has three sections: the sex worker's claims (3:16–22), the king's verdict that testifies to his discernment (3:23–27), and the people's praise of Solomon's wisdom and justice (3:28).

3:16–22 Sex Worker's Claims

The two sex workers find favor with Solomon and stand before him for a verdict (3:16). The first one narrates the case: both the women live in the same house and both have babies just three days apart (3:17–18a). There is no one else living with them to be their witnesses (3:18b). One of those nights, while she is asleep, the next lady's baby dies because she accidentally lies on him (3:19). That second sex worker gets up in the middle of the night, takes her dead son and places him next to the first sex worker, and takes her son and puts him next to her breast (3:20). Only the next morning when the first lady wakes up to nurse her son, she realizes he is dead (3:21a). When she looks closely, she realizes that it isn't her son (3:21b).

As she finishes her narrative, the other sex worker objects saying, "No! The living one is my son; the dead one is yours" (3:22a). The first lady objects, and a fight breaks out (3:22b). Each claims the living child as her own in front of Solomon. Since there are no witnesses, Solomon has to identify the culprit on his own.

3:23–27 King's Verdict

Solomon listens and repeats their claims: "This one says, 'My son is alive and your son is dead,' while that one says, 'No! Your son is dead and mine is alive'" (3:23). Both are stern in their claim. So, he commands a servant to bring a sword to him (3:24) and gives an order: "Cut the living child in two and give half to one and half to the other" (3:25). While inanimate objects can be easily divided, dividing a living child is not a good solution. Solomon is not intending to cut the child into two pieces, but he is saying this to find the real mother. As soon as the mother of the living child hears this verdict, she begs the king not to divide the child; moved by her love for her child, she asks the king to give the living child to the other woman (3:26a). The phrase, "deeply moved out of love for her son," shows the biological and psychological attachment of the mother to her child.[3] A mother conceives and carries her child within her womb, and she is attached to her child every moment, thinking of the child, enjoying the feeling of the child growing and moving in her womb, and anticipating the day she will deliver the child. This phrase, "deeply moved" is not merely a metaphor, but an expression of the deep sorrow

---

3. J. B. Jeyaraj, "Biblical Perspective on Children and their Protection," *Children at Risk: Issues and Challenges*, eds. J. B. Jeyaraj, C. Gnanakan, et al. (Delhi, India: SPCK, 2009), 5–18.

and pain that mothers experience when they see their children die in front of them or in an accident or war.

On the other hand, the other woman says, "Neither I nor you shall have him. Cut him in two!" (3:26b). She does not have the same emotion the mother has for her living baby. Hearing her, the king knows what to do: "Give the living baby to the first woman. Do not kill him; she is his mother" (3:27). The scene vividly contrasts the real mother with the one who tells lies. The real mother wants her child to live, even if he will be handed over to the other woman, because she does not want her innocent child to be a victim of dispute. The jealous woman in this event, however, wants the child to be killed. She is envious of the woman who still has a child because her own child has died. The king notices the women's feelings, expressions, and words, and he discerns the real mother and orders his servants to give the living child to her. This scene confirms that God has granted Solomon his request for a listening heart (3:12).

3:28 People's Praise of Solomon

When the news about Solomon's just verdict reaches the public, they praise the king for giving the child to the real mother through the wisdom given to him by God (3:28). This concluding verse justifies Solomon for seeking wisdom from God and practicing it in his judgment among the people. It also illustrates how Solomon, a young king, began his rule following God just as David did.

1 KINGS 4:1–34

SOLOMON'S ADMINISTRATION AND FAME

1 Kings 4 traces Solomon's ongoing steps to reorganize his administration along with the development of his gift of wisdom. This chapter has two units: lists of chief officials (4:1–19); a description of the peaceful life in Israel and Solomon's growing wisdom and fame (4:20–34).[1]

4:1–19 LISTS OF OFFICIALS

When people come to power and take over a top position, they typically try to bring about changes in the administration. As soon as Solomon was enthroned as king, he removed key adversaries who had worked against David and him (ch. 2). Now, he establishes officials to help him rule the nation of Israel (4:1) with orderliness (4:2–19) and prosperity (4:20–34).

4:1–6 Chief Officials

The narrator gives a brief overall statement: "So King Solomon ruled over all Israel" (4:1). Then, he lists the names of the officials within Solomon's administration in order of importance. The highest position is the high priest: Azariah, son of Zadok (4:2). After him are the official secretaries and recorder: Elihoreph, Ahijah, Jehoshaphat (4:3). Commander in chief of the army is Benaiah, son of Jehoiada (4:4a). Benaiah joined Nathan the prophet and Zadok the priest in siding with appointing Solomon as the king and opposed Adonijah (1:8). Later Solomon sent Benaiah to strike down Adonijah (2:25). Solomon repays him by appointing him as the commander in chief. Zadok and Abiathar serve as priests (4:4b) under the high priest of Azariah (4:2). Abiathar was demoted to a simple priesthood and expelled from Jerusalem because he sided with Adonijah (1:7; 2:26–27). In addition, Solomon appointed another Azariah in charge of the district governor (4:5a, 7–19), Zabud as his

---

[1]. The Hebrew text of chapter 4 ends with verse 20. Verses 21 onwards are part of chapter 5. For a discussion, see Gina Hens-Piazza, *1–2 Kings*, 47–48, and John Gray, *I and II Kings: A Commentary*, 129–132.

personal priest and advisor (4:5b), Ahishar as palace administrator (4:6a), and Adoniram in charge of forced labor (4:6b). These men help Solomon rule the people in wisdom and justice.

4:7–19 Districts and Governors

Solomon created twelve districts and appointed governors over each district. The district governors are named in verses 8–19. The land of Canaan had already been divided into twelve territories when the Israelites settled in it. Moses allotted territories to each tribe, except for the tribe of Levi, according to the size of the tribe (Num 26:52–56). Later, Joshua implemented this same scheme of allotment (Joshua 13–19). These territories were not enclosed with a fence or wall, but marked by placing stones engraved with the name of the tribe on the four corners of the border or entrance to the territory.[2] The purpose of creating these twelve districts was to supply provisions for the king and his royal household; each district was responsible to provide all the necessary resources for one month (1 Kgs 4:7). The governors in charge of the districts were required to collect and send these provisions to Jerusalem.

It would be difficult to alter the original borders of the tribal territories and set new boundaries for each tribe, and so Solomon created the new districts within these original territories, identifying certain towns as districts for revenue purposes. These new districts were no longer known by the names of the tribes, but instead by the names of the principal cities and the governors. Though the new districts did not change the borders of the original territories, the significance of the original borders diminished over the years.[3] The new districts became prominent in Solomon's administration, and the burden of supplying provisions and labor for the king developed ill-feelings among the northern tribes towards Solomon (12:4).

The narrator gives descriptions of some of the governors. Ben-Hesed owned Sokoh and all the land of Hepher (4:10). Early readers would have understood the significance of this statement. Ben-Abinadab was married to Taphath, one of the daugthers of Solomon (4:11). Ben-Geber had a large territory under his care: the settlements of Jair, the region of Argob, and "its sixty large walled cities with bronze gate bars" signifying their wealth (4:13). Ahimaaz married another daughter of Solomon, Basemath (4:15). Some of

---

2. For the history of these allotments, see Bright, *History of Israel*, 126–139; Norman K. Gottwald, *The Tribes of Yahweh* (New York: Orbis Books, 1981), 220–227.
3. Bright, *History of Israel*, 217.

the governors were, then, his own sons-in-law. Geber, son of Uri, had the countries of Sihon and Og (4:19), kings whom Moses defeated (Deut 1:4).

India faced a similar situation during the British rule, who divided the land into provinces and districts and introduced a new revenue system that would benefit their rule.[4] They reduced the powers of the local *Zamindars* (landlords) and required them to pay taxes and supply provisions and raw materials for the imperial rule.

4:20–34 LIFE IN THE KINGDOM

In this section, the narrator describes the life of prosperity in the land of Israel. He does so by explaining the carefree lives the people lived in Solomon's vast kingdom (4:20–21), by listing the quantity of provisions that each district provided for the monarchy (4:22–28), and by describing how Solomon's wisdom and fame expanded throughout the nations (4:29–34).

4:20–21 People's Leisure Living

God had promised to Abraham saying, "I will make you a great nation" (Gen 12:2a). As promised, "The people of Judah and Israel were as numerous as the sand on the seashore" during Solomon's reign (1 Kgs 4:20a). In addition, they lived carefree lives: "They ate, they drank and they were happy" (4:20b, 25). Their lives reflect the peace and prosperity the king and the people enjoyed. Solomon's kingdom extended beyond the land of Canaan, touching the borders of the Euphrates, Philistines, and Egypt (4:21a, 24). These kingdoms beyond Israel brought tributes to the king, which might have included money, gifts, and materials, since they were his subjects (4:21b).

4:22–28 Prosperity in the Land

The twelve districts with the governors provided for Solomon's daily provisions (4:22–28). They gave 30 *cors* of the finest flour and sixty *cors* of meal (4:22a). A "*cors*" is equivalent to five metric tons (220 liters).[5] The phrase, "all who came to the king's table" (4:27) suggests that the huge supply was not only for the king and his family, but also for the officials in the administration. They also sent "ten head of stall-fed cattle, twenty of pasture-fed cattle and a hundred sheep and goats, as well as deer, gazelles, roebucks and choice fowl" (4:23).

---

4. B. P. Tyagi, *Agricultural Economics and Rural Development* (Meerut, India: JaiPrakash Nath and Company, 1990), 215–219.
5. The NIV footnote.

Once again, these gifts reflect the prosperity the nation enjoyed. The writer reflects that by listing the vastness of his kingdom (4:24) and the prosperity and calmness of the nation – everyone "lived in safety, everyone under their own vine and under their own fig tree" (4:25).

In addition, Solomon had twelve thousand horses and four thousand chariot horses (4:26). These horses may have been for his army. The Deuteronomic law warned against accumulating horses for one's personal pomp or a temptation to return to Egypt to get more (Deut 17:16). Yet having horses and chariots is unavoidable in the midst of powerful nations that also have their own horses, chariots, and military. Perhaps that was why Solomon had those horses.

Today, many nations spend 50–60 percent of their budget on the military rather than the welfare of the people. In some South Asian countries, basic services, such as health, education, food, and shelter for the poor, are diverted to fund nuclear research and amass weapons for the military. Yet both the Deuteronomic law and the prophet Samuel discourage military buildup and instruct both the leaders and the people of Israel to trust the Lord for their protection and safety and also to let the people enjoy the fruits of their own labor.

People in Solomon's kingdom lived leisurely and prosperous lives: "They ate, they drank and they were happy" (4:20) and they "lived in safety, everyone under their own vine and under their own fig tree" (4:25). Grapes and figs are important food items in the society (see Mic 4:4). A vine is a symbol of prosperity and is also used metaphorically to refer to the chosen Israelites (Isa 5:1–6). Figs are not only used in food, but also to make oil. Fig trees are cultivated alongside grapevines (Luke 13:6), and so the branches of a fig tree and the cluster of green leaves on a grapevine are used together in an idiomatic expression of sitting under one's own vine and fig tree. This idiom expresses a life of peace, prosperity, long life, and security. All these blessings were provided by the able administration of King Solomon, who enabled the people to enjoy their labor without any political threats from outside or any internal conflicts. These statements praise the king and give credit to his policies and administration. However, these verses do not reveal the dangerous situation of the people in Solomon's kingdom. Very soon, their society will face a difficult period (12:1–19). The huge needs and expenses of the administration, along with the burden on the citizens of supplying provisions and labor, resulted in the division of the kingdom. Nevertheless, if a king rules well, then the people will also enjoy prosperity (4:20). The governors of the districts saw to it that "nothing was lacking" in Solomon's kingdom (4:27), including provisions for the livestock in Solomon's barns (4:28). People and leaders lived in peace and prosperity.

4:29–34 Solomon's Growing Wisdom and Fame

This section gives credit to the wisdom and understanding of Solomon for creating revenue districts, appointing chief officials and governors, and developing the country through his able administration (4:29a). His wisdom and knowledge are vast, like sand on the seashore, and cannot be compared with the wisdom of anyone in the four corners of the surrounding region (4:29b). The phrase, "people of the East," refers to those living in Mesopotamia on the eastern side of his country. The "wisdom of Egypt" refers to those living southwest of Israel. Even the people of Ezrahite in the south of Transjordan cannot match the wisdom of Solomon (4:31). Ancient Israelites knew the countries in their surrounding area and those countries in the Mediterranean region that they could reach for trade. Within this limited geographical space, there were many people and schools who were famous for wisdom in places such as Egypt, the eastern countries of Assyria, Babylon, Persia, and Teman in Edom. Yet because of God's gift of wisdom and understanding, Solomon was known to be wiser than anyone in the surrounding region.

By using God's gift of wisdom, Solomon developed a stronger administrative structure than any of the surrounding nations. Three thousand proverbs and more than a thousand songs are attributed to him (4:32). The proverbs of Solomon include parables, similes, metaphors, and riddles. Solomon spoke knowledgeably about plants and trees that grew in the region from Lebanon to Israel, and he had many insights about animals, birds, and fishes (4:33). Some of his proverbs speak about the beauty of flowers, the behavior of animals, and the ethical life of human beings (Prov 30:24–31). It is also possible that he created parks and gardens (Eccl 2:5) and enjoyed their beauty and fragrance (Song of Songs 1:14; 2:3; 6:2).

Rulers and people from all the nations in the surrounding region came to Jerusalem to listen to Solomon's wisdom (1 Kgs 4:33). In summary, God faithfully fulfilled the promises he gave to Solomon. Solomon's administration maintained peace and security for the people and also nurtured the development of knowledge and literature in the society. God also fulfilled the promises he made to Solomon in the dream at Gibeon by blessing him with riches, fame, and long life. Solomon used God's wisdom to develop Israel as a powerful nation in that region and to become one of the greatest kings in Israel.

1 KINGS 5:1–18

PREPARATION FOR BUILDING THE TEMPLE

Solomon's kingdom has peace and prosperity. As such, Solomon sets out to build the temple in Jerusalem (1 Kings 5). Although David desires to build this temple, Solomon carries out the actual building of the temple (5:3–4). The first half of the chapter summarizes the correspondences between Solomon and Hiram, the king of Tyre, from whom Solomon wants to buy timber (5:1–9). The second half explains the results of such conversations (5:10–18).

The narrator describes Solomon's initiative in continuing the international treaty with Tyre in order to build the temple as another example of Solomon using God's gift of wisdom. The narrator reminds us that the theme of building the temple is connected with God's promise to David that his son would build the temple (2 Sam 7:11–14). We can anticipate that this promise will be fulfilled because the preparation is already taking place. The theological significance of this chapter appears in verses 3–5, where Solomon states his reasons for building the temple. On the one hand, he is carrying out the plan of his father, David, based on Nathan's prophecy (2 Sam 7:11–14). The narrator anticipates the fulfillment of this prophecy. On the other hand, Solomon says that he is building the temple "for the name of the Lord," which connects to Deuteronomic theology (Deut 12:11). Building the temple "for the name of the Lord" indicates Solomon's obedience in following the law. He is doing what God wants him to do.

5:1–9 CORRESPONDENCES BETWEEN HIRAM AND SOLOMON

Building logs of cedar did not grow in Jerusalem; they grew in Tyre, in Hiram's territory. Solomon needs those logs to build the temple. But Hiram too needed Solomon's alliance. So, Hiram starts diplomatic discussions with Solomon. This first part of the chapter has three sections: a description of the good relationship between Solomon and Hiram, the king of Tyre (5:1); Solomon's rationale and proposal for building the temple (5:2–6); and Hiram's agreement to and revision of Solomon's proposal (5:7–9).

5:1 Relationship between Solomon and Hiram

The narrator first describes the long-standing relationship between Hiram, the king of Tyre, and David (5:1; compare 2 Sam 5:11–12). Tyre, the capital of the Phoenician kingdom, is located on the coast of the Mediterranean Sea on the west and borders the land of Israel on the north. In the ancient Near East, Tyre was an ally of Israel and maintained a good relationship with Israel. It was customary practice during this time to renew treaties anytime a new king came to power, since a treaty expired after the death of either party to the agreement. After hearing about David's death and Solomon's enthronement, Hiram sends his envoys to Solomon to find out if the good relationship between Tyre and Israel will continue (1 Kgs 5:1). Hiram may also want to know more about this new king and his plans for peace or war as well as his wisdom, which has been praised by those who have visited Jerusalem. 1 Kings 5:1 connects 4:34 that says people from other nations came to Solomon. Hiram was one of them.

5:2–6 Rationale and Proposal for Building the Temple

We are not told about the discussions between Solomon and Hiram's servants ("envoys" in modern terms), but Solomon is pleased with Hiram and wants to continue the good relationship between the nations. He sends a message (probably in writing, 5:2) to Hiram about his plan to build the temple, explaining his rationale for such a huge project. In his message, he identifies three convincing reasons for the need for a temple in Jerusalem.

5:3 David Couldn't Build

First, Solomon says that David could not build the temple, although he wanted it, because of all the wars he fought (5:3). David wanted there to be a permanent center of worship in the capital of his kingdom because of the Deuteronomic law (Deut 12:11–14). For David, building the temple would ensure Yahweh's presence in his kingdom and earn the blessings of the Lord for the nation. The temple would be a center for worship, prayer, offering sacrifices, and a repository for the ark of the covenant. Those who lived in different regions of the nation could be united by this central sanctuary even as they worshiped at their own local sanctuaries. However, David had not been able to build the temple because all his energies and resources had been spent fighting against his enemies and protecting Israel from enemy attacks.

5:4 Solomon Has Rest

Second, Solomon explains that God "has given him rest on every side," with no adversaries or disasters, implying he has the time to build the temple (5:4). The Hebrew term (*nuh*) used here to mean "rest" is different from *sabbath* and *shalom*, as it means settling down quietly or enjoying a peaceful situation away from any political threat. The noun of this root word (*menuha*) means peace of mind or soul from all fears and is similar to the Indian term "*shanthi*" (peace). Solomon is sure that all the adversaries against his kingdom have been crushed. The Hebrew word (*satan*) that is used here refers to anyone who is doing wicked and evil things. Moreover, Solomon cannot envisage any possible disaster (Heb. *ra*, which means evil), such as a political attack, in the immediate future since the surrounding places are all controlled by the Lord. He attributes this sense of rest to the Lord because the Lord has granted it. Thus the peaceful situation is a divine signal to move forward with the plans to build the temple.

5:5 Right Time to Build

Third, Solomon says that it is the right time to begin the work and "I intend, therefore, to build a temple for the Name of the LORD my God, as the LORD told my father David" (5:5a). He is referring to both Deuteronomy and 2 Samuel. The words "a temple for the Name of the LORD" echoes the words from Deuteronomy, "a dwelling place for his name" (Deut 12:11). And, the phrase "to build a temple" echoes the words of the Lord to David, "build a house for my name" (2 Sam 7:13). In addition, Solomon quotes what God said to David through Nathan, "Your son whom I will put on the throne in your place will build the temple for my name" (1 Kgs 5:5). Building the temple will fulfill the prophecy given to David (2 Sam 7:12–17). Solomon is obeying a divine command.

By using the word "name," Solomon is referring to the personality and the name of Yahweh. He claims that Yahweh is the God of his father, David, as well as his own God. Quite often, the name of a deity reveals the character or function of that deity. For example, in the name *Muthumari Amman* (a goddess of the Tamils), the word "muthu" refers to the small round boils of smallpox or chickenpox on the skin, and the word "Amman" refers to a female deity. The temple for the goddess "Amman" is built at the entrances to villages in South India to block smallpox or chickenpox from entering the villages and spreading the disease. The name "Yahweh" means "I AM WHO I AM" (Exod 3:14). It is the personal name for God, which is holy (Exod 20:1–7).

The people of Israel used "Adonai" (which means "my Lord") in the place of Yahweh, out of respect. Adonai (Yahweh) was the God of Abraham and Jacob, the God of promise and blessing. He sets the Israelites free from their long bondage. Solomon, knowing these past histories of the Israelites, wants to build a temple where the "Name" of the Lord, "Yahweh" and "Adonai," will abide forever (1 Kgs 5:5).

5:6 Request for Timber

After stating the reasons for building the temple, Solomon orders Hiram to cut down the necessary trees in Tyre (5:6). The phrase, "give orders," means that Solomon commands Hiram to supply the wood. The "cedars of Lebanon" are famous – just like the teak and rosewood of Kerala and the Andaman Islands of India. The cedars of Lebanon can grow to a height of one hundred feet because of the suitable soil and climate. Cedar wood is also strong and good for polishing. Solomon offers incentives for supplying the timber. First, he offers to provide manpower from his kingdom to work alongside with the laborers of Hiram, since his men lack the skill to cut trees properly. Second, he offers to pay the wages of the laborers as set by Hiram.

5:7–9 Hiram Agrees and Revises the Deal

Hiram is happy to receive this message from Solomon and replies positively to the plan to build the temple. First, he thanks God for continuing the cordial relationship with Israel (5:7a). Then he praises the Lord for giving David a son to rule over the nation (5:7b). How can the king of Sidon, who worships other gods, offer praises to Yahweh, the God of Israel? In a polytheistic religious culture, people accept and even worship other gods and goddesses. Hiram can recognize that Solomon's God is helping his people, and so Hiram can give credit to Yahweh without feeling the need to worship Yahweh alone. Many polytheists believe that gods and goddesses help the communities that worship them.

We can notice a revision of Solomon's proposal in Hiram's reply (5:8–9). First, Hiram adds juniper logs to Solomon's request for cedar (5:8). Second, Hiram does not want Solomon's men to help cut the trees. Instead, "My men will haul them down from Lebanon to the Mediterranean Sea" (5:9a). Hiram tells Solomon that all the cutting and transporting of the logs through the Mediterranean Sea will be done by his men. When the logs are delivered to a point closer to Israel, Solomon's men can collect them and transport them inland. Finally, he requests that Solomon will supply food for his royal court (5:9c).

5:10–18 RESULTS OF THE CORRESPONDENCES

Their conversations resulted in actions, which the narrator tells in this second half of the chapter. It has two sections: the treaty with Hiram for the necessary material and Solomon's payment for the same in offering food for the king's household (5:10–12) and the gathering of the laborers, that is, enlistment of people to do the service for the government (5:13–18).

5:10–12 The Treaty with Hiram

1 Kings 5:10–12 summarizes the terms and conditions for the treaty between Hiram and Solomon. Solomon will supply twenty thousand *cors* of wheat and twenty thousand *baths* of pressed olive oil. Solomon supplies these quantities year after year, which suggests that this supply will last for one year. A *cor* is roughly five metric tons, making the annual supply of wheat 100,000 tons or more, and 440,000 liters of oil a year (5:10).[1] The phrase "pressed olive oil" does not refer to crude oil but oil that has been finely crushed and purified. Solomon agrees to supply 440,000 liters of pure olive oil (5:11). These quantities show the prosperity of the land. The two leaders agree to this treaty as two equal partners. Solomon did not make this agreement foolishly; "The LORD gave Solomon wisdom, just as he promised" (5:12). His trade was based on the GDP of Israel, which reflects how the Lord had blessed Solomon's kingdom. The narrator concludes, "There were peaceful relations between Hiram and Solomon" (5:12), implying this treaty was fair and within their means.

5:13–18 The Gathering of Laborers

After the treaty is made, Solomon collects the laborers for the building project from all over Israel. The NIV's terminology "conscripted" meaning "forced laborers" assumes too much. In Hebrew, the verb is "go up" or "gather together." Similarly, in the Greek translation of the Old Testament, the LXX, the verb is "to raise up." In other words, Solomon gathered or raised up 30,000 men, the natural-born Israelites. Then he divides these men into three batches of 10,000 each (5:13). Each batch of laborers go to Lebanon for a month and spend two months at home. What they did in Lebanon is unclear since Hiram promised

---

1. NIV footnote.

to cut the trees and transport them by sea himself. Maybe, they supervised the cutting and the shipping. Adoniram supervised the entire project (5:13).

In Jerusalem, Solomon has 70,000 carriers of the wood from the seashore to the land and 80,000 stone cutters to supply stones for the temple (5:15). Israel is known for mountains, rocks, and hills filled with stones, and so stone was the main construction material. Solomon appoints 3,300 supervisors to oversee the stonework (5:16). As Solomon commanded, they removed large blocks of high-grade stones to be placed as the foundation stones for the temple (5:17). The skilled workers from Israel, Tyre, and Byblos cut, shaped, and prepared the timber to build the temple (5:18). The "Byblos" in the English translation refers to "the Gebalites" in the Hebrew text, and they lived in the coastal region north of Tyre and were skilled craft workers.

The number of laborers who are engaged in the various aspects of building the temple is staggering. When a king undertakes a major building project, laborers have to serve the project. Because the temple is a national project that is supposed to serve the interests of Israel, the people do not question the king's orders. They are glad to oblige.

Taj Mahal was built as a monument of love by Shah Jahan in memory of his wife, Mumtaz, in AD 1632. The oral tradition says that almost the entire male force in his kingdom worked for twenty-two years, along with skilled men from other countries. Precious stones and marble were imported from the Middle East and Italy.[2] Similarly, in South India, the Meenakshi Temple, a temple for a goddess, was built by the Nayak Kings between AD 1559–1655. It has five towers that are three hundred feet tall and includes a compound wall that is forty feet high and stretches between five hundred and six hundred feet on each side.[3] The temple and wall were built with large blocks of stones that were quarried from nearby mountains and transported to Madurai. The temple took more than a hundred years to complete, and those who failed to work for this project were punished by the kings.

Solomon built such a temple for the Lord, not because he wants to compete with other nations. Instead, he wants to centralize worship so that all Jews will come to Jerusalem to worship God in the temple where he chooses to place his name. David envisioned such a temple, and Solomon built it.

---

2. NIEE, 1541.
3. Kriti Saraswat Satpathy, "Did You Know These Interesting Facts About the Meenakshi Amman Temple?" (February 4, 2020) in India.com. See https://www.india.com/travel/articles/did-you-know-these-interesting-facts-about-the-meenakshi-amman-temple-3235163/, accessed on October 4, 2021.

THE SIGNIFICANCE OF *YHWH*

When Solomon had peace in the land, he wanted to build the temple that his father, David, had vowed to build for the Lord God. In that context, the Scriptures refer to God placing "my Name" in the temple (1 Kgs 5:5; 8:16, 18, 19, 29). This is a reference to Yahweh, in Hebrew, for the letters YHWH (known as the tetragrammaton). In Hebrew, the name "YHWH" simply means "to be" and is the name that God revealed to Moses when he asked for God's name and God said, "I am who I am" (Exod 3:14). This name is incomprehensible, for God alone can name himself. To understand its significance, it is necessary to highlight four background aspects of the theology of God's name.[1]

First, there is no point in praying to a god without knowing the god's name. Thus Moses asked for the name of the God who sent him to deliver the Israelites from their bondage in Egypt. Before Moses, others called God various names. Abraham called God, "Sovereign Lord" (Gen 15:2), and God revealed himself as *El-Shaddai* or "Al-mighty" (17:1). Hagar called the Lord who spoke to her, *El-Roi*, meaning, "You are God who sees me" (16:13). From these narratives, we know that these names reflect each person's experience with God. The phrase, "God of Abraham, Isaac, and Jacob," which appears repeatedly in the OT, suggests that the personal name of God had not yet been revealed and also makes a historical connection with these ancestors, affirming that the God who revealed himself to them is one and the same. When God reveals his personal name to Moses as "Yahweh," (Exod 3:15), the name of the God of Israel becomes known, and later Solomon prays to "Yahweh" for help.

Second, this name signifies the nature, qualities, and actions of Yahweh. These attributes are manifested when enemies attack or famine ravages the land and when God punishes the Israelites or shows them love and compassion. These attributes can all be seen in the stories of the kings. Solomon's prayer at the dedication expects God to act and to show mercy and forgiveness.

Third, God's name is a holy name because Yahweh is holy. The Israelites must not misuse God's name, which is made clear in the warning of the prophets (Zech 13:3; Mal 1:6). The temple, which was built for the name of Yahweh, is also holy because he dwells there. Solomon did not affix a name placard with the inscription, "Temple of Yahweh," on the

---

1. For discussion on "Name Theology," see John Goldingay, *1 and 2 Kings for Everyone* (Louisville: Westminster John Knox Press, 2011), 36–38.

temple door because Yahweh's name is revealed through his actions. Yet an inscription to the "Unknown God" was written on the altar at Athens (Acts 17:22–23). In India, name boards are affixed to temples to identify the names of the deities. In later periods, the Israelites referred to God as *Adonai* ("my Lord") to avoid pronouncing the personal and holy name, Yahweh.

Fourth, God appears to Solomon to affirm his acceptance of the temple. Then God assures Solomon that he has heard Solomon's prayers and gives him a warning (1 Kgs 9:1–8). For Yahweh, obedience to the Deuteronomic law is more important than the temple. The king and the people cannot worship other gods and disobey the commands and decrees. If they do, God will reject the temple that was consecrated for his name and destroy both Israel and the temple.[2] His name will only continue with the temple as long as he dwells within it. The temple will not be useful without his presence, but will stand like any other building. His name, "Yahweh" ("I am who I am"), implies that he will exist forever, whether or not there is a temple. He existed before the tabernacle, and he continues to exist after the fall of Jerusalem and the destruction of the temple. He lives among people, whether they have a building for him, or not.

---

2. See Amos 5:21–25; Jeremiah 7:1–15.

1 KINGS 6:1-38
MAGNIFICENCE OF THE TEMPLE

From ancient times to modern days, people have been interested in visiting centers of worship that have been constructed as expressions of faith and culture by different religious communities. Temples, cathedrals, synagogues, *guruduwaras*,[1] and mosques continue to attract tourists, irrespective of their religious faith. Visitors pay attention to the year of construction, its structure, the materials used, and how it has been maintained as a religious center.

1 Kings 6 details the construction of the temple in Jerusalem, describing its foundation, walls, and the sanctuary. The chapter has two sections describing the construction of the outer temple (6:1–10) and the inner temple (6:14–38) with an interlude of God's word affirming his presence in the midst of Israelites (6:11–13). Though many Israelites never saw the first temple built by Solomon, the details in this chapter can help readers glimpse its magnificent construction.

6:1–10 THE FIRST SET OF DESCRIPTIONS

Once peace reigned in Solomon's kingdom, he began the construction of the temple, his palace, and the wall of Jerusalem that he had neglected until now (3:1). Whereas chapter 5 outlined his gathering the timber needed for the construction of the temple, this chapter outlines the construction of the temple, its architecture.

6:1 Temple Construction Begins

Solomon began the construction of the temple during the fourth year of his rule (6:1).[2] He may have started the construction between 968–967 BC.[3] The text says that the construction began in the "four hundred and eightieth year after the Israelites came out of Egypt" (6:1). Since Exodus does not mention

---

1. The worship center of the Sikhs.
2. Scholars have different opinions about the exact period of Solomon's rule. Bright dates Solomon's reign 961–922 BC; Wiseman suggests 970–930 BC. Bright, *History of Israel*, 478–481; Wiseman, *1 and 2 Kings*, 30. Musa Gotom suggests 960 BC could be the year of beginning the construction. *ABC*, 422.
3. Gray, *I and II Kings: A Commentary*, 160–161. House suggests that the construction could have begun in 966 BC. Paul R. House, *1, 2 Kings: An Exegetical and Theological Exposition of Holy Scripture*, 127.

the exact year that the Israelites left Egypt (Exod 12:31–50), it is difficult to fix the year for the construction upon this date.[4] Any proposed date would be an educated guess.

Nevertheless, it would have been a monumental building. It is difficult to visualize the architecture today even after seeing the wooden model of the temple in a museum. This section speaks of the temple measurements (6:2–6); the custom for cutting and shaping the stones (6:7–8); and the completion of the main building (6:9–10).

6:2–6 Temple Measurements

The measurement of "one cubit" is roughly .45 meters.[5] As such, the size of the main building was 27 meters long, 9 meters wide, and 14 meters high (6:2).[6] To modern eyes – having seen mega-malls, towers, and high-rise buildings – the temple might not seem very large, but it was a magnificent building for the ancient period. It had a portico in the front that was 9 meters long and 4.5 meters wide, which was supported by pillars (6:3). Narrow windows were placed high up on the walls of the main building to let light into the main hall and sanctuary (6:4). A structure went around the building that housed side rooms (6:5). Around the outsides of the temple, the structures extended three floors: lower, middle, and upper floors (6:6).

6:7 Temple Sanctity

Verse 7 describes an important custom in constructing a temple. Stone blocks were cut, shaped, and polished in the quarry. This was to maintain the sanctity of the temple. The size of these stone blocks differed according to their position in the temple, such as above the foundation, along a straight wall, at the corners, or to support the roof. Once the stones were brought to the building site, no hammer, chisel, or other iron tool were used to cut or shape them further.

This method reflects traditional building in India, where anyone who visits the ancient temples will notice the custom of treating the main hall as sacred. Even today, some temples – particularly the inner sanctuaries – in India are constructed without any metal tools.

---

4. For a discussion see Bright, *History of Israel*, 121–122. Genesis 15:13 in the Hebrew text says the Israelites were in bondage for 400 years in Egypt, but the Greek text mentions 440 years of bondage.
5. Or, 1.5 feet. See R. J. McKelvery, "Temple," in *NBD*, 1168–1172.
6. The NIV footnote.

6:8–10 Temple Construction

Access to the three floors were on the south side (6:8a). Whereas an "entrance" (probably a slope) went to the lowest floor, stairways led to the middle and third floor (6:8b). To finish the main building, Solomon covered it with beams and planks of cedar (6:9). He also had several rooms built around the main hall (6:10). The text says that these rooms were 7.5 feet or 2.2 meters high, though it does not describe their purpose. These additional rooms were connected to the main building with cedar beams.

6:11–13 GOD'S PROMISES

So far, the narrator has been describing the exterior structure (6:2–10). And before he describes the interior structure of the temple (6:14–18), he reminds readers about God's revelation to Solomon regarding God's promises and conditions (6:11–13). The Lord spoke to Solomon (6:11) to follow all God's laws and statutes – instructions he gave David concerning the temple structure (6:12; compare 1 Chr 28:19). Just as God instructed Moses to make the tabernacle according to the plans shown to him on the mountain (Exod 25:8; 26:30), David received the blueprints for the temple from God (1 Chr 28:19). Solomon is to build the temple according to God's blueprints, and this verse reminds him of that (1 Kgs 6:12).

When he obeys and builds the temple as God instructed, then he will fulfill his promise: "I will live among the Israelites" (6:13a). This phrase affirms that Yahweh prefers to dwell among the people. God is always "people oriented," but he allows the building of a tent (Exod 25:8) or a temple as a meeting place where people can worship.

Unlike gods of other nations and religions, God's tent or temple does not have an idol within it; since the Israelites are forbidden from worshiping any idols (Exod 20:3–4). This restriction contrasts the belief of many Hindus in India, Nepal, Sri Lanka, and Malaysia. By placing an idol or image of their god or goddess in a temple, followers believe that their deity will dwell there, listen to their prayers, and accept their *poojas* (worship). In Athens, Paul was "greatly distressed to see that the city was full of idols" (Acts 17:16). The Lord Jesus taught that God is not to be worshiped in Jerusalem or Mt. Gerizim (John 4:22); instead, "the true worshipers will worship the Father in the Spirit and in truth" (4:23).

When Solomon constructed the temple as instructed by God, he will not only live with them (1 Kgs 6:13a), he "will not abandon [his] people Israel" (6:13b). If the temple is the dwelling place of Yahweh, it will remind the people that he lives among them and wants to be in relationship with them. When Yahweh calls the Israelites "my people" (6:13), he expects them to follow him faithfully (Deut 7:7–9).

God wants the temple to remind the people that God dwells with them and that his presence is meant to bless the nation. Verses 11–13 also remind the people about God's earlier promise to David that his son would build a temple for God (1 Kgs 3:3).

God's relationship with the people is interrelated with their relationship to the temple. If God rejects and abandons the Israelites, their country will be destroyed, and the temple will also be attacked and destroyed. The covenantal relationship between Yahweh and Israel binds together the people, their land, and the temple. The theme of the temple is central to the life of the Israelites, as it connects the exodus tradition (1 Kgs 6:1), to the exile (Ezek 37:27), to the people's return from exile in order to rebuild the temple (as prophesied in Ezekiel 40–43 and Zech 8:9).

6:14–38 THE SECOND SET OF DESCRIPTIONS

Now the narrator outlines the interior temple work (1 Kgs 6:14–38). This section describes the overall structure of the inner temple (6:14–18), the Most Holy Place (6:19–28), decorations on the walls (6:29–30), the doors of the sanctuaries (6:31–35), and the inner courtyard (6:36). It concludes with a summary statement about the time it took to construct the temple (6:37–38).

6:14–18 Structure of the Inner Temple

When the exterior structure is finished (6:14), Solomon focused on the interior work. He lined the walls with cedar boards from floor to ceiling so that the exterior stone walls could not be seen and covered the floor with planks of juniper (6:15, 18). He created the inner sanctuary, the most holy place, by partitioning twenty cubits of space from the rear of the temple and making it a separate section inside the main sanctuary (6:16). The Most Holy Place, in Hebrew *ha-qodesh*, is a place for the presence of Yahweh. The remaining forty cubits in the front of the sanctuary functioned as the main hall (6:17). The cedar planks covering the interior walls of the temple were carved with the designs of open flowers and gourds, a type of creeping and trailing plant (6:18). Such decorations are also carved into the interior walls of some ancient Hindu temples.

6:19–28 Most Holy Place

Solomon prepared the inner sanctuary at the rear of the temple to set the ark of the covenant of the Lord in it (6:19). It was twenty cubits long, twenty cubits wide, and twenty cubits high (6:20a). Solomon overlaid the inside of this chamber and the altar with pure gold (6:20). Chains of pure gold were stretched across the front of the inner sanctuary, perhaps so that people would not step inside the holy of holies by mistake (6:21). Basically, the entire Most Holy Place was covered by pure gold (6:22).

The temples in India, the inner sanctuary is a square of equal length, width, and height. The idol of the deity is kept in this inner sanctuary, which is also called the "holy of holies" (*moolasthanam*). The few steps leading into the inner sanctuary are used by the priest alone in order to offer rituals (*pooja*) for the deity. Most inner sanctuaries are small and dark, and so the walls are often adorned with brass or gold plates to reflect light on the idol. Oil lamps are hung outside the inner sanctuary to shed light on the steps leading up to the inner chamber. In a way, they resemble Solomon's temple.

Remembering the instruction given to Moses to make two cherubim out of gold and place them at either end of the ark of the covenant, facing one another, with their outstretched wings covering the ark (Exod 25:17–22), Solomon placed two cherubim inside the inner sanctuary (1 Kgs 6:23–28). He made the cherubim of olive wood (6:23). He positioned the cherubim so that they were facing one another, with one wing of each touching the wall of the inner sanctuary and the other wing touching the wing of the other cherub (6:24). The Hebrew word for cherubim (*keruvim*) refers to a symbolic and celestial "being," whose function is to guard the tree of life (Gen 3:24) or protect the tablet of the Ten Commandments inside the ark of the covenant (Exod 25:18–22).[7] Positioned in this way, their large wings spread open to protect the ark (1 Kgs 6:26–27), similar to an eagle spreading its wings over its eaglets. Finally, Solomon overlaid the olive wood cherubim with pure gold (6:28).

Some religions in India use similar images of gods and goddesses being protected by the wings of birds, five-headed cobras, dragons, or celestial beings with human faces and wings. Visitors to Hindu temples will notice these designs.

---

7. R. K. Harrison, "Cherubim," in *NBD*, 185–186.

6:29–30 Decorations on the Walls

Solomon then decorated the walls of these sanctuaries (6:29–30). He carved cherubim, palm trees, and open flowers (6:29). Cedar, juniper, and olive woods are good for carving and last longer than many other sources of timber. The palm is a tall, slender, and unbranched tree, and its leaves were used to decorate interior spaces or to celebrate victory (John 12:13).[8] The open flower blossoms might have been a reminder of God's beautiful creation, bringing back the memory of the Garden of Eden. In addition, he covered the floors of both the inner and the outer rooms of the temple with gold (1 Kgs 6:30). These illustrate his prosperity and devotion to God.

6:31–35 Doors of the Sanctuaries

Solomon made doors of olive wood for the entrance of the inner sanctuary (6:31a). The doors were one-fifth of the width of the sanctuary (6:31b). He then carved cherubim, palm trees, and open flowers on them (6:32). Both these doors as well as the floors of the entire building were overlaid with hammered gold (6:32). In the same way, Solomon made doorframes of olive wood, one-fourth the width of the hall for the main hall (6:33). He then made two doors of juniper wood (with "two leaves that turned into sockets"), carved with similar designs, and overlaid with hammered gold (6:34–35). Solomon may have used gold to decorate the walls, doors, cherubim, and floors to make them more valuable, to protect them from erosion, or to make them shine distinctively. His choices certainly replicated the tabernacle that was constructed during the period of Moses.

6:36 Inner Courtyard

After building the two sanctuaries, Solomon also built an inner courtyard (6:36a). It had "three courses of dressed stone and one course of trimmed cedar beams" (6:36b). The narrator does not explain the purpose of this courtyard.

6:37–38 Construction is Complete

This section states the year that the temple construction began (6:37) and then the year it was completed (6:38). Solomon laid the foundation during his fourth year of reign in the month of *Ziv* (compare 6:1); the building was

---

8. Leaves of mango trees are used in temples and houses in South Asia to decorate the entrance and doors as an auspicious sign and blessing.

completed during the eleventh year of his reign in the month of *Bul* (6:38a). It took seven years for Solomon to construct the temple (6:38b).

1 Kings 6 outlines the vast resources used for the construction of the temple, its magnitude, and glory. The temple must have served as a symbol of pride for the nation of Israel. Solomon fulfilled the prophecies and instructions that God gave to his father, David.

In South Asia, temples play an important role in the lives of many Hindus, Jains, and Buddhists. Their temples are magnificent buildings that required enormous resources and labor. People go there to worship their deity.

For the Israelites, the temple was a visible representation of God's presence in their midst (6:13a). It reminded them that he has not abandoned them (6:13b). He was with them and he would help them in their daily and political struggles. That was why Solomon, as soon as he had peace in the land, built the temple of God.

THE HEBREW CALENDAR AND THE TEMPLE

During the ancient period, Egypt, Canaan, Assyria, and Babylon produced their own calendars according to their religious beliefs, cultures, and social needs. Most of the ancient calendars are based on a lunar system or connected to an agrarian life. The Canaanites, who worshiped Baal and Asherah (the nature god and goddess of the fertility cult), emphasized the agricultural seasons of spring, dry summer, rains, ploughing, sowing, and harvest. The Israelites borrowed the Canaanite calendar and seasons for their own agriculture but they oriented it to God's liberation from Egypt during the exodus period. The first month, *Nisan*, has thirty days and marks the people's liberation from bondage of Egypt and the celebration of the Passover.[1] It roughly falls in the Gregorian months of March and April. The second month, *Iyyar*, has twenty-nine days and marks the dry season after the barley harvest. It falls roughly in our months of April and May, which is a suitable month to do construction in the ancient Near East. During this month, in the fourth year of the reign of Solomon, the workers began digging and laying

---

1. J. B. Jeyaraj, "Festivals, Communication and Development," *Journal of Dharma* 28 no. 3 (July–September): 340–365.

the foundation for the temple (1 Kgs 6:1).[2] The third month, *Sivan*, has thirty days and falls within May-June of the Gregorian months. *Tammuz* is the fourth month (roughly falling between June-July months), and it has twenty-nine days. The fifth month is *Av*, and it has thirty days. It roughly falls within July and August. The name comes from Babylon. *Elul* is the sixth month with twenty-nine days. It falls within August and September of the Gregorian months. The seventh month is *Tishrei* or *Tishri*. It falls within the September and October months and has thirty days. The eighth month, *Cheshvan* or *Marheshvan*, has twenty-nine or thirty days (depending on the year it is celebrated). It roughly falls within October and November of the Gregorian calendar. Solomon finished building the temple during the eighth month of his eleventh year (6:38) – seven years and six months after he began the construction.

This temple stood for nearly 370 years (957–586 BC) before the Babylonian king, Nebuchadnezzar's commander, burned it to the ground. The work on the second temple began around 516 BC. Herod the Great magnified that second temple, which lasted until AD 70, when Roman Titus destroyed it.

---

2. D. J. Wiseman, "Calendar," in *NBD*, ed. J. D. Douglas (Leicester: IVP, 1987), 157–159.

1 KINGS 7:1–51

BUILDING PALACES AND FURNISHING THE TEMPLE

1 Kings 7 continues the story of Solomon's building projects. It has two sections: building the palaces (7:1–12); furnishing the temple (7:13–51). The brief narrative about the palaces compared with the detailed description of the temple implies that Solomon considered the temple as more important than his palaces.

Both stories of the temple and palace are connected by the same Hebrew word for "house," *bayit*. The temple is the house where the God of Israel dwells (6:37), and the palace is the house where the king and his family dwell and carry out the administration of the kingdom (7:1). The temple signifies the religious dimension; the palace signifies the political dimension.

In the ancient monarchical period in Asia, kings represented both the religious and political authority. The king was the guardian of the religion and needed to perform all the worship and rituals through the priests. He was also the guardian of the people and needed to protect them, administer justice for them, and seek their welfare. In turn, the royal family and their descendants needed to be protected in a secluded place, a palace, to perform the responsibilities of the king. Thus, the construction of the temple and the palace were both necessities that would have been understood by the nation. Solomon kept both the religious and political needs side by side. As such, the temple and palace were located in the same complex or vicinity.[1]

7:1–12 BUILDING THE PALACE

The story of building the palace begins with an introductory note, which says that the construction by Solomon continued for thirteen years (7:1). Just as the temple was the "house" (*bayit*) of God (6:3, 17), the palace was the "house" (*bayit*) of Solomon. The palace was built with cedar logs from Lebanon. It was one hundred cubits long, fifty cubits wide, and thirty cubits high, roughly

---

1. Gray, *1 and II Kings: A Commentary*, 159.

45 meters long, 23 meters wide, and 14 meters high.² The palace was very large, with four rows of cedar pillars supporting the main structure and forty-five beams placed on top of the pillars as a roof (7:2–3). Windows were arranged in sets of three, facing each other for light and air circulation (7:4). The doors were also placed in sets of three, facing each other (7:5).

Solomon also constructed a colonnade in front of the palace (7:6). It was fifty cubits long and thirty cubits wide. Before it was a portico. And in front of that, there were pillars and an overhanging roof. All of these would have given the palace a magnificent look.

Next to the palace, Solomon built the throne hall or "the Hall of Justice," where he judged the people (7:7a). It was covered with cedar from floor to ceiling (7:7b).

A hall of justice is called a *darbar* in India. A king used a throne hall, where he sat on his throne in a royal outfit, to appear before the officials and public on festival or celebration days and to judge the people. Foreign dignitaries and kings also met the king in the throne hall to pay homage. Ancient poets praised the king in the throne halls. In this hall, the king also discussed policy matters, laws, and plans for war or how to defend the country from enemy attack.

Solomon's palace, that sat farther back from the hall of justice, was similar in design (7:8). The king lived with his family in that palace.

In addition, Solomon built a palace, in the same vicinity, for Pharaoh's daughter, whom Solomon had married (7:8). Most likely, it was for the queen and her consorts to have privacy away from the public and the political leaders, many of whom were men.

Solomon built all three structures – "from the outside to the great courtyard and from fountain to eaves" – with blocks of high-grade stones that his masons cut to size in the quarries (7:9). They all had smooth surfaces so as not to harm the people. The foundations of these buildings rested on large stones of enduring quality (7:10). Some were as large as 4.5 meters. The buildings themselves were made of high-grade stones and cedar beams (7:11). Chariots, horses, elephants, and people all traveled across the courtyard, and so the dressed stones were paved to bear immense pressure. And for safety, the great courtyard was surrounded by three courses of walls, with finely dressed stones and cedar beams (7:12a). In many ways, these palaces and justice hall, resembled "the inner courtyard of the temple of the LORD with its portico" (6:12b).

---

2. The NIV footnote.

7:13–51 FURNISHING THE TEMPLE

After explaining the construction of the palaces and the hall of justice, the narrator returns to describe the furnishing in the temple. First, he speaks of the bronze furnishings (7:13–47) and then the gold (7:48–50).

7:13–47 Bronze Furnishings

King Solomon wanted bronze furnishings for the temple, in addition to the gold that covered the entire inside of the Most Holy Place. So, he made preparations to do the same. The best of the bronze craftsmen was in Tyre by the name of Huram.

7:13–14 Huram the Craftsman

King Solomon sent his messengers to Tyre and brought Huram (7:13). Huram's mother was a widow from the tribe of Naphtali, and his father was from Tyre (7:14a). Huram was a "skilled craftsman in bronze," filled with wisdom (*hokmah*), understanding (*tevunah*), and knowledge (*da'at*) of all kinds of bronze work (7:14b). These three words describe him as an expert in metallurgy and refer to his practical knowledge. "Wisdom" is not academic knowledge that can be gained in a school. In Israel, wisdom refers to the practical knowledge and skill needed to lead a good ethical life or to accomplish a task well. "Understanding" refers to Huram's ability to discern what Solomon wants in order to furnish the temple in bronze. "Knowledge" underlines Huram's empirical insights in terms of design. To furnish the tabernacle, Yahweh chose Bezalel and Ohaliah, who were filled with the spirit of wisdom, understanding, and all kinds of skills (Exod 35:30–35). Similarly, Huram was filled with wisdom, understanding, and knowledge to do all kinds of bronze work for the temple of the Lord (1 Kgs 7:13–14). Both Moses and Solomon took precise care to construct and design a dwelling place for God.

In India, any Hindu temple construction should be done by a Hindu leader or expert, preferably someone who belongs to the upper caste and not a Muslim or Christian. Similarly, mosques should be constructed and furnished only by a Muslim contractor. While the contractors can employ others, it is preferable for the laborers to belong to the Muslim religion and culture in order to preserve the sanctity of the building and to prevent the leaders and workers from being polluted by a person of another religion and culture.

Solomon, however, picked Huram of Tyre because of his expertise not because of his birth or religion. The future generations of Israel, particularly the priests and officials in the court, are to accept Huram's work irrespective of his status.

7:15–22 Two Bronze Pillars

The bronze work for the temple included two hollow cast pillars that were eighteen cubits high, with a circumference of twelve cubits (7:15). If this modern equivalent to ancient cubits is correct, then these pillars were huge.[3] Two bronze capitals that were each five cubits high were placed on top of these pillars (7:16). The shape of the capitals may have replicated a royal crown. Each capital was adorned with seven interwoven chains and decorated with pomegranates (7:17–18). The stone pillars of some temples in India depict a banana with its skin opened, and its stem connected to a crown. In south Indian culture, banana bunches with stems and leaves are a symbol of prosperity. Similarly, pomegranates are a symbol of agricultural fertility in many ancient Near Eastern countries, including Israel. During a wedding in Arab families, pomegranate seeds are thrown on the bride,[4] just as we throw rice on the bride in Indian and western cultures as signs of blessing. Bronze capitals were also placed on top of the pillars for the portico, but they were only four cubits and were decorated with lilies (7:19). These "lilies" may have been lotus flowers, which is commonly used in Egypt as a symbol of life and purity. The portico pillars were also decorated with pomegranates (7:20). Huram then placed these pillars at the north and south entrances at the portico of the temple (7:21). The south pillar was named "Jakin," which means "firm" or "solid," and the north pillar was named "Boaz," which denotes "strong" or "strength." From these names, we can infer that the pillars gave strong support to the portico. After he planted the pillars, then he placed the lilies on top of them; that completed the work of the two bronze pillars (7:22).

7:23–26 Sea of Cast Metal

After completing the work on the bronze pillars, Huram made a "sea" of cast metal in a circular shape that was ten cubits wide and five cubits high (7:23a). Its circumference was 14 meters (7:23b). The Hebrew word, *yam*, means "sea" in a figurative sense to refer to water. This metal basin could hold "two thousand baths," which is equivalent to ten thousand gallons (nearly 38,000

---

3. Wiseman, *1 and 2 Kings*, 122. The NIV footnote says, "That is, about 27 feet high and 18 feet in circumference or about 8.1 meters high and 5.4 meters in circumference."
4. Gray, *I and II Kings: A Commentary*, 185.

liters) of water, and so it would have looked like a sea of water (7:26), like an infinity pool. The rim of the basin had shapes of two rows of gourds encircling it, ten gourds in a circle to a cubit (7:24).

This basin was placed on top of twelve oxen, which were designed to bear the weight of the massive tank (7:25a). The oxen were arranged in groups of three, with one group facing north, south, west, and east (7:25b). The large quantity of water in the basin (7:26) may have been used by the priests for ceremonial cleansing and to rinse offerings. Or, it could have been for aesthetics.

7:27–37 Ten Bronze Stands

Next, Huram made ten movable stands of bronze that were affixed with panels and wheels (7:27–37). They were smaller than the two large pillars, but nevertheless, they were big: 1.8 meters long and wide, and 1.4 meters high (7:27). These stands had side panels with depictions of lions, bulls, and cherubim (7:28–29). The stands rested on four bronze wheels with bronze axles so that they could be easily moved around (7:30). Both the stand and the transporter had wreaths of hammered work (7:29–30). Although the stand was square, inside the stand was a circular opening (7:31). The wheels themselves were hidden by the side panels for aesthetics (7:32) and they were made with the same vigor and quality as that of chariot wheels – "the axles, rims, spokes and hubs were all of cast metal" (7:33).

These movable bronze stands also had four handles, one on each corner (7:34). The top of the stands had a circular brand from which the supports and panels were attached (7:35). Then the entire stands had several art engravings of cherubim, lions, palm trees, and wreaths testifying they were more than functional; they were beautiful art pieces (7:36). Since Huram used molds to make these stands, they were identical in size and shape (7:37).

7:38–39 Ten Bronze Basins

The ten bronze movable stands held ten bronze basins, each holding fifty baths, 880 liters, of water (7:38). These movable basins were not small by any means. After casting them, Huram placed five of those stands on the south side of the temple and five on the north (7:39a). In addition, he placed the Sea on the south side, at the northeast corner of the temple (7:39b). All of these would have given the temple, the portico, the courtyard, and the palaces a majestic look. With sun shining on these bronze and gold structures within the temple, it would have been magical.

7:40–47 Summary of All Bronze Furnishings

Verses 40–47 summarize the bronze work completed by Huram for the temple of the Lord, including the pots, shovels, sprinkling bowls that he made. They also say that the metal furnishings were molded, polished, coated, and finished between Sukkoth and Zarethan in the plain of the Jordan, most likely because the casting and finishing required clay and a lot of water (7:46). Solomon could not calculate the total weight of all these metal furnishings because there were so many and they were so heavy (7:47).

7:48–50 Gold Furnishings

After listing all the bronze furnishings Solomon made for the temple of the Lord, the narrator lists all the gold furnishings Solomon made for the temple of the Lord (7:48–50). It included a golden altar, table (on which was the bread of the Presence), ten lamp stands of pure gold, floral work, lamps, tongs, pure gold basins, wick trimmers, sprinkling bowls, dishes, censers, and gold sockets for the doors of the main hall and inner sanctuary, the Most Holy Place. These gold furnishings were made for rituals within the sanctuary, as gold was considered more sacred than other metals and could withstand stains and erosion.

By creating a central sanctuary in Jerusalem, Solomon paved the way for centralizing the worship, as commanded by God (Deut 12:11–12). Worshiping within the temple in Jerusalem, the people would gain identity as the people of Yahweh and unite as a nation, forgetting all their tribal divisions. The explicit reason for building the temple was to establish a dwelling place for the name of Yahweh. Worshiping Yahweh in only one place contrasts sharply with the Canaanites who worshiped Baal and Asherah with idols and altars, shrines and temples in various places of their choosing all over the land of Canaan.

7:51 Setting Up the Treasuries

Once the temple construction was furnished and the bronze and gold furnishings that Huram made were set in place, Solomon brought all the silver and gold furnishings that David had collected and placed them in the treasury (1 Kgs 7:51). Although God would not allow David to build the temple for him, David collected these items out of his love for the Lord. Solomon now placed them in the treasury. Usually, the treasury was a chamber that was constructed within the temple to hold the things used for worship. The precious things that David had collected included gifts that he had received from his vassals, spoils of war that had been dedicated to Yahweh, and the vessels used during worship by the priests.[5]

In India today, most of the gold vessels used in worship, along with the jewels used to decorate gods and goddesses, are kept in a chamber inside the temples. Some ancient kings not only used the temple for worship, but also to store their gold, silver, and jewels. In the Padmanath Swamy Temple in Trivandrum, Kerala, which was constructed by the Maharaja of Travancore, an ancient king, archaeologists discovered gold and diamonds inside an inner chamber. This treasure is now in the custody of the government.[6]

In verses 40b and 51, the narrator repeats that all the work was "done for the temple of the Lord." It was not built to fulfill David's vision or for Solomon's glory. Instead, it was built for "the name of the Lord."

---

5. Gray, *I and II Kings: A Commentary*, 202.
6. This discovery was broadcast on the TV news in 2010.

1 KINGS 8:1–66

DEDICATION OF THE TEMPLE

Any dedication – whether a house, shop, or dam across a river – is an important event to local communities. Even more important is the dedication of a temple, church, or mosque because these spaces are set aside for worship and provide unity and identity to those who belong to that religion. In the Asian context, there are various rituals for dedication.

1 Kings 8 narrates dedication of the temple in Jerusalem, which has four sections: bringing the ark of the covenant to the temple (8:1–21), prayers of petition (8:22–54), blessings on the people (8:55–61), and a dedication ceremony (8:62–66). The prose styles used to narrate the story of the dedication include direct speeches from Solomon (where political and religious concerns overlap), prayers from Solomon (which include elements of praise, petition, and thanksgiving), and historical sketches within Solomon's speeches and prayers (which reveal his retrospective outlook and acknowledge the fulfillment of God's promises).

8:1–21 BRINGING THE ARK TO THE TEMPLE

The law required all Israelites to come together to celebrate the Feast of Unleavened Bread (Passover), the Feast of Weeks, and the Feast of Tabernacles (Deut 16:16). This last feast (Heb. *Succoth*) is also known as the Feast of the Tent or the Festival of Booths to remember the exodus, when Israelites wandered and lived in tents. After the Israelites settled in Canaan, they lived in permanent houses, but they were to remember their early history, when they lived in tents and Yahweh dwelled with them inside the tent of the meeting, where the ark of the covenant was kept. Now, Solomon brings the people together to Jerusalem for a special occasion, the dedication of the newly built temple.

8:1–2 Gathering of the People

After furnishing the temple, Solomon summoned first all the elders of Israel, heads of the tribes, and chiefs of families with the intention of planning together with him about bringing the ark of the covenant from Zion, the City of David, to Jerusalem, where the temple was (8:1). The people are not left alone. Instead, King Solomon established a festival in the month of Ethanim, the seventh month, and brought the entire nation together in Jerusalem (8:2).

8:3–5 Transporting the Ark

When the elders, the selected representatives arrive, the priests take the ark of the Lord, the tent of meeting, and all the sacred furnishing in it and bring them to Jerusalem, to the newly built temple (8:3–4). The priests and Levites alone carry these sacred objects (8:4b). As the procession begins, the entire assembly of Israel, with King Solomon, precede the procession while sacrificing sheep and cattle of unaccountable number to the Lord (8:5). The general word "sacrifice" refers to cutting the animals, but the purpose for offering the sacrifices is not stated clearly in the text. The sacrifices may have been a peace offering to God so that he would not punish them for carrying the ark, as he punished Uzzah for touching the ark during the time of David (2 Sam 6:6–13). The people would have wanted God to be pleased by their efforts in carrying the ark safely to the temple.

This procession resembles some of the processions in India,[1] with one difference. In Indian processions only the upper caste is allowed to join in the dedication of a temple, while the lower caste have to remain on the outskirts and watch. In the dedication of the temple in Jerusalem, however, the entire assembly of Israelites joined the procession and participated as the assembly of God while only the priests carried the ark.

8:6–9 Placing the Ark in the Temple

After transporting the temple from the City of David to Jerusalem, the ark was placed inside the Most Holy Place, beneath the wings of the cherubim (8:6). The large wings of the cherubims overshadowed the ark and the poles that were used to carry the ark (8:7). Those poles occupied the entire Most Holy Place so that those who entered the main hall could see it (8:8a). Parenthetically, the narrator says that it could be seen even at the time he was writing this document (8:8b), that implies that this document was written a short time after the placement of the ark in the Most Holy Place. The ark contained only the two tablets of the commandments within it, which were originally placed

---

1. Some temples in south India have a tall wooden structure called a "temple-car," which has four giant wheels. The deities are brought out of the temple and placed in this temple car, which is tied with big, long ropes that the people can use to pull the car along the road during Car-festivals.

there by Moses at Horeb, the place where the Lord made a covenant with the Israelites, as they came out of their bondage in Egypt (8:9). The rod of Aaron and the pot of manna that were traditionally kept in front of the ark seem to be missing (Exod 16:33; Num 17:10), although no reason is stated.

Tourists who visit the large temples in India will notice a decorated throne that is placed on two long poles.[2] The idol god or goddess of the temple is placed on the seat of the throne, and then two priests in the front and another two priests at the back lift up the poles and carry the throne on their shoulders through the streets.

8:10–11 Glory of Yahweh

As the priests leave the Holy Place, the cloud fills the temple of the Lord (8:10). This is a most significant event, because Yahweh came into the temple in the form of a cloud (8:11b), just as in the days of Moses (Exod 40:34–35), which would have reminded the people of God's glory filling the tabernacle. Since God does not reveal his face to people, he manifests his presence through the form of fire, thunder, a sound, or a cloud (Gen 15:17; Exod 13:21; 40:36–38; Num 6:15–21). The presence of the cloud confirms his presence in the temple with his people.[3] When the people saw the cloud, they recognized the glory of their God. This event is theologically important because a tent or temple cannot become holy unless God comes and dwells in it. The cloud was so thick that the priests could not perform their rituals until it settled (8:11a).

In the South Asian context of dedicating temples, after carrying around the deity on a throne and setting the deity upon the altar in the holy of holies, the priests continue to perform their *pooja* (worship) until it is finished.[4] No cloud or fire fills the holy of holies, and the people can still see the idol of the deity from the courtyard. In rural India, the priests go into ecstasy and dance with a long sharp spear. Then the priest plants his spear into the altar, symbolically pinning down the spirit,[5] which will remain so long as the spear is not removed. After pinning the spirit to the altar, the priest asks the people to sacrifice goats to the deity and offer fruits, vegetables, flowers, and liquor in worship.

---

2. The throne is called the *Pallacku* or *Chapparam*.
3. H. Wheeler Robinson, *Corporate Personality in Ancient Israel* (Philadelphia: Fortress Press, 1980), 25–37.
4. Since the term *pooja* is associated with worship and rituals to Hindu deities, Christians use the term *aradhana* for their worship and service.
5. Different spirits represent different gods and goddesses.

8:12–21 Blessing of Solomon

Solomon then delivers a speech to the people (8:12–21). His first two statements frame the rest of his prayers and blessing (8:12). First, he remembers the words of Yahweh, who said that he was dwelling in a dark or thick cloud (8:12a; Exod 40:34–38). Second, he has built a magnificent temple for God to dwell in their midst forever.

As the whole assembly of Israel stood, Solomon turned to them and blessed them (1 Kgs 8:14). Then he praised the Lord, the God of Israel, who blessed his father David with the promise to set his name in and among his people, in Jerusalem (8:15–16). Then he narrates how David wanted to build this temple but God wanted Solomon to build it instead (8:17–19; compare 2 Sam 7:1). Finally, he thanks God for giving him the opportunity to build the temple for him and acknowledges that he has fulfilled the wish of his father (8:20–21).

The scene then shifts to the temple itself where Solomon stands before the altar of the Lord and speaks to the people. Until the glory of the Lord descends on the Most Holy Place, the people have access to the temple, to even see the Most Holy Place.

8:22–54 PRAYERS OF PETITION

Within the temple, in front of the altar, spreading his hands towards the heavens, Solomon offers a prayer of several petitions before God (8:22–54). Before praying, Solomon stands, faces the altar, and spreads out his hands towards heaven (8:22). These actions demonstrate his genuine spirit of pleading to God. In this prayer of dedication, sometimes he prays (*tephillah*, 8:29–30), sometimes he pleads (*tehinna*, 8:45), and sometimes he cries (*rinna*, 8:28).

8:23–30 Praises to God

Solomon's prayer begins by saying Yahweh is the God of Israel and there is no other God like Yahweh in heaven or on earth (8:23a), asserting that Yahweh is superior to any god (Exod 15:11; 20:2; Deut 4:39; Ps 86:8–10). He then acknowledges Yahweh is a faithful God who is committed to his covenantal promises to those who obey him (1 Kgs 8:23b). As such, God has been faithful to his promises to David (8:24) and to his descendants (8:25–26).

Solomon speaks of God's imminence and transcendence (8:27a). He knows that the earth, the vastness of the heaven, and even the entire universe cannot contain God. So if God, who dwells everywhere, cannot be localized in a building or limited to a space, then the temple Solomon built is far too small (8:27b). After making this acknowledgment, Solomon pleads with God to listen to his cry and prayer (8:28). He asks God not to turn away his eyes from the temple, but to keep his attention on it day and night so that God will hear his prayers and the prayers of the people (8:29). Finally, he asks God to hear his supplications and the people's prayer, especially when they offer those prayers looking towards the temple (8:30).

8:31–32 Forgiving Individuals

After these prayers, Solomon makes a series of petitions. First, Solomon pleads with Yahweh to vindicate individuals when they come to the temple if they acknowledge their innocence or confirm that they did not commit wrong against another person (8:31). During the exodus and settlement period, the parties in a dispute put forth their case to the local elders, who decided whether a person was guilty or innocent (e.g., Exod 22:7–12). The guilty person was punished by the priests and elders, according to their law and custom, and the innocent person was vindicated. In this petition, Solomon asks the God of justice to listen to anyone who declares himself or herself to be innocent and swears before the altar in the temple (1 Kgs 8:31). After hearing the case, God must punish the guilty parties directly and declare the righteous to be free (8:34). This petition emphasizes each person's responsibility to be accountable to God.

8:33–51 When Israel Sins

Solomon then sets up a series of hypothetical cases where the nation of Israel might sin against God. In each of these cases, he wants God to forgive them. These include sins committed both in wartime and in peacetime.

8:33–34 When Nations Defeat Them

Throughout the history of Israel, they were attacked by the Philistines, Edomites, Moabites, Midianites, and other neighboring nations. God and the prophets attributed their failure to their sin of forgetting their covenant with God. But, whenever the people repented, God raised his messengers to deliver the people and help them reclaim their territory. This history echoes the laws of blessings and curses in the book of Deuteronomy, where Yahweh promises that the nation of Israel will be restored to their land from captivity if they return to him and follow his ways (Deut 30:1–5).

Solomon draws on this history and asks God to hear from heaven the cries of the people and forgive their sins and restore them to their land when they pray towards the temple after they have sinned and been caught in their sins (8:33–34). He wants God to extend his mercy and grace to the nation if they are taken captive in war because of their sin.

8:35–36 When Rain Fails

Rain from heaven is needed for the land to prosper. God can withhold the rain if Israel sins (see Deut 28:21–24). Solomon pleads that if they sin and God shuts the rain from heaven, that when they pray towards the temple, he should listen to them – for his name's sake – and forgive the people's sin and let the land have rain (1 Kgs 8:35–36).

8:37–40 When Famine or Plagues Comes

Solomon then prays that whenever the land suffers from plagues and diseases, and the people look towards the temple and plead for his mercy, God should forgive the people, teach them to fear God, and bless them to live in the land (8:37–39). Then they will fear him all the days of their lives (8:40).

8:41–43 When Foreigners Visit

Every nation hesitates to take refugees or non-citizens into their countries. The refugee crises, hostility towards immigration, and ethnic cleansing worldwide attest to this. But God wanted Israel to be a nation that showed hospitality to refugees and foreigners. So, Solomon pleads on behalf of the foreigners, especially when they look towards the temple and ask for help (8:41–43). For Solomon, Yahweh could not be limited to the Israelites or the borders of the land of Israel, because the God of Israel is sovereign over all the nations and powerful to answer all prayers. Missiologists might perceive this as a "centripetal" trend of evangelism, where the foreigners come to Israel, encounter the living God, and receive answers after they pray in the temple of Yahweh. This could be contrasted with a centrifugal trend, when the Israelites go out to the foreigners and tell them about the uniqueness of Yahweh. In a way, Solomon anticipates that Israel might sin by not showing hospitality to foreigners and makes this plea.

8:44–45 When Going to War

Sometimes, the enemies will come against them (8:33–34), and sometimes Israel will go to war against enemies, even to conquer their land. In those days, Solomon wants God to show mercy towards Israel, especially when they look towards the temple and pray in the Name of the Lord (8:44–45).

1 Kings 8:1–66

8:46–51 When Israel Enters Captivity

In the last plea for sins Israel might commit, Solomon pleads for release from captivity. "There is no one who does not sin" against God (8:46a). As such, the people will sin, God will become angry with them and give them over to their enemies who will take them into captivity (8:46b). But if they repent while in captivity, look towards the temple and pray for deliverance, in God's Name, Solomon wants God to listen to their prayers and show mercy to them (8:47–50). Just as he brought them from Egypt, Solomon wants God to keep on delivering his people from any captivity, provided they pray towards the temple in Jerusalem.

In all of these pleadings, Solomon highlights the importance of repentance and prayer towards the temple in Jerusalem. This practice is held in other religions where someone will look towards a place of religious significance to pray. Even the Samaritan woman asked the Lord, "Our ancestors worshiped on this mountain, but you Jews claim that the place where we must worship is in Jerusalem" (John 4:20). She wanted to know if the Samaritans or the Jews were correct. Solomon's answer would have been that the Jews were correct – they should look towards Jerusalem and pray and then God will hear them. Solomon saw the temple as the place of God's residence on earth, although he is transcendent.

8:52–54 Conclusion

Solomon concludes the petition by asking one more time for God to be gracious to the pleas of the people, especially when they cry out to him (8:52). He listens because he himself chose the Israelites to be his special people, delivered them from Egypt, and set them apart from the rest of the people in the world as God's inheritance (8:53; compare Deut 7:7–11). After praying, Solomon rose up from his kneeling position in front of the altar, where he had his hands spread out toward heaven (8:54).

8:55–61 BLESSINGS FOR PEOPLE

Solomon then stood towards the whole assembly of Israel and blessed them in a loud voice (8:55). In the blessing, he gives due credit to God for giving rest to his people just as he promised (8:56). He blesses the people saying God will be with them and never forsake them as he has been with their ancestors (8:57). Solomon, with a blessing, challenges them to obey God and keep his commandments, laws, and decrees (5:58). He prays and blesses saying that they'll remember the words that they heard today and obey them so that "all the people of the earth may know the Lord is God and that there is no other" (5:59–60). He concludes by blessing them: "May your hearts be fully committed to the LORD our God, to live by his decrees and obey his commands, as at this time" (5:61). By declaring that Yahweh is the sovereign Lord, Solomon strengthens the faith of his audience and affirms that the God of Israel is the only true and living God, who can both transcend earth, heaven, or any place and also dwell immanently in a temple.

These affirmations can still be used in dedication liturgies for church buildings today. Our churches need to praise God while also proclaiming theological truths about our history and faith.

8:62–66 DEDICATION CEREMONY

After bringing in the ark to the temple, and making prayers of petitions, and pronouncing blessings on the people, Solomon has the dedicatory ceremony. This dedication had three stages: dedication of the temple of the Lord (8:62–63), consecration of the courtyard in front of the temple (8:64), and celebration festival for fourteen days (8:65–66).

8:62–63 Dedication of the Temple

Solomon began the dedication ceremony by offering sacrifices to the Lord (8:62). It was an elaborate sacrifice of fellowship offering with 22,000 cattle and 120,000 sheep and goats (8:63a). The fellowship offering was similar to a communion service in that it was shared by the king, priests, and the people, signifying their unity as they dedicated the temple. In this way, the king and all Israelites dedicated the temple to the Lord (8:63b).

8:64 Consecration of the Courtyard

On the same day, Solomon consecrated the courtyard in front of the temple (8:64). He did that by offering burnt offerings, grain offerings, and the fat of the fellowship offering. He chose the courtyard to do these sacrifices because the bronze altar that stood before the Lord was too small to hold these offerings. That tells us the number of offerings would have exceeded the offerings given during the dedication of the temple (compare 8:63).

8:65–66 Celebration Festival

The dedication of the temple and the consecration of the courtyard followed fourteen days of celebration (8:65–66). People from as far as Lebo Hamath in the north to the Wadi of Egypt in the south came for this celebration and celebrated it before the Lord God for fourteen days (8:65). On the fifteenth day, Solomon dismissed them. Having witnessed the temple dedication, heard Solomon's prayers, and participated in the celebration, the people blessed the king for his achievements and then returned to their homes joyfully (8:66a). Their hearts were glad because of all the good things the Lord had done for his servant David and his people Israel (8:66b). Even though Solomon built the temple and dedicated it to the Lord, the people acknowledged this was God's faithfulness to David, a man after God's heart.

1 KINGS 9:1–28

GOD'S APPEARANCE AND SOLOMON'S ACTIVITIES

After Solomon built the temple and the royal palace, God appeared to him, as he had earlier in Gibeon. This divine visitation would have boosted Solomon's image as a religious person and communicated to the people that he had a direct connection with God. The first part of this chapter narrates how the Lord appeared and spoke to Solomon a second time (9:1–9); the second part highlights Solomon constructing buildings, developing towns, building ships to develop commercial trade across the sea, observing the required religious festivals, and offering sacrifices (9:10–28). In all these achievements, Yahweh warns Solomon to remember his covenantal relationship with him.

9:1–9 GOD'S APPEARANCE TO SOLOMON

God's first appearance is reported in 1 Kings 3:5; the second appearance happens after Solomon completes the temple and palace (9:2). As the account unfolds, it becomes clear that the economic and social situation that had developed in Israel as a result of Solomon's building projects prompts Yahweh to take the initiative to appear to Solomon and warn him.[1]

In both appearances, God uses the word "servant" to refer to David and Solomon. Both dreams highlight the conditional nature of God's promises to David: God will remain faithful *if* Solomon obeys the Lord and practices the commandments (3:14; 9:3–4). At Gibeon, God invites Solomon to ask for whatever Solomon wants (3:5); at Jerusalem, Yahweh speaks, and Solomon listens without responding (9:1–3). In this speech, Yahweh makes four affirmations. Yahweh confirms that he has heard Solomon's prayers. He has "consecrated this temple," which means it is sacred and holy. Yahweh promises that he will place his name in the temple, thereby assuring Solomon that the presence of God will continue in there forever. His eyes and heart will be in the temple, looking at the king and people, seeing their needs, answering their prayers, and showing love and compassion to them. Yahweh also wants

---

[1]. Gray, *I and II Kings: A Commentary*, 237; Wiseman, *1 and 2 Kings*, 134.

Solomon to know that all these confirmations, affirmations, and assurances are conditional. God requires any ruler of Israel to administer justly and to stand firm in obeying the law and following God's statues. God wants Solomon to know that the one God of Israel will never compromise his attributes. God promises to establish Solomon's rule over Israel, confirming that his throne will be secure. Solomon will have descendants who will be his successors to the throne, and so his kingdom will continue through his family.

This promise of an everlasting rule of David's dynasty is unique to Israel when compared with the historical and religious backgrounds of other nations. Babylon practiced the festival of Marduk annually to renew the kingship each year. On the fifth day of this celebration, the priest removed the signet ring from the finger of the king and placed it on the altar. The king had to fall in front of the idol on the altar and promise that he would rule the nation in justice. Then the priest offered sacrifices, after which he put the ring back on the king's finger, symbolically renewing the kingship.[2] Indian kings practiced similar religious traditions where the king's rule was restored annually before a deity.[3]

Although David's rule is assured, the kings must walk faithfully, with integrity and uprightness in all they do (9:4). Then God's promise to David will be fully fulfilled (9:5).

Verses 6–9 echo the main teaching of Deuteronomy (Deut 28:11–15), which is that obedience to the Lord brings blessing and disobedience brings curses and punishments. The list of punishments for disobedience includes losing the land to enemies. If the Israelites disobey, they will be removed from their land. Moreover, they will be rejected and the temple will be destroyed. In consequence, the nation will become an object of ridicule and will lose its reputation as the chosen people of Yahweh (1 Kgs 9:6–7). If the people forsake Yahweh, who brought them out of bondage in Egypt, and worship other gods and goddesses with sacrifices and offerings, they will be cut off from their land and ridiculed by other nations (9:7–9). The exodus tradition is mentioned here as a reminder of the Sinai covenant, which commands the Israelites to worship Yahweh alone.

These verses also warn us that observing God's law and practicing his values are more important than any building projects (9:7). This warning needs to be remembered by those who put more importance on the architecture, towers, bells, or paintings of church buildings rather than genuine worship and the ethical life demanded by the Bible.

---

2. "Akkadian Rituals," in *ANET* (New Jersey: Princeton University Press, 1969), 334–335.
3. *Cilappathigaram*, an ancient Tamil literature, narrates the evaluation of King Pandian.

9:10–28 SOLOMON'S OTHER ACTIVITIES

After receiving Yahweh's confirmation through the dream, Solomon continues to build the kingdom (9:10–28). He gave towns to King Hiram as payment for building materials (9:10–14); he constructed additional buildings and developed towns throughout the kingdom of Israel (9:15–24); he offered sacrifices at the temple according to the religious requirements (9:25); and he built a fleet of ships to develop commercial trade with other countries (9:26–28).

9:10–14 Towns as Payment

At the end of twenty years, Solomon gave twenty towns in Galilee to King Hiram of Tyre as a payment for the cedar, juniper, and gold that Hiram had supplied for the construction of the temple and palace (9:10–11). This payment did not satisfy Hiram (9:12). After seeing the towns, which may have been situated near Tyre, Hiram described them as the "Land of Kabul," which means "not worth" anything, "defective," or "good-for-nothing" (9:13). In spite of this criticism, Hiram supplied more resources: 120 talents of gold (9:14).

9:15–24 Constructions

Solomon engaged in several building constructions (9:15–24). In addition to the Lord's temple and his own palace, he built the terraces, the wall of Jerusalem, and the cities of Hazor, Megiddo, and Gezer (9:15). Gezer was a wedding gift to Solomon from his father-in-law, the king of Egypt; Solomon rebuilt it (9:16–17a). Solomon built up Lower Beth Haron, Balath, and Tadmore in the desert region within his boundary (9:17b–18). Solomon gave some of these towns and cities more attention because he wanted to strengthen them to secure the northern, central, and southern borders. He built storehouses in some cities and towns, where he could store agricultural produce for the royal families, court officials, commanders, and army (9:19). He stationed his chariots and horses in various towns so that he would be ready for war.

To complete these building projects, Solomon needed a large labor force. Verses 20–23 describe the two kinds of laborers that Solomon used. First, he used the forced labor of Canaanites who had been left in Israel as slaves (9:20–21). Second, Solomon used labor from the Israelite community, but they were not slaves because the law of Moses did not allow one Israelite to make another Israelite a slave (9:22; compare Deut 15:12–15). The Israelites served as his "fighting men, his government officials, his officers, his captains, and the commanders of his chariots and charioteers" (9:22). In addition, 550 of them served as supervising officials in charge of Solomon's projects (9:23).

Solomon was careful not to use Canaanites in his army or as officials who supervised the construction projects. Instead, he made sure that all of his Canaanite workers were overseen by Israelites to avoid hampering the work and also to prevent treason. Similarly, Sri Lanka changed its policy to employ only the Sinhalese in the army and police force.[4]

9:24 Gezer

Gezer was a Canaanite city. The king of Egypt, Solomon's father-in-law, defeated it and killed all its inhabitants (9:16). When he gave his daughter to Solomon as a wife, he gave Gezer as her dowry. His daughter, Solomon's wife, remained there until Solomon built a palace for her in the City of David, and then the supporting terraces (9:24).

9:25 Annual Festivals

Although Solomon was busy with building projects, he did not forget his religious obligations, as the Lord instructed. Three times every year, he offered burnt offerings and fellowship offerings on the altar he had built for the Lord along with burning incense (9:25). Most likely these were the festivals of Passover, Festival of Weeks, and the Festival of Booths (Exod 23:14–17; Deut 16:16).[5] Solomon fulfilled his religious duties and kept the temple and priests busy in the service of the Lord.

9:26–28 Shipping and Trade

Solomon also ventured into building ships to develop commercial trade with other countries (1 Kgs 9:26–28). Since the Phoenicians, who lived near the Mediterranean Sea, were skilled boat builders and sailors, Solomon once again sought help from King Hiram in Tyre. The main dockyard for building ships was Ezion Geber, which was near Edom on the coast of the Red Sea (9:26). With the help of Hiram's sailors, Solomon's servants sailed to Ophir and brought back 420 talents of gold (9:27–28). The exact location of Ophir is not known, but scholars suggest that it is in the region of South Arabia, possibly Oman or Yemen.

---

4. TV news during the time of civil war in Sri Lanka between LTTE (Liberation Tigers of Tamil Elam) and the Government. One can infer from the lengthy report of civil war between LTTE and Sri Lankan Government, Tamil soliders were not involved in the war since it was against the Tamils. See https://en.Wikipedia. org/wiki/Sri Lankan Civil War, accessed on August 6, 2021.
5. Roland de Vaux, *Ancient Israel: Its Life and Institutions* (London: Darton, Longman and Todd, 1978), 484–506.

1 KINGS 10:1–29
SOLOMON'S WISDOM AND WEALTH

A good leader's fame and popularity grow and spread based on his or her achievements. The person could be a king, political, leader, business person, religious leader, or an activist. If the person is accepted and appreciated by people, he or she can become famous at the global level. Mother Teresa and other recipients of the Nobel Prize are such examples. 1 Kings chapter 10 tells us that Solomon rose to this level of greatness because of the wisdom and wealth he had accumulated. His greatness was not achieved by his own efforts but by his request for a wise and discerning heart and God fulfilling his request (3:11–15). This chapter can be divided into two distinct literary sections: the visit of the queen of Sheba (10:1–13) and Solomon's wealth (10:14–29).

10:1–13 VISIT OF THE QUEEN OF SHEBA

Though the name of the queen is not mentioned, she was the ruling monarch of Sheba. Women often ruled a kingdom. Cleopatra of Egypt, Sobekneferu of Egypt, Neferneferuaten Nefertiti of Egypt, Theodora of Rome, Empress Wu Zetian of China, and Olga of Kiev are some of them. Rani Lakshmi Bai (AD 1828–1858) was a ruler and freedom fighter in India, from the state of Jhansi in North India. Scholars are not sure of Sheba's location, but some suggest it was Yemen.[1] This section has the following divisions: the arrival of the queen of Sheba (10:1–3), her visit with Solomon (10:4–5), her affirmation of his wisdom and wealth (10:6–9), and her gifts (10:10–13).[2]

10:1–3 The Queen of Sheba's Arrival

The queen of Sheba arrived at Solomon's court in Jerusalem after hearing about his fame. Without electronic media to show the splendor of a king in those days, the fame of a king spread through the people who travelled to various places, such as traders, sailors, and those who worked on building projects. The queen particularly wanted to know and test Solomon's wisdom

---
1. Hens-Piazza, *1–2 Kings*, 98.
2. Hiram was included to say that riches were coming from visitors and allies. Wiseman, *1 and 2 Kings*, 141.

and his relationship with his God. The term "test" (Heb. *nasah*) refers to answering riddles and puzzles.[3] Most likely she did not come to start a trade route between the two nations or to maintain security and peace in the region of Red Sea.[4] She wanted to raise some questions about ethical issues to hear how Solomon will respond. "Solomon answered all her questions; nothing was too hard for the king to explain to her" (10:3). She did not come empty handed: she came "with camels carrying spices, large quantities of gold, and precious stones" (10:2).

10:4–5 Seeing is Believing

The queen of Sheba not only notices Solomon's wisdom, but also the splendor of the palace, the quantity and quality of food on the table, the seating of his officials according to their ranks, the robes of the officials attending his court, the dress of the cupbearers, and the burnt offerings offered at the temple. The report says that she was overwhelmed by all she witnessed (10:5).

10:6–9 The Queen of Sheba's Affirmation

After seeing Solomon's wisdom and achievements, she responds by acknowledging that what she has heard about Solomon is true (10:6–7). She is struck by the happiness of the people and officials (10:8). Solomon's achievements are measured by the happiness of the people in the country. And, she acknowledges God as the real source of Solomon's success: "Praise be to the LORD your God, who has delighted in you and placed you on the throne of Israel" (10:9). She realizes God's eternal love for Israel has made Solomon the king in order to maintain justice and righteousness (10:10; compare Deut 7:7–9). She might not have accepted Yahweh as her God or converted to the worship of Yahweh. She is only saying that the God of Israel, who is delighted in Solomon, should be appreciated and praised. Solomon's prosperity is the result of God fulfilling his promises to Solomon. As a queen who belonged to the faith of another god, Sheba recognized the abundant blessings that had been showered upon Solomon by his God. This implies that Yahweh is a living God, who is powerfully acting in the history of his people to fulfill his promises and keep his covenant with them.

---

3. The term "test" (*nasah hidoth* – testing with hard questions) does not refer to an academic test or political matters but answering riddles and puzzles that Solomon had to prove himself wise. Hens-Piazza, *1–2 Kings*, 98.
4. Wiseman, *1 and 2 Kings*, 139.

10:10–13 Exchange of Gifts

After responding with this speech, the queen gives Solomon gifts of gold, a large quantity of spices, and precious stones (10:10). These gifts were not rewards for answering her questions, but a good gesture of alliance, hospitality, and appreciation. She was not alone in giving Solomon gifts: Hiram, his ally in Tyre, did the same (10:11). In addition to gold, Hiram's ships brought almugwood, which is a red wood found in India, Sri Lanka, and some parts of Lebanon that is durable and good for polishing, shining, and musical instruments.[5] Solomon used this wood to make supports for the temple of the Lord and for the royal palaces (10:12a). In addition, he made musical instruments like harps and lyres (10:12b). As a customary practice, Solomon reciprocates this gesture to the queen of Sheba – "all she desired and asked for, besides what he had given her out of his royal bounty" (10:13a). With her questions and riddles answered and with abundance of gifts, the queen of Sheba returns to her country (10:13b).

10:14–29 ACCUMULATION OF WEALTH

The second section describes how Solomon used his wisdom to accumulate more wealth for the kingdom (10:14–29). He spent his riches to construct and decorate more buildings and to maintain a cavalry with chariots and fortifying cities. Solomon accumulated a large wealth, 23 metric tons of gold, through trading, collecting taxes from merchants, and receiving tributes from vassals and governors (10:14–15). Part of the gold was used for making shields of two kinds – a bigger one to cover the entire body and a smaller one to cover the chest. Some shields were also kept as showpieces, which were used during ceremonies to display Solomon's riches (10:16–17). This was a common practice among the kings of powerful nations in those days, just as powerful nations today display their fighter jets, modern tanks, and missiles during national celebrations.

Another custom of the period was to set the throne of the kings on a stage and decorate its steps with gold, brass, ivory, and fine wood (10:18). Putting the throne six or seven steps higher than the people enabled the king to view all his officials in the court as well as the people who were coming with their grievances and seeking solutions (10:19). Ancient Babylonian mythology considered these seven steps up to the throne to represent the seven layers of the divine cosmos, and the king who sat on the throne reflected an assurance of

---

5. Wiseman, *1 and 2 Kings*, 141.

God's power on the earth.[6] The Israelites might have altered the custom to six steps to reflect God creating the cosmos in six days.[7] In addition to the gold-plated ivory throne, Solomon asked the craftsmen to fix images of golden lions on both sides of the steps and the armrests of the throne (10:20). The lion is famous for roaring and being powerful enough to subdue its prey or attack any other animal coming into its territory, as we see in the stories of Samson (Judg 14:5–6) and David (1 Sam 17:34–35). Solomon preferred the image of lion on the armrests of the throne as a symbolic expression of his power and authority. The paintings of some ancient Hindu kings in south India depict the throne with a picture of a tiger, fish, or bow and arrow behind the seat, all symbols of courage and valor. These can be seen in the paintings of flags carried by kings and walls of temples in Madurai and Nellai.[8]

The household articles were also made of gold to reflect the status of the royalty (1 Kgs 10:21a). Silver was not preferred since it was not as valuable as gold (10:21b). Because Solomon had an abundant supply of gold through trade, he could afford this luxury. Verse 22 highlights his accumulation of wealth through his fleet of small ships, which sailed in the region of the Red Sea. The term "ships of Hiram" may indicate a type of long ship[9] used for trade between the Mediterranean Sea and different port cities in west Asia, and returned with enormous loads of goods once every three years. Moreover, kings and vassals from many nations came to Jerusalem to hear the wisdom of Solomon and to see his splendor, bearing tributes and gifts that added to his wealth (10:23–25). Solomon's trade was for territorial expansion or to colonize countries to get their wealth.

In addition, Solomon strengthened his defense by accumulating chariots and horses (10:26a). He had 1,400 chariots and 12,000 horses in Jerusalem (10:26b). He imported chariots and horses from Egypt and Kue[10] (10:28–29). Solomon bought a chariot for six hundred shekels of silver and a horse for a hundred and fifty shekels of silver, which may have been used for ceremonies. He sold some of the horses he bought to the Hitties and Arameans, which brought him additional wealth (10:29). Verse 27 highlights the economic boom that took place during Solomon's period: the silver that circulated was

---

6. Gray, *I and II Kings: A Commentary*, 266.
7. Gray, *I and II Kings: A Commentary*, 263.
8. See https://tamilandvedas.com/2012/6/21, 'Flags of Ancient Indian Kings.' See also en.wikipedia.org/wiki/List of Tamil Flags, accessed on July 26, 2021.
9. Provan, *1 and 2 Kings*, 89.
10. This may refer to Cilicia. Wiseman, *1 and 2 Kings*, 144.

as abundant as stones and rocks, which are found everywhere in Jerusalem. The idiomatic expression, "cedar as plentiful as sycamore-fig," also refers to the abundant resources that were circulating through trade (10:27). Some preachers of prosperity theology in India quote Solomon as an example and tell people that money, wealth, and property are not evil – only the love of them. While we cannot live without money, Jesus taught that we cannot serve God and wealth (Matt 6:19–24). We have many good examples including Sadhu Sunder Singh, Amy Carmichael, and Mother Teresa who led simple lifestyles and spent their income for the poor and needy.

1 KINGS 11:1-43

SOLOMON'S DECLINE

Those who reach the pinnacle of greatness and fame can quickly slide downhill due to a scandal, thereby losing their reputation and power. This pattern can be noticed in the lives of many politicians and religious leaders today. This would not happen if these leaders were more careful in both their personal and public life. Unfortunately, after reaching the pinnacle of greatness (as recounted in 1 Kings 8–10), Solomon experiences a reversal of events because of his own mistakes.

1 Kings 11 narrates this decline in four sections. First, Solomon marries foreign wives, promotes idolatry within Israel, and incurs God's punishment (11:1–13); second, God brings adversaries against Solomon (11:14–25); third, Solomon faces internal strife within Israel (11:26–40); fourth, Solomon dies (11:41–43). The story of Solomon's progress begins with 1 Kings 3 and ends with Solomon's decline in 1 Kings 11. This pattern of a king rising to power, committing sin, facing failure, and ending in decline is part of the Deuteronomic theology, which can be noticed in the stories of Saul, David, Solomon, and other kings who came after Solomon.

11:1-13 WIVES, GODS, AND IDOLATRY

The opening phrase, "King Solomon . . . loved many foreign women" (11:1), signals Solomon's downward trend, connecting it with Yahweh's warning, "You must not intermarry with them" (11:2). God forbid all the Israelites, including the leaders, from marrying foreign wives because he wanted his people to worship him alone, the living God, and not worship the gods and goddesses of the Canaanites (Deut 7:1–4). This condition was stipulated in the Ten Commandments (Exod 20:1–3).

1:1-8 Wives from Different Religions

Solomon's wives were from the Moabites, Ammonites, Edomites, Sidonians, and Hittites, in addition to the daughter of Pharaoh, whom Solomon had married earlier (1 Kgs 11:1). The theme of inter-religious marriage began when Solomon married Pharaoh's daughter (3:1; 9:24), and it runs throughout the story of Solomon's reign, appearing again in this list of wives from foreign nations (11:1). Solomon fell into the custom of having many wives and concubines like other kings. "Solomon held fast to them in love" (11:2), implying he could not resist the clutches of lust and sex. The number – seven hundred wives and three hundred concubines – could reflect a literary style that expresses having too many women or reality (11:3).

In his younger years, Solomon resisted their tug to promote foreign religions, but "as Solomon grew old, his wives turned his heart after other gods" (11:4). Rather than using the usual Hebrew word for "turn" (*sub*), which means to turn in the opposite direction, the narrator uses the Hebrew word *natah*, which means to turn away his heart from walking on the right path. As a result, "his heart was not fully devoted to the LORD," drawing a comparison with David's full commitment to Yahweh (11:4).[1] Yet Yahweh's expectation is that his people will "love your God with your full heart, mind and strength" (Deut 6:4).

Instead, Solomon followed Ashtoreth, the goddess of the Sidonians, and Molek, "the detestable god of the Ammonites" (1 Kgs 11:5). Ashtoreth was worshiped in Canaan as one of the consorts of Baal. As a nature and fertility deity, she was worshiped to bless the land with prosperity. She is like the Indian *Lakshmi*, the goddess of money and prosperity, often portrayed with gold coins pouring from one of her hands. Worshiping "Lucky Lakshmi" is supposed to bring wealth to her devotees. For the Israelites, however, worshiping the creation rather than the Creator God is idolatry.[2] Solomon went after Molek, the god of the Ammonites. The worshipers of Molek sacrificed young boys and girls while making a vow, believing that their vows would be fulfilled because of the sacrifices. Yahweh forbid such practices and considered Molek a "detestable god" (11:5). Unlike his father David who walked worthily before the Lord God, Solomon did evil in his eyes by worshiping Ashtoreth and Molek (11:6).

Solomon also promoted the worship of Chemosh, the detestable god of Moab, a warrior god. The Moabites worshiped and offered sacrifices to this god, believing that he would bring them victory in battle (Num 21:29; Jer 48:46). Instead of trusting the mighty God of Israel to protect his people, Solomon trusted Chemosh. Solomon worshiping foreign gods and goddesses

---

1. There is a play on words here. The narrator uses "fully" which in Hebrew is *shalem* with the consonants (*sh–l–m*), which is identical to the consonants in Solomon's name (*sh–l–m*). Solomon is not living "fully" up to his name.
2. D. F. Payne, "Baal," in *NBD*, 109–110; J. A. Motyer, "Idolatry," in *NBD*, 503–505.

from Sidon in the west to the region of Ammon and Moab in the east implies that Solomon polluted the entire land of Israel with these deities. He built high places for these gods (1 Kgs 11:7) and helped his wives burn incense and offer sacrifices to their national deities in the land of Israel (11:8). Basically, "Solomon did evil in the eyes of the Lord" (11:6).

Solomon's idolatrous actions are a contrast to his earlier efforts to build a temple for Yahweh. Just as Solomon sacrificed at the temple for Yahweh, he allowed his wives to sacrifice to foreign gods. He is solely responsible for polluting his country with the worship of the deities of different nations. Those who are covenanted with the Lord must remain loyal to Yahweh and cannot practice idolatry. Inter-religious marriage is a problem for those who follow the Lord, as it can lead to syncretism. Solomon's sin was not polygamy but his marriage to foreign wives, who worshiped other gods and goddesses. Ancient kings who had unlimited wives and lived an extravagant life often became spiritually bankrupt (Deut 17:17–18). Credible leaders must integrate faith, prayer, and public life in order to bring honor to God. Yahweh stands by his character, and he will not compromise with disobedient leaders.

11:9–13 God's Punishment

Yahweh's verdict is declared in the second section (11:9–13). "The Lord became angry with Solomon because his heart had turned away from the Lord" (11:9a). God had appeared to Solomon twice in dreams (11:9b), and in both incidents, God firmly told Solomon not to follow other gods (3:14; 9:6–7; 11:10). In addition to these warnings, Solomon already knew this commandment from the law of Moses. Because Solomon broke his covenant with Yahweh, God judges him by saying that he will tear away Solomon's kingdom (11:11). The image of tearing connects with the symbolic action in the next section, when Ahijah tears his new garment into twelve pieces and gives ten pieces to Jeroboam (11:29–31). Tearing usually means dividing something into pieces. First, God says that he will tear the rule from Solomon's hands and give it to one of his subordinates (11:11). The word "servant" in this verse refers to an official in Solomon's court who has the potential for leadership. Second, God has to maintain his promise to David while also maintaining the condition he gave to Solomon. God cannot make compromises with anyone who violates the norms of the covenant, but God can show compassion for the sake of David, who was humble and followed the Lord and wanted to establish a dwelling place for Yahweh in Jerusalem (11:12–13). Thus God assures Solomon that he will not tear away his kingdom while Solomon is alive.

God will allow Solomon to continue on the throne as the king of the united Israel, and he will not face humiliation through a coup or attack from enemies.

11:14–25 ADVERSARIES

After announcing judgment, God raises adversaries against Solomon. The narrator mentions two in particular: Hadad the Edomite (11:14–22) and Rezon son of Eliada (11:23–25). Hadad and Rezon come against Solomon because they had suffered under the rule of David. God raises them against Solomon because Solomon violated the law (Deut 7:3–5; 17:17). Solomon's kingship is coming to an end. Whenever the leaders of Israel failed to correct themselves and reform their religion and society, God brought external forces to punish them so that they would repent and follow their God again (Judg 2:11–20; Isa 44:28; Jer 25:8–14; Amos 3:11–15). The theology of retribution links together causes and consequences.

11:14–22 Hadad the Edomite

God raises Hadad, an Edomite from the royal family, to threaten Solomon's control over Israel (11:14). The past history of Hadad's flight to Egypt (2 Sam 8:13–14) recalls David's defeat of the Edomites through Joab and his control over them so that they had to pay tribute and would not rise up against Israel again (1 Kgs 11:15–18). Yet the Lord leads Pharaoh to support Hadad through a marriage alliance (11:19–20). Pharaoh's support of Hadad is not a betrayal of the agreement he had made with Solomon, who had married and loved Pharaoh's daughter. Pharaoh may have been planning to extend his political alliance to Edom. When Hadad heard that David and Joab died, he wants to return to his country to take revenge on Solomon (11:21). Pharaoh doesn't understand the logic and yet permits him to return (11:22).

1:23–25 Rezon Son of Eliada

God also raises up Rezon as an adversary against Solomon (11:23–25). Rezon was a military leader of Hadadezer, the king of Zobah (11:23). When David defeated the king of Zobah, Rezon fled to Damascus and strengthened his army (11:24; compare 2 Sam 8:3–8). After the death of David, Rezon started threatening Solomon (1 Kgs 11:25). Thus the last period of Solomon's life was filled with threats from both the north and east.

1 KINGS 11:1–43

11:26–40 JEROBOAM, AN INTERNAL STRIFE

Along with these external threats, internal problems started mounting within Israel. It began with Jeroboam.

11:26–28 Introduction of Jeroboam

Jeroboam hailed from the town of Zeredah, which was located in the northwest of Bethel and belonged to the tribe of Ephraim. His mother, Zeruah, was a widow (11:26). He was one of Solomon's officials. His name meant, "may he contend for the people," and is confirmed in the statement, "he rebelled against the king" (11:27). He didn't rebel against the king until he met Ahijah, the prophet, who prophesied about the divided kingdom. In fact, Solomon appreciated the work of Jeroboam and placed him in charge of the whole labor force (11:28).

Jeroboam was an official as well as "a man of standing" (11:28). This phrase means that he was trustworthy and loyal in the job. As a result, Solomon made him the overseer of the entire labor force for the house of Joseph. The term "house of Joseph" refers to the tribes of Ephraim and Manasseh, who had settled on the west side of the Jordan. The narrator provides this background information to inform the reader that Jeroboam was part of Solomon's administration and knew well the progress, burden, suffering, and criticism of the people.

11:29–39 Prophecy of Ahijah

Throughout the biblical narrative, God raises up prophets to speak the truth to leaders. Ahijah, the prophet of Shiloh, puts on a new cloak and meets Jeroboam on the road to communicate God's plan through a symbolic action (11:29). Ahijah tears his new cloak into twelve pieces and asks Jeroboam to pick up ten pieces. Then Ahijah explains the meaning of this symbolic act (11:30–32).

First, he says that God will tear the kingdom from Solomon's hands and give ten tribes to Jeroboam (11:31). According to the geographical settlement of the twelve tribes, the tribes of Benjamin and Judah settled in the extreme south, and the other ten tribes were in the north and the Transjordan region (Num 32–34; Josh 13–19). However, when Solomon changed the borders of the tribal territories, he joined some towns from one tribal area to another tribal territory for the sake of revenues and taxes. As a result, the tribe of

Benjamin gradually merged with the tribe of Judah forming just "one tribe" (1 Kgs 11:32).[3]

Second, even though God will divide the nation and make Jeroboam the king of the ten northern tribes, Solomon's successor will rule over the southern territory of Judah and Benjamin. The tribes of Judah and Benjamin will be given to Solomon's family because of God's promise and the covenant he made with David for choosing Jerusalem as his dwelling place (11:32). On the other hand, he will divide the tribes and give Jeroboam the northern ten tribes because of Solomon worshiping Ashtoreth, Chemosh, and Molek (11:33).

Third, this division will not happen until Solomon had died because of God's promise to David (11:34). Only after Solomon's son starts reigning will the kingdom be divided (11:35). God will let Solomon's son continue to reign because of his faithfulness to David so that "David my servant may always have a lamp before me in Jerusalem, the city where I chose to put my Name" (11:36). This verse means that one of David's descendants will continue to rule in Jerusalem. A lamp is a symbol for a descendant or successor continuing the family or dynasty.[4]

Fourth, God will appoint Jeroboam as a ruler over "all that your heart desires," that is, he will be a king over Israel (11:37). But he must continue to obey "whatever I command you and walk in obedience to me and do what is right in my eyes by obeying my decrees and commands, as David my servant did" (11:38a). And, God will be with him and build his dynasty. It too will last as David did. Kings may be changed one after another to rule the kingdom, but the divine conditions for ruling God's people are unchanging, from the time of David to Solomon to Jeroboam.

Finally, God will humble David's descendants in this way, but not forever (11:39). God promises to humble the dynasty of Solomon before him, but it would not be forever. This promise ultimately finds fulfilment in Jesus, the son of David, a descendant of Solomon.

11:40 Solomon's Reaction

Ahijah's prophetic message prepares Jeroboam to lead the country after Solomon. When Solomon learns that the Lord had prepared the next leader through a prophet, Solomon seeks to kill Jeroboam (11:40). This trend echoes Saul's attempt to kill David after God had selected David to be the king. God

---

3. Bright, *History of Israel*, 217–218.
4. Wiseman, *1 and 2 Kings*, 149.

protects Jeroboam; Jeroboam escapes to Egypt and becomes a fugitive under the rule of King Shishak (ca. 945–924 BC) until the death of Solomon.

11:41–43 DEATH OF SOLOMON

The death of a king is normally reported using a formula that has four elements: first, the number of years that a king ruled; second, his death and burial; third, the name of his successor; fourth, a reference to the annals of his activities and war. The narrator begins with the fourth element and says that his activities are recorded in "the annals of Solomon" (11:31). Many kings appointed chroniclers in their court to record the discussions, decisions, and all the religious, social, and political activities of kings. These documents were preserved in special record rooms. Then he says Solomon ruled for forty years (11:42). Solomon then "rested with his ancestors," a polite way of referring to the demise and burial of an elderly person within the culture of ancient Israel (11:43). The polite phrase in Hindu culture is to say that the person has "reached the feet of god," implying that the body is burnt but the *atman* (soul) has reached Brahma (godhead in Hinduism). Christians use the expression, "asleep in the Lord," to describe the time between a funeral service and the expected resurrection (1 Thess 4:13–17). Finally, the narrative says that Solomon's son, Rehoboam, succeeded him to the throne (ca. 932 BC).

1 KINGS 12:1–33
REHOBOAM AND JEROBOAM: A DIVIDED MONARCHY

A new chapter in the history of Israel begins in 1 Kings 12, which narrates the tension between the ruling monarch, Rehoboam, the son of Solomon, and his rival, Jeroboam. This rivalry resulted in the separation of ten tribes from the united nation of Israel to form the northern kingdom of Israel. The house of David and Benjamin formed the southern kingdom of Judah.

The narrative can be divided into two main sections: the events leading up to the division of Israel into two kingdoms (12:1–24) and the reign of Jeroboam in the north kingdom (12:25–33).

12:1–24 EVENTS LEADING TO THE DIVISION

As prophesied by the prophet Ahijah (11:29–39), soon after the death of Solomon, events took place toward dividing the kingdom into the northern Israel and the southern Judah. This section has four events: Rehoboam and the people's request (12:1–5); Rehoboam's rejection of the people's request (12:6–15); the northern tribes' decision to separate (12:16–20); and Rehoboam's encounter with the prophet that averts a civil war (12:21–24).

12:1–5 Rehoboam and the People's Request

Following Solomon's death, Rehoboam succeeded as the king of the united Israel (933–917 BC). He went to Shechem to be coronated as the king. Shechem was an ancient town and had a historical significance. After settling in Canaan, Joshua gathered all the tribes at Shechem and renewed the covenant (Josh 23:25). It was in the territory of Ephraim, a central place that connected the north and south. All Israel joined Rehoboam there to make him the new king (1 Kgs 12:1). His coronation could have resembled that of David's and Solomon's with the people affirming, "Hail the king" (1 Sam 10:1–24; 1 Kgs 1:30–40).[1]

---

1. Bright, *History of Israel*, 183.

While Rehoboam was made king, Jeroboam son of Nebat returned from Egypt (12:2). He had fled there when Solomon tried to kill him and took shelter with King Shishak (11:40). When he returned, being a former official of Solomon, he became one among the spokepersons for the people (12:3). The people made a collective request to Rehoboam to lessen the burden of labor that had been imposed by his father, Solomon (12:4). The harsh labor that burdened the people was connected with all of Solomon's building projects. The people did not object to serving the king by producing food, promoting agriculture, working in the palace, or defending the country in times of attack; rather, they objected to the burden of forced construction. Today, the problems of bonded slavery continue in quarry and construction projects in South Asia. The building records for the huge temples in Asia also indicate how people were forced into labor by the kings. The people asked Rehoboam to lighten their forced labor. After all, Solomon's building projects had lasted for twenty long years (9:10). And, it might have demanded all the men's time and energy, and so they could not devote attention to their households, wives, and children.[2] Though the text does not explicitly mention this reason, it remains true even today. In addition, they might have paid high taxes and revenues to meet the costs of constructing and furnishing the temple and palaces. After hearing the people's request, Rehoboam asked the people to return in three days to receive his response (12:5).

12:6–15 Rejection of the Request from the North

During this three-day waiting period, Rehoboam consulted with his elders for advice (12:6). This is a good approach for any leader. Leaders should consult wise and capable people who will give them good advice, and then they should listen to the advice, evaluate it in the light of divine values, and implement it. The elders whom Rehoboam consults were experienced and able officials who served Solomon in the court and offices (12:6). They knew the ground reality, and so they advised Rehoboam to grant the people's request and win them over to his side, saying, "give them a favorable answer, they will always be your servants" (12:7).

Unfortunately, Rehoboam rejected their advice and consulted with young people who had grown up with him (12:8–9). This verse indicates that Rehoboam wanted to continue to rule just as his father had ruled. When the young people supported Rehoboam without any disagreement, it suited

---

2. Hens-Piazza, *1–2 Kings*, 122.

his interests. The young men advised the king to tell the people that he would make their burdens even heavier than the labor that Solomon had imposed on them. The reply that the youth scripted for Rehoboam conveys both arrogance and contempt. The first phrase, "My little finger is thicker than my father's waist" (12:10), could be a vulgar cultural expression to express disrespect.[3] This figurative way of comparing someone to a little finger is intended to humiliate the person for his or her minimal status, power, or wealth. The second phrase, "I will scourge you with scorpions," recommends a form of torture that is even more cruel than his father's whips, which were used to beat the people and make them obey (12:11). When scorpions sting people, they inject their poison into the skin, which makes people cry out in pain and may even cause death.

Three days later, Rehoboam called the people and spoke harshly to them (12:12–13). Instead of following the advice of the elders, he followed the advice of the young men and repeated what they had said to him (12:14). A leader must be careful to keep administrative issues separate from friendships. Close friendships have misled many leaders to commit blunders and promote corruption. Regardless, Rehoboam's stubbornness and decision were to fulfill the prophesy of Ahijah that God would tear apart the kingdom of Israel because of Solomon's sin (12:15). God works his plans in mysterious ways to fulfill his purposes. Even Rehoboam's rebellious heart was to fulfill God's plan to separate the kingdoms.

12:16–20 Decision to Separate from the Union

When the people received this harsh and humiliating reply from Rehoboam, they were upset and decided to separate and refuse to serve the king. They express their decision in a poetic style:

> "What share do we have in David,
> What part in Jesse's son?
> To your tents, Israel!
> Look after your own house, David!" (12:16)

The first two lines uses the rhetorical device of the question, "What?" They are poetical parallelism expressing their decision that they do not want to have any "share" in the kingdom of David, and so they are severing the relationship with the kingdom hereafter. The phrase, "to your tents," is a formula for bidding farewell and departing that is used to express the action that the people will

---

3. Hens-Piazza, *1–2 Kings*, 123.

take now that they have decided not to be part of the kingdom. They instruct the house of David to look after their own affairs, meaning that the people of the north are leaving Rehoboam and will work out their kingdom under another leadership. Soon after saying this, the people went home.

The people's decision to separate from Judah left Rehoboam to rule over the towns of Judah (12:17). Unable to tolerate the revolt, Rehoboam sent Adoniram, an official in charge of forced labor, to control the rebellion of the ten tribes, but the people stoned him to death (12:18a). Hearing of his death, Rehoboam fled to Jerusalem in his chariot (12:18b). This rebellion continued for a long time, until the time of the composition of this book (12:19), 721 BC.

Soon after Rehoboam fled to Judah, the Israelites made Jeroboam as the king over the northern tribes, Israel (12:20a). He had been with the people in Shechem and had represented their collective request to Rehoboam to lessen the people's burden. The people invited Jeroboam to the assembly to confirm him as king (933–912 BC). But the tribe of Judah (including Benjamin) remained loyal to David and kept Rehoboam as their king (12:20b).

12:21–24 Rehoboam and the Prophet

Arriving in Jerusalem, Rehoboam gathered 120,000 men from the tribes of Judah and Benjamin to take military action against the northern tribes to subdue and control them (12:21). Once again, God intervenes by sending the prophet, Shemaiah, to ensure that the prophecy foretold by Ahijah about how God would tear apart the kingdom of Israel would be fulfilled (12:22–24). The phrase, "man of God," describes Shemaiah as a prophet (see 17:24). Rather than sending Ahijah to speak to Rehoboam, God sent Shemaiah, who told the people of Judah and Benjamin that the separation and Jeroboam's confirmation as a king was God's doing and will, and so they should not go to war against the northern tribes. If they went to war, they would be fighting against God's plan and would not be successful (12:24a). In this way, the prophet played a political role in stopping the civil war and so avoided much bloodshed. Rehoboam obeyed the word of God and sent the people back to their homes (12:24b). Rehoboam's obedience at this point in the story contrasts with Jeroboam's disobedience in the following narratives.

12:25–33 JEROBOAM'S REIGN

Jeroboam starts ruling the northern kingdom of Isarel (12:25–33). The section describes how Jeroboam consolidated his position as king of the ten tribes in the north (12:25), his unwarranted fear (12:26–27), and his installation of idolatry as that of Solomon (12:28–33).

12:25 Consolidation

When a king begins to rule a new territory, his first step is often to strengthen the borders. Thus Jeroboam fortified Shechem as his capital and dwelt there (12:25a). Then he built up Peniel in Gilead to guard against invasion from the Amorites (12:25b).

12:26–27 Unwarranted Fear

Unfortunately, he was disturbed by a fear that the people would abandon him and return to Rehoboam (12:26). He was worried that if their allegiance to Rehoboam began to grow, they would create political trouble. Instead of overcoming this fear by trusting in God's plan for him to rule over the ten tribes in the north, as prophesied by Ahijah, Rehoboam began to plot how he could stop the people from going to the temple in Jerusalem for festivals and offering sacrifices (12:27). He feared that any visit to Jerusalem would develop relationships between the northern tribes and the people of Judah and Benjamin, and so he wanted to end these regular trips to the south.

12:28–33 Installation of Idolatry

After consulting with his officials, Jeroboam decided to install the worship of golden calves (12:28a). Whereas Rehoboam consulted his elders but decided to ignore their advice, Jeroboam's advisors gave him the wrong decision in the first place. Jeroboam made two golden calves and presented them as the gods who brought them out of Egypt (12:28b). Idols of golden calves were not new to the Israelites, because Aaron had introduced this form of worship during the exodus (Exod 32:1–6). The head of Apis, one of the gods of Egypt, was represented in the form of a bull. Baal, the Canaanite deity, was depicted as a bull in their myths. The bull is a symbol of the power to procreate in fertility cults or to attack enemies in other cults. In India, cows and bulls are worshiped as gods because they have the power of procreation and supply milk. Jeroboam used the symbol of a golden calf to represent Yahweh's image, and he echoed the words that Aaron had spoken to the Israelites in the wilderness. This act violated God's commandment to the Israelites, which forbids them from making images for their worship, because God cannot be represented by any image (Exod 20:4; Lev 26:1; Deut 5:8). Jeroboam connected the idols with the historical tradition of Yahweh liberating Israel so that the Israelites would believe in the idol as a powerful god. This lie was wrong and reveals how Jeroboam was trying to use religion for his own political gain. Instead of Jerusalem, he made two alternative cultic centers in Bethel, at the southern border of his kingdom, and Dan, at the northern border, so that people would not need to cross the border into the southern kingdom of Rehoboam and to the temple in Jerusalem (12:29).

After putting the idols inside the cultic centers at Bethel and Dan, Jeroboam built shrines for idols all over the country so that people would have easy access to worship them (12:31a). Next, Jeroboam appointed non-Levites as priests in these shrines, violating the Levitical tradition that God had ordained (12:31b). Instead of following the pattern of having altars to offer sacrifices for Yahweh and priests to minister from the tribe of Levites, as in the early settlement period to which the Israelites were accustomed, Jeroboam introduced a new religious system to suit himself. Next, he changed the calendar and chose the months when the Israelites should offer sacrifices (12:32). He also instituted new festivals so that the people would not go to Jerusalem, the chosen place of Yahweh, to celebrate the old required festivals (12:33a). Finally, he visited the shrines himself, promoting the worship of idols to the Israelites (12:33b). All these actions went against Yahweh's plan to centralize worship in the temple of Jerusalem and to avoid building shrines and offering sacrifices on the high places for other gods.

Jeroboam should have guided the people in the north towards the proper worship of Yahweh, but instead he promoted all the new idols and shrines with non-Levitical priests and his new festal calendar, leading the people to go to Bethel and Dan to worship the golden calves. The verdict, "this thing became a sin," judged Jeroboam as responsible for the people's idolatry (12:30). His sins against God are referred to again in 1 Kings 13:34 and 2 Kings 17:21. The phrase, "sin of Jeroboam," based on his introduction of idolatry in Israel (1 Kings 12) became a reference point that was used by the narrator to evaluate the rule of some kings.

1 KINGS 13:1–34

THE CONSEQUENCES OF JEROBOAM'S SIN

Jeroboam's idolatry had consequences. First, a man of God came and prophesied against the false altar, which led to conflict between Jeroboam and the man of God (13:1–10). Second, the man of God himself was deceived and killed by another man of God who lied to him (13:11–32). Third, Jeroboam continued in his sins despite repeated warning resulting in his ultimate downfall (13:33–34).

13:1–10 THE KING AND THE MAN OF GOD

Jeroboam continued his idolatrous worship in Bethel. So God sent a man of God, a prophet, to warn him. The phrase, "by the word of the LORD," authenticates that the message he is proclaiming is from the Lord (this phrase appears eight times in this chapter: 13:1, 2, 5, 9, 18, 20, 26, 32). The prophet came from Judah, the land of David and Rehoboam. While he reached Bethel, Jeroboam was standing by the altar ready to make an offering (13:1). So he spoke and said, "Altar, altar! This is what the LORD says: 'A son named Josiah will be born to the house of David. On you he will sacrifice the priests of the high places who make offerings here, and human bones will be burned on you'" (13:2). It is strange that the man of God cried against the altar rather than against Jeroboam. Usually, prophets address an individual (2 Sam 12:7–13), a city (Amos 1:3, 6, 9), or the people of Israel or Judah, calling them to listen. The man of God addressed the altar directly, calling out, "Altar, altar" (1 Kgs 13:2). This is an indirect way of communicating with the king, who was standing by the altar burning incense (13:1). Josiah, a king, will be born in the family of David, implying the continuation of the dynasty in the southern kingdom. And, Josiah will not tolerate the priests offering sacrifices to the idols, and so he will sacrifice those priests on the same altar. Human bones will be burnt on the altar next to Jeroboam (13:2). Because the pagan priests of the high places offered human sacrifices to Molek and other burnt offerings to the idols, they will be burnt alive on altars. This could have been a warning for the priests, who were standing by the altar with Jeroboam.

Josiah becomes a king 295 years after this prophesy (638–608 BC). So the man of God also declares a sign from the Lord to endorse the genuineness of God's message with the certainty of its eventual fulfillment (13:3). The sign is that the altar will be split apart and the ashes on it will be poured out by the mighty power of God. This sign happened on the same day, and the king and priests all witnessed the destruction of the altar and the ashes pouring out of it (13:5). This sign proved that the man of God's prophecy was from the Lord and also previewed what would happen during the future rule of Josiah.

After seeing the sign, instead of repenting and abandoning the worship of idols, Jeroboam became angry and ordered the people around him to seize the prophet. Then the king stretched out his hand to capture the man of God and kill him (13:4). After Jeroboam stretches out a hand, however, he could not bring it back. At the same time, the altar was split apart and its ashes fell on the ground, as prophesied by the man of God (13:5). Once Jeroboam realized that the power of God was making him unable to stretch out his hand to harm the prophet, he pleaded with the man of God to pray for his hand to be restored (13:6a). The man of God graciously interceded with the Lord to restore the king's hand (13:6b). Though God selected Jeroboam to bring about God's plan for the separation of the ten tribes under the ruthless rule of Rehoboam, here he is condemned for failing to honor the conditions of the prophetic word given to him by Ahijah (11:38). He disobeyed the commandments and statutes of the Lord, and so the kingdom will be taken from him, just as it was torn from Rehoboam.

As the king witnessed the signs and wonders of the Lord performed through the man of God, he knew that the prophet was a genuine servant of God whose prophecies were true. So, Jeroboam invited the man of God to return to the king's home for a meal so that the prophet could receive a gift for restoring the king's hand (13:7). But the man of God refused, repeating the instructions the Lord had given him (13:8–9). The man of God rejected the king's offer in order to obey the Lord. His obedience here contrasts with Jeroboam's disobedience.

13:11–32 THE OLD PROPHET AND THE MAN OF GOD

Jeroboam's sin of idolatry resulted in a judgment against him and the death of a man of God through false prophesy. This section narrates that latter story.

As news about the signs and message from the man of God from Judah spread, the sons of an old prophet living in Bethel reported the event to their father (13:11). Bethel had been a cultic center for a long time, where people would go to consult prophets. Some were professional prophets who earned their living from these cultic centers, and so they defended the cultic centers and their rulers (Amos 7:10–15). This old prophet of Bethel wanted to meet the man of God, and so he asked his sons to help him arrange his journey (1 Kgs 13:12–14). After confirming the man of God's identity, the old prophet invited the man from Judah back to his home for meal (13:15). The man of God gave the prophet the same reply that he had given to the king that he could not eat anywhere in the land of Israel as instructed by God (13:16–17).

The old prophet had not been sent by God to meet the man of God from Judah, and yet he introduced himself as a prophet (13:18a). Then he told a lie, saying that an angel had appeared to him and told him to invite the man of God to his home for food and drink (13:18b). The old prophet was not supposed to tell lies. Yet, he purposefully misled the man of God. So the man of God returned with the old prophet to his house to share a meal (13:19). The man of God may have assumed that Yahweh had changed his earlier instruction through this old man. A prophet should always analyze the words of another prophet to discern if he is speaking the truth in the name of the Lord. The man of God should have noticed the contradiction between what Yahweh had said to him and what the old prophet was saying in the name of God. The man of God from Judah could have asked the Lord to confirm whether this prophecy was false or true. Without that confirmation, the man of God should have chosen to obey God's command rather than the words of the old prophet. Instead, the man of God returned with the old prophet and ate and drank in his house (13:19).

Now, the word of the Lord came to the old prophet and he cried out against the man of God asking why he defiled the word of the Lord and didn't obey him (13:20–21). As a punishment of his disobedience his body "will not be buried in the tomb" of his ancestors (13:22), a cultural expression that means that he will not be buried with his ancestors or have proper funeral rites. This implies he will not reach his home but will die on the road. Even today, some villagers in India believe that their relatives should be buried along with their ancestors in the garden of their families, and so they bring the dead body to the family's burial ground so that the dead person will not be alienated from his ancestors. When the dead person is buried in the family graveyard, his community believes that they have honored him by returning him to his own soil. For if his body was cremated in a city far away from his village, he would be cut off from his native soil and ancestors.

The man of God finished eating and drinking (13:23a). Then the old prophet put him on the saddled donkey and sent him off to his hometown (13:23b). On the way home, a lion killed the man of God and left his body on the road, neither eating his body nor attacking his donkey (13:24). The lion stood there, as if guarding the dead body from other animals or eagles. Some people passed by, saw the lion guarding the body of the prophet, and reported the incident to the people in Bethel (13:25). The lion's behavior implies that God sent it to fulfill the old prophet's prophecy. When this news about the man of God reached the old prophet at Bethel, he remembered God's prophecy about his death (13:26). The prophet felt sorry for this sad demise of the man of God, and so he went and took the body and buried it in his own tomb in Bethel (13:27–30). His gesture of burying and mourning could be regarded as respecting another prophet, but it also fulfilled the curse that the man's body would not be taken to Judah and buried in his own land with his ancestors.

Then the old prophet instructed his sons to bury his own dead body in the same grave with the man of God (13:31). He also told his sons that the prophecy of the man of God from Judah against the altars and shrines in Bethel and Samaria was true and would be fulfilled (13:32).

Commentators give several explanations why the old prophet asked his sons to bury him in the same grave with the man of God.[1] First, the prophet from Bethel may have wanted to identify himself with a true prophet of God, whose prophecies are genuine and will be fulfilled. Second, the prophet may have wanted to express unity between the prophets from the north and south, at least in death. Third, he may have wanted to preserve the history of this encounter between the man of God from Judah, King Jeroboam, and his own experience so that future generations would hear the story about this event at Bethel. Fourth, the prophet may have wanted to sanctify his death through contact with a true prophet whose prophecy had come from God.[2] In 2 Kings, we learn that Josiah did not destroy this grave when he destroyed the shrines and altar of Bethel in order to preserve the history of this event (2 Kgs 23:17–18). Regardless, Jeroboam's idolatry resulted in the death of the man of God and the false prophecy of the old prophet.

---

1. Hens-Piazza, *1–2 Kings*, 136.
2. Simon J. DeVries, *1 Kings*, 171.

13:33–34 THE KING CONTINUES IN SIN

In spite of all these incidents, Jeroboam did not turn away from his wrong activities (13:33a). Instead, he continued to appoint priests for the high places to conduct worship at the altars he had built there (13:33b). These priests were not from the tribe of Levi. Both his sin of idolatry and setting aside the house of Levi resulted in his downfall and the destruction of his dynasty from "the face of the earth" (13:34). This, too, is a prophecy as the total exile of the northern kingdom will not happen until several hundred years after this prophecy.

THE PRIESTHOOD

One of Jeroboam's many sins was appointing priests for the high places of other gods (1 Kgs 13:33). The writer continues, "This was the sin of the house of Jeroboam that led to its downfall and to its destruction from the face of the earth" (13:34). Israel shouldn't worship other gods or have priests for other gods because they were God's chosen people (Exod 2:1–10; Num 1:47–54). Although the OT considers the entire people of Israel as special people of God, the tribe of Levi was set aside as a kingdom of priests (Exod 19:5–6), and these Levitical priests had the vital role of representing God before the people. This did not mean that they were superior to the people; rather, they were set apart for the ministry of God in order to represent him to the people and to represent the people to him. Therefore, when Jeroboam appointed priests to serve other gods, he committed a great sin that brought about the downfall of his family.

In Indian Hinduism, two kinds of priesthood exist. At the popular level, anyone from any community can be a Hindu priest for their family or village deities, and they do not need to have knowledge of Sanskrit or training in telling slogans and *mantras*. They do need to know how to make sacrifices to idols and how to demonstrate their ecstasy to foretell the fortunes of the worshipers. On the second level, the priesthood is limited to the upper caste of Brahmins, who know Sanskrit and can recite slogans and *mantras* from their sacred books.

In a way, this resembles the Israelites' worship pattern. Although everyone was called a priest, there were specialized Levitical priests to serve before God. It was considered sinful to replace them voluntarily, ask them to worship other gods, or appoint others as priests to serve foreign gods. When Rehoboam did these things, he angered God.

> The New Testament also speaks of the priesthood of believers (1 Pet 2:4–5). At the same time, Paul says, "There is one God and one mediator between God and mankind, the man Christ Jesus" (1 Tim 2:5). Our priesthood should never try to replace the priesthood of Christ. Anyone who exalts himself to replace Christ as the priest is sinful.

1 KINGS 14:1–31
END OF JEROBOAM AND REHOBOAM

1 Kings 14 brings down the curtain on the reign of Jeroboam in the north and Rehoboam in the south, concluding with the names of the new kings for these kingdoms.[1] The first section narrates the fall of Jeroboam (14:1–20); the second section narrates the last days of Rehoboam (14:21–31).

14:1–20 THE FALL OF JEROBOAM

The prophet Ahijah, who predicted God's plan for Jeroboam to rule over the ten northern tribes of Israel, now predicts God's punishment on Jeroboam and his family. This prophecy is centered around the illness of Jeroboam's son, Abijah.

14:1 Abijah's Illness

Abijah means "my father is Yahweh." He was Jeroboam's heir apparent to the throne of Jeroboam. But he became deadly ill (14:1). In those days, prophets were consulted on health matters and were sought for their prayers for miraculous healing (see 2 Kgs 4:18–36; 5:3). The king knew that Ahijah was a true prophet, whose words had been fulfilled in his lifetime, and so the king knew that the prophet would tell the truth concerning Abijah's fate.

14:2–9 Jeroboam's Wife Hears the Prophecy

Jeroboam asked his wife to disguise herself and sent her to Ahijah to find out what would happen to their son, Abijah (14:2). She took ten loaves of bread, some cakes, and a jar of honey as an offering to the prophet (14:3–4). Jeroboam wanted her to hide her identity as his wife so that she would receive an unbiased report from the prophet. Using a disguise is never a good practice since it is impossible to hide from God. Though Ahijah was losing his sight because of his age (14:4), God spoke to him before Jeroboam's wife arrived at his door and told him what to tell her. The Lord revealed both the identity

---

[1]. For the chronological year of the kings in Judah and Israel, see the chart in *South Asia Bible Commentary*, 475–476.

of Jeroboam's wife and the message that Ahijah was supposed to declare to her (14:5).

As soon as Jeroboam's wife arrived at Ahijah's house, he identified her and said that he had "bad" (Heb. *qasheh*) news for her (14:6). Then, the prophet recalled God's part in tearing away the kingdom from Solomon and raising Jeroboam to rule over the ten northern tribes (14:7). This blessing included the condition that Jeroboam obeyed the Lord and kept his commandments, just as King David had done (14:8). But Jeroboam had not obeyed God; instead, he was doing evil in the eyes of the Lord by erecting idols made out of metals, referring to the two golden calves (14:9). This aroused the Lord's anger since Jeroboam "turned your back on me," an idiomatic phrase that means that the king had treated Yahweh with disdain.

14:10–16 Four Verdicts

After charging the king for his disobedience to Yahweh's commandments, the prophet pronounced four verdicts as punishment from God (14:10–16). The first verdict was against Jeroboam's family and the entire male population of his house, including the sons of his slaves and servants (14:10). The entire male population in his household will be destroyed so there will not be an heir in his family. The phrase about burning up Jeroboam's family "like cow dung" is a figurative expression for destroying them to ashes, without leaving a trace. Moreover, when the male population of his house die, their corpses will be eaten by dogs and birds (14:11). This verse echoes Elijah's verdict against Ahab and Jezebel (21:23–24). The prophetic formula, "the Lord has spoken," confirms that this prophecy will surely happen (14:11). Usually, kings in ancient south India who went to war after worshiping their gods and goddesses were assured that they would return with victory. The priests only gave good omens and spoke of the support of their gods and goddesses. If a king was killed in the battle, his death was regarded as a sign of valor and martyrdom. If he returned in defeat, it was regarded as shame. This understanding contrasts with Jeroboam's death, which is God's punishment for his disobedience.

The second verdict is related to Jeroboam's son, Abijah. As soon as Jeroboam's wife sets foot in her city, the boy will die (14:12). All the people of the northern kingdom would mourn for the boy and bury him (14:13a). Unlike all other descendants of Jeroboam who will die in the city or the country and will be eaten by dogs or birds, Abijah will be buried. Abijah will have an honorable burial "because he is the only one in the house of Jeroboam in whom the Lord, the God of Israel, has found anything good" (14:13b).

Unlike his father, Abijah might have followed the Lord and kept a covenantal relationship with Yahweh.[2] The dynasty of Jeroboam is in trouble because his heir is going to die. God is gracious to Abijah, and he will not experience a horrible death like the rest of the males in Jeroboam's house.[3] The Lord will do good because he has found something good in this boy, which contrasts with his punishment for Jeroboam, who has done evil.

The third verdict was that another king would be raised up for the north and fight against the family of Jeroboam (14:14). He would kill all the descendants of Jeroboam and take over the throne, leaving none to succeed him in the future. Jeroboam's dynasty would be uprooted because of Jeroboam's sins in promoting the worship of foreign gods and goddesses, appointing priests from any family, worshiping in the shrines, and offering sacrifices at the altars.

The fourth verdict was against the people of Israel in the north who followed the idol worship promoted by Jeroboam (14:15). Any sin committed by a king not only affects him and his family but also his nation. The Lord will "strike" Israel, which means he will smite the people as one who shakes a reed in the water. A reed is a plant that roots in shallow water in a river, pond, or marshy area, which waves as the wind blows. This imagery of a reed is used in various places throughout the OT (Isa 9:14; Ezek 29:6). It is a wonderful sight to see reeds swaying in the wind alongside water, but unlike a deeply rooted tree, such as an oak, they convey instability (2 Kgs 18:21; Matt 11:7). In 1 Kings 14:15, the narrator says that God is going to destabilize Israel by sending an enemy to destroy them and make the kingdom unsteady. Then, the Lord will uproot Israel from the land that was given to their ancestors, as promised by Yahweh and scatter the people beyond the Euphrates River (14:15). They will be deported by the enemy to a far country, where they will live in exile. This prophecy was fulfilled by the Assyrians.

The people of Israel will be devastated, humiliated, and alienated from the Promised Land because of their sin of making "Asherah poles" (14:15). Goddess Asherah was the counterpart of Baal. The Canaanites erected thin, long stones on both sides of the statue of the idol of Asherah, representing the fertility of the mother goddess. Similar pillar stones can be seen in villages throughout India today. A red or yellow woman's skirt is tied around the pole, and a red mark (*tilak*) is placed on top of the stone to depict the goddess. Many women worship these stone pillars, bringing offerings to them and garlanding

---

2. DeVries, *1 Kings*, 179.
3. Paul House, *1, 2 Kings: An Exegetical and Theological Exposition of Holy Scripture*, 192.

the pole in order to increase their fertility. This kind of worship, which was initiated by Jeroboam, aroused God's anger, and so he abandoned Israel into the hands of its enemies (14:16).

14:17–20 Fulfillment of Ahijah's Prophecy

After hearing Ahijah's prophecy and God's verdicts, Jeroboam's wife returned to Tirzah (14:17a). This is the first time that the name Tirzah appears in the story. When Jeroboam's wife entered the house, her son died, just as the prophet had prophesied (14:17b). This episode began with Jeroboam's wife stepping over the threshold of the prophet's house and receiving the word of God from Ahijah and concludes with the fulfillment of Ahijah's prophecy as she enters the threshold of her house. This scene closes the curtain on Jeroboam's dynasty. Just as prophesied, the people buried Abijah and mourned for him (14:18).

Jeroboam's reign, rule, and wars were written in the books of the annals of the kings of Israel (14:19). He reigned twenty-two years and rested with his ancestors (14:20a). Upon his death, Nadab, his surviving son, succeeded him as king (14:20b).

14:21–31 LAST DAYS OF REHOBOAM

After narrating the end days of Jeroboam, the king of the northern kingdom of Israel, the author returns to speak of the end days of Rehoboam, the son of Solomon and the king of Judah. This section begins with a biography (14:21), continues to talk about how Rehoboam did evil in the eyes of the Lord (14:22–24), his political loss (14:25–28), and his death (14:29–31).

14:21 Biodata

The narrative about Rehoboam begins with a brief biodata, stating that he became a king of Judah at the age of forty-one after the death of his father, Solomon, and that he reigned for seventeen years in Jerusalem (14:21). The phrase, "the city the Lord has chosen . . . to put his name," is in contrast to Jeroboam's actions to *stop* the people from going to the temple in Jerusalem, by establishing the cultic centers at Bethel and Dan. Rehoboam's mother's name is Naamah, which means "pleasant." Solomon married Naamah, the Ammonite, to establish political peace between his kingdom and the Ammonites. The narrator mentions Naamah at the beginning of this section (14:21) and again at the end (14:31). In between, he describes everything that Rehoboam did (14:22–30).

14:22–24 Rehoboam's Evil

Just as Jeroboam led Israel to commit adultery, Rehoboam led Judah to do "evil in the eyes of the LORD" that stirred up God's anger against them (14:22). The evil includes setting up high places for worship of other gods, sacred stones of remembrance, and Asherah poles on every high place and tall trees (14:23). In addition, they even had temple prostitution (14:24). The phrase "male shrine prostitutes" refers to men who were dedicated as holy within the cultic center so that people could use them for sexual pleasure. This ritual was considered to be a way to improve one's fertility. Rehoboam brought in all the detestable practices of the nations, though the Lord had ordered the Israelites to destroy such altars in the land.

14:25–28 Political Loss

As a result of their sin, God judged the people of Judah. Shishak, the king of Egypt, attacked Jerusalem around 925 BC, during the fifth year of Rehoboam's rule (14:25). Shishak took the gold shields of Solomon and the valuable treasures of the royal palace and temple (14:26). When Rehoboam lost the gold shields to Shishak, it was a source of humiliation, and now his body guards had to use bronze shields (14:27–28). In those days, whenever a country was defeated by an enemy, the looting of gold from temples and royal palaces was commonplace.[4] Though the nation of Judah had been blessed with prosperity, and its temple and palaces were famous for their elaborate and costly decorations, it was all plundered by their enemies as punishment for their disobedience to God.

14:29–31 Rehoboam's Death

The concluding section describes that all the works of Rehoboam were recorded in the annals of the king of Judah (14:29). It also narrates the continuous tension and war between Jeroboam and Rehoboam (14:30). When Rehoboam died, he was buried with his ancestors in the city of David (14:31). Abijah, Rehoboam's son, succeeded him as the next king of Judah (14:31). His name meant "my father is Yahweh."

---

4. For example, in AD 1000–1026, Muhammad Ghajini attacked the temple in Somnath in northwest India several times and plundered the valuables. Romila Thapar, *A History of India*, vol. 1 (London: Penguin Books, 1965), 231–232.

1 KINGS 15:1–16:34

JUDAH AND ISRAEL: TWO KINGDOMS

After the story of the division of the united monarchy under the leadership of Jeroboam and Rehoboam (930–922 BC), the narrator reports how these two kingdoms continued under the leadership of different kings.[1] The history of the two kingdoms is a single story of the people of Yahweh. These stories continue to testify how their kings fail to keep God's laws and sin against him and yet God continues to show them his covenantal faithfulness.

By reading 1 Kings 15–16 in continuous sequence, we will get a bird's-eye view of the successors to the throne in these two kingdoms during the reigns of Jeroboam, Nadab, Baasha, Elah, Zimri, Omri, and Ahab in the north and the reigns of Rehoboam, Abijah, and Asa in the south. All stories begin with a brief biodata, summarizes their activities (including wars, victories, and defeats), evaluates their reign with respect to David, details their punishment by God, and concludes with a formula about their death and successors.

15:1–8 ABIJAH, KING OF JUDAH

Abijah became the king of Judah, the southern kingdom, in the eighteenth year of Jeroboam's reign of Israel, the northern kingdom.[2] Abijah's rule lasted only three years (15:2a). His mother was Maakah, the daughter of Abishalom (15:2b), who worshiped Asherah (15:13).[3] Either by her or his father's influence, Abijah "committed all the sins his father had done before him; his heart was not fully devoted to the LORD his God" (15:3a). He didn't follow David (15:3b). But God remained faithful and "gave him a lamp in Jerusalem" (15:4a). That meant, he had a descendant to sit on the throne after him and

---

[1]. The chronology list of different years of the kings is taken from the commentary of *Africa Bible Commentary*, 412–413. The same list is reprinted in *South Asia Bible Commentary*, 475–476. John Bright's list vary slightly from the list given in *Africa Bible Commentary*. Bright, *History of Israel*, 481–483.
[2]. The name Abijah (2 Chr 11:20; 12:16; 13:1) is written as "Abiyam" in the Hebrew text of 1 Kings 15:1 and as "Abiyom" in the Syriac version. Both are regarded as variants of the same name.
[3]. According to 2 Chronicles 13:2, Maakah was the granddaughter of Uriel of Gibeah, who possibly married Tamar, the daughter of Absalom (a variant of Abishalom). If so, then Maakah is a descendant of the family of Absalom.

Jerusalem itself remained strong (15:4b). Once again, David is praised for following God with his heart and soul, "except in the case" of committing adultery with Bathsheba, the wife of Uriah the Hittite, and killing him (15:5). David's sin was not idolatry but adultery and murder, and he was punished and then forgiven after his repentance. God showed mercy to David because he never wanted to abandon Yahweh and go after other gods. Rather, he wanted to build a temple for the Lord, and he demonstrated his ambition by bringing the ark of the covenant to Jerusalem. The temple of God's presence in Jerusalem is meant to be a lamp that will guide the people. The reference to David's loyalty to Yahweh is meant to remind any king in the dynasty of David to be committed to the covenantal conditions with Yahweh.

Throughout Abijah's reign, wars and tensions persisted between Abijah and Jeroboam, the king of Israel (15:6). The details about this war are narrated in 2 Chronicles 13:2–20, and the author of 1 Kings simply says, "Are they not written in the books of the annals of the kings of Judah" (15:7). Abijah died and was buried in the City of David (15:8a). As a testimony to God's faithfulness, Asa his son succeeded him (15:8b).

15:9–24 ASA, KING OF JUDAH

Asa became the king of Judah in the twentieth year of Jeroboam in the north (15:9). He reigned for the next forty-one years in Jerusalem (15:10a). His grandmother was Maakah daughter of Abishalom (15:10b).

Asa's kingdom lasted forty-one years because he did what was right in the eyes of the Lord, just as David did (15:11). He expelled the male shrine prostitutes from the land (15:12). Jeroboam had brought them into the land (14:23–24). Asa also removed all the idols of gods and goddesses that his ancestors had made and worshiped (15:12). In his zeal to serve God, he deposed his grandmother, Maakah, from her position as queen-mother because she had established images of Asherah for worship (15:13a). Further, he cut down all the Asherah poles and burned them in the Kidron valley (15:13b). However, Asa could not complete his actions throughout the land, and he left some high places with pagan deities (15:14b). But his heart was "fully committed to the Lord all his life" (15:14b). Finally, he dedicated the silver and gold vessels he and his father had and brought them into the temple (15:15).

He didn't, however, have peace during his reign: Baasha king of Israel was a constant threat to Asa (15:16). Baasha crossed the border of Judah and captured Ramah, which was situated nine kilometers north of Jerusalem, fortifying it to blockade the trade route and to prevent people from crossing the border between the northern and southern kingdoms (15:17). This intrusion into the territory of Judah was intended to make Asa surrender to Baasha's terms and conditions. As an act of political diplomacy, Asa sought support from Ben-Hadad, a Syrian king living in Damascus, to cancel the treaty between Baasha and Ben-Hadad so that Baasha would not be able to capture all of Judah. Ben-Hadad was the son of Tabrimmon, who was the son of Hezion (15:18–19).[4] To gain Ben-Hadad's favor, Asa took all the silver and gold in the treasury of the temple and his palace and sent them with his officials as gifts to Ben-Hadad. After receiving these gifts, Ben-Hadad agreed to support Asa and sent his troops to attack the towns of northern Israel. He captured Ijon, Dan, Abel Beth Maakah, and Kinnereth (Galilee) along the northern border and Naphtali, which was east of the Sea of Galilee and south of Damascus (15:20). To counter these attacks from Ben-Hadad, Baasha abandoned his attacks on Judah (15:21). After the Syrian king attacked northern Israel and Baasha withdrew from Ramah, Asa issued an order to all the people in Judah to remove the blockade that Baasha had built around Ramah and use the timber and stones to strengthen the borders of Geba in the territory of Benjamin (which was situated thirteen kilometers north of Jerusalem, just east of Ramah) and Mizpah as new frontiers of defense (15:22).

Just as with other king's achievements, Asa's achievements (including the cities he built) were written in the annals of the kings of Judah (15:23a). As Asa became old, his feet became diseased, possibly because of diabetes or gout (15:23b). Asa died and rested with his ancestors. He too was buried in the city of his father David. Jehoshaphat, his son, succeeded him as the king of Judah, the southern kingdom (15:24).

15:25–28, 31 NADAB, KING OF ISRAEL

After recounting the history of Judah during this period, the narrator turns to the six kings of northern Israel. This history begins with Nadab. He became the king of Israel in the second year of Asa, king of Judah and ruled over Israel for two years (15:25). Nadab did evil in the sight of the Lord, just like his father, Jeroboam (15:26). But his life was shortlived as Baasha – son of Ahijah from the tribe of Issachar – had conspired against him and killed him at Gibbethon, a Philistine town, in the southwest Galilee (15:27). This happened during the

---

4. The word *Tabrimmon* means "good is Rimmon," referring to the "thunderer-god," which was a title for Baal known in Aram (i.e., Syria). Wiseman, *1 and 2 Kings*, 168.

third year of Asa's reign over Judah (15:28). The short achievements of Nadab were written in the book of the annals of the king of Israel (15:31).

15:27–16:7 BAASHA, KING OF ISRAEL

After killing Nadab, Baasha son of Ahijah from the tribe of Issachar appointed himself as the king of Israel (15:27–28). Then, Baasha killed all the descendants of Jeroboam's family and household, fulfilling the prophecy of Ahijah (15:29). Baasha's action against Jeroboam's family was due to their sin, which had aroused the anger of the Lord (15:30). During his whole reign, he fought with Asa, the king of Judah (15:32).

Baasha reigned over Israel, with his base in Tirzah, for twenty-four years (15:33). Just as the other kings of Israel, Baasha "did evil in the eyes of the Lord," with the inevitable end of his reign (15:34a). Of course, his sin was the sin of idolatry (15:34b).

God raised another prophet, Jehu the son of Hanani, to receive a message about Baasha's punishment (16:1). The message reminded Baasha that God had lifted him up from the dust – meaning not from the royal family, but from a low position – and appointed him to rule over Israel (16:2a). But instead of following God and his laws, Baasha followed "the ways of Jeroboam and caused my people Israel to sin" (16:2b). Therefore, God would wipe out Baasha's family, just as he had wiped out Jeroboam's family (16:3). Dogs will eat those who die in the city and birds will eat those who die in the country (16:4). In Israel, God's justice always delivered appropriate punishment for one's sin. A similar idea is conveyed by the proverb, "What you sow, you reap."

The same concluding formulas are used at the end of this section to mention how the acts of Baasha were recorded in the chronicles of the kings (16:5). Baasha, too, died and Elah, his son, succeeded him as the next king of Israel (16:6). The narrator added one more reminder that Baasha's punishment came as a result of his sin against God (16:7).

16:8–10, 14 ELAH, KING OF ISRAEL

In the twenty-sixth year of Asa king of Judah, Elah became the king of Israel (16:8a). He was Baasha's son. He reigned in Tirzah for two years (16:8b). He faced a violent death at the hands of his commander of chariots, Zimri (16:9–10). Elah's achievements were written also in the annals of the kings of Israel (16:14). Elah reigned over Israel for only two years.

16:11–13, 15–20 ZIMRI, KING OF ISRAEL

Zimri, one of Elah's officials, succeeded Elah as the next king of Israel. Zimri is an Aramaean name. He was the commander of half of Elah's chariots. He took the kingdom by violence. Elah was in Tirzah at the house of Arza, the palace administrator. He was drunk (16:9). Zimri came in, struck him with a sword, and killed him (16:9). This happened in the twenty-seventh year of Asa king of Judah. Soon after killing Elah, Zimri made himself the king of Israel (16:9).

As soon as he began to reign, he killed off Baasha's whole family and friends, as the prophet Jehu prophesied (16:11–12). Baasha and his family led Israel to worship other gods, arousing Yahweh's anger, and thus they fell into the hands of Zimri (16:13). The term "worthless idols" means they were created by human hands and did not have the power to protect the people or provide agricultural fertility for the land.

Zimri's reign was short-lived. The phrase, "Zimri reigned in Tirzah seven days," conveys the tragic nature of Zimri's short reign (16:15). When the Israelites in the camp heard that Zimri had plotted and killed Elah, they made Omri, the commander of the army, as the king over them (16:16). They were fighting in Gibbethon, but they withdrew from there and laid siege to Tirzah where Zimri was (16:17). Then Zimri went into the citadel of the palace and set it on fire (16:18). He may have decided to commit suicide rather than be captured by Omri. Ultimately, he died because of "the sins he had committed, doing evil in the eyes of the LORD" (16:19). He lived as Jeroboam, the founding king of Israel, who introduced the worship of the golden calves at Bethel and Dan. Zimri's reign and the rebellion he carried out against Elah are written in the annals of the kings (16:20).

16:21–28 OMRI, KING OF ISRAEL

After the seven short days of Zimri's reign of Israel, the people were split into two factions. Half the people supported Tibni son of Ginath for king. The other half supported Omri (16:21). Of these two, Omri's followers were stronger than Tibni's. As a result, Tibni died and Omri became king (16:22).

Omri spent his first six years ruling from Tirzah (16:23). Then he bought the hill of Samaria and built a city there, calling it "Samaria" after the name of the former owner, Shemer (16:24). Since the city was at the top of the hill (which was a hundred meters high), Omri had a strategic viewpoint of the trade route to Tyre and Sidon. He may have wanted to establish a new capital for the northern kingdom, since the palace at Tirzah had been burnt down by Zimri.[5] Extra biblical evidence points that he expanded his territory into Moab.[6]

Omri did evil in the eyes of the Lord, just as his forefathers did (16:25). He imitated everything Jeroboam did and led the people to worship foreign gods. Because Omri followed the sin of Jeroboam and did even more evil than any other king in Israel, God punished Omri (16:26). His achievements were written in the book of the annals of the kings of Israel (16:27). After his death, he was buried in Samaria, and his son, Ahab, succeeded him to the throne (16:28).

16:29–34 AHAB, KING OF ISRAEL

The name "Ahab" means "my brother is Abba," which is a reference to the "Father god."[7] Other suggestions for the meaning of this unique name are "the brother of the father" or "resembling the father."[8]

When Ahab, son of Omri, became the king of Israel, Asa was still ruling Judah; it was his thirty-eighth year of reigning (16:29a). Ahab reigned over northern Israel from Samaria for twenty-two years (16:29b). The narrator will return to a detailed account of Ahab's life and rule after he introduced Elijah in chapter 17. But for now, he tells the readers that "Ahab son of Omri did more evil in the eyes of the LORD than any of those before him" (16:30). Then he listed two: he excelled the sins of Jeroboam and he introduced the worship of Baal because of the influence of his wife Jezebel daughter of Ethbaal, king of the Sidonians (16:31). The word "Jezebel" in the Phoenician language means "Prince" or "Where is the Prince?" (carrying connotations of Baal). The people shouted out this name as they cried for Baal.[9] The name "Ethbaal," the father of Jezebel, means "Baal is alive" or "Baal exists" in the Phoenician language. Because of him and Jezebel, Ahab introduced the worship of Baal in Israel, which God explicitly forbade.

Ahab built altars for Baal and set up Asherah poles (16:32–33). Ahab misled the nation by promoting Baal and ignoring Yahweh, just as Jeroboam and his successors had done. Because he was responsible for the sins of the country, he aroused the anger of the Lord (16:33).

---

5. Bright, *History of Israel*, 240.
6. Wiseman, *1 and 2 Kings*, 174.
7. Wiseman, *1 and 2 Kings*, 174.
8. Gray, *I and II Kings: A Commentary*, 367.
9. Gray, *I and II Kings: A Commentary*, 368.

In addition, Ahab had done what was totally abhorred by God: he allowed his generals to sacrifice their children to their gods. One of his generals was Hiel of Bethel. He decided to rebuild Jericho, the city Joshua destroyed (compare Josh 6:26). In order to do that, he sacrificed his firstborn son Abiram before laying the foundation (16:34a). Before setting up the city gates, he sacrificed his youngest son Segub (16:34b). Most likely, these sacrifices were made to Baal. And since Ahab allowed it in his kingdom, God's anger aroused against him. A secret ritual in ancient Indian culture involved cutting off the head of a male child and then shedding his blood on the foundation stone of tall temples, water reservoirs, or fort walls to drive away evil spirits and make them safe. This pattern resembles what Hiel did, an act that did not please Yahweh. God forbids all forms of idolatry, especially those that harm the innocent like the women and children.

1 KINGS 17:1–24

THE PROPHETS OF ISRAEL

In the stories of the previous kings, from Solomon to Omri, the narrator recounts what they did for the country and the God of Israel. Some of the stories begin with brief information about their background and identify their wrong actions. All kings are compared with either David or Jeroboam. The evaluation sometimes includes a communication from the prophets to the kings and nations about God's punishment for their sins and usually ends with the formula, "the rest of the actions are written in the annals of the kings." In these stories, the kings are the central figures. The narrative between 1 Kings 17 and 2 Kings 9 shifts to focus on the life and ministry of the prophets – Elijah, Obadiah, Elisha, and Micaiah – and their relationship and conflict with the kings and the nation of Israel.

17:1–24 STORY OF ELIJAH

Elijah is unique and extraordinary, both in terms of his prophetic role and the miracles he performed by the power of Yahweh. His zeal for God and for justice is demonstrated in the stories of 1 Kings 17 through 2 Kings 2. Elijah was a courageous and compassionate prophet who confronted the royal power, stood on the side of the poor, widows, and peasants, and championed the cause of justice with courage and faith in the Lord. Elijah is one of the rare prophets who is mentioned by name in the later recording of the OT (Mal 4:5–6) as well as the NT (Matt 17:1–13; Mark 9:1–13; Luke 1:17).

There are several memorable events in the life and ministry of Elijah: he is fed by ravens (1 Kgs 17:1–6); he miraculously provides food for the widow of Zarephath (17:7–16); he miraculously raises her son from death (17:17–24); he sends Obadiah with a message to Ahab (18:1–16); he proves Yahweh is the only true God on Mount Carmel (18:17–46); he flees to Horeb and receives a revelation of Yahweh (19:1–18); he calls Elisha (19:19–21); he condemns Ahab's injustice to Naboth (21:1–29); he prophesies against Ahaziah (2 Kgs 1:1–18); and he is taken up to heaven in an amazing way (2:1–18).

Several stories in the history of the two kingdoms of Israel are inserted within Elijah's narrative because they happened during Elijah's lifetime. These narratives include the role of another prophet in the matter of the war with Ben-Hadad (1 Kgs 20:1–43), the prophecies of Micaiah against Ahab (22:1–40), and stories about the kingdoms continuing under the rules of Jehoshaphat in Judah and Ahaziah in northern Israel (22:41–53). All these stories became part of the historical writings in 1 and 2 Kings rather than the prophetic books of the later recordings of the OT, because they include events about what the prophets said and their interactions with kings and people. The narrator uses several literary forms: stories (1 Kgs 17:2–6; 7–24), questions (18:9, 16), reports (18:16), miracles (17:22–23), taunting (18:27), and dialogues (19:9–18).

The life of a true prophet did not include walking on red carpet or sleeping on a bed of roses. Prophets had to struggle and face life-threatening situations while proclaiming God's word and seeking to help others. All three stories in 1 Kings 17 are connected by this theme of facing hard situations and risking one's life, a challenge for us as well.

17:1–6 Famine in the Land

The narrator introduces the prophet by his name, "Elijah," which means, "My God is Yahweh." He is identified as "the Tishbite," coming from the village of Tishbe, which was located in Gilead on the Transjordan region, thirteen kilometers north of the Yarmuk River.[1]

The phrase, "as the LORD, the God of Israel, lives" (17:1) is a formula for making an oath or swearing in the name of Yahweh. Elijah is proclaiming that his prophetic predictions are valid by swearing in the name of Yahweh. God can swear by his name (Jer 51:14; Amos 4:2; 6:8) because he alone is the living God. Usually, the Israelites were cautioned against swearing by the name of God (Lev 19:12; Num 30:2; Matt 5:34–36) because such an oath bound the person to death if he or she disobeyed the vow or failed to fulfill the oath. When Elijah came to Ahab and declared that there would not be any dew or rain for the next few years, he used two key phrases. First, the phrase, "except at my word" (1 Kgs 17:1), means that the rain will not fall unless God says that it can come on the land. Elijah is not asserting his own authority, but the prophetic word that was given to him by Yahweh. Second, Elijah claims his identity, status, and responsibility with the phrase, "whom I serve." Proclaiming that he is a servant of God is a dangerous claim to make in front of the king, as the majority of the people of Israel were serving Baal, the national god who had been approved by the king and queen. As a servant

---

1. Wiseman, *1 and 2 Kings*, 164.

of God, Elijah is saying, "God will stop the rain. I confirm this by swearing in the name of the LORD."

The Canaanites, who worshiped Baal, regarded Baal as the rain or thunder god, who gives rains to the land that then produces food. Ahab and his people had come to believe that only Baal, the god of fertility, could bring rain and the abundance of the agriculture field. They forgot their God as the Lord of all creation, who created plants and brought rain. Thus Elijah is saying that he will stop the rain based on the prophecy he received from God, which will result in drought and famine throughout the land until the Israelites realize that Baal cannot bring forth rain.

When a country suffers disaster, the people including the ministers of God, suffer. In this story, the prophet was threatened by the severe famine, but God made a special provision to supply him with water and food. The Lord asked Elijah to go eastward and hide in the Kerith ravine where he would provide him water and food (17:2–4). This description suggests that Kerith was a small brook and that water probably only flowed in it during the monsoon season. The early monsoon rains in Israel normally fell between late-October and early January, and the late rains normally fell between April and May. Though the exact location of this ravine is not clear, commentators suggest it was east of the Jordan or west of Jericho.[2] Elijah obeyed God and stayed in Kerith Ravine until further instruction (17:5). This place was in a location that Ahab could not reach easily to capture Elijah. While Elijah camped at Kerith, God ordered the ravens to bring him meat every morning and evening (17:6). In Indian stories about ravens, the black crows steal food from others rather than giving it to them. Yet God uses birds that prey on others to deliver meat for his servant every day. This story echoes God's wonderful provision of manna and meat for the Israelites during their journey in the wilderness (Exod 16:8, 19). As Elijah was in hiding, he watched the lack of rain and how it was resulting in famine.

17:7–16 Elijah and the Widow of Zarephath

Sometime later, the brook Kerith dried up because of the drought, and so Elijah had to find drinking water some other way (17:7). God knew about Elijah's problem and commanded him to go to Zarephath, a village that was thirteen kilometers south of Sidon (17:7–8). This territory on the border of northern Israel had also been affected by drought and famine. This territory was famous

---

2. Hens-Piazza, *1–2 Kings*, 163; Y. Aharoni, *The Land of the Bible: A Historical Geography*, trans. A. F. Rainey (London: Burns and Oats, 1979), 256.

for its worship of Baal, but Baal could not bring rain to his own region, and the people there were counting their last days before death.

The word of the Lord directed Elijah to go to the house of a widow in Zarephath, whom he had commanded to give him food and drink (17:9). As instructed, Elijah went to Zarephath and met the widow at the gate of the city (17:10a). She was gathering sticks to build a fire to make a small piece of bread. Elijah asked her for a drink and a piece of bread (17:10b–11). She answered, "As surely as the LORD your God lives . . . I don't have any bread – only a handful of flour in a jar and a little olive oil in a jug. I am gathering a few sticks to take home and make a meal for myself and my son that we may eat it – and die" (17:12). She greeted Elijah in the name of his Lord God. Her reply suggests that she did not know that Elijah was a prophet from Israel but assumed that he was a sojourner asking for food. She told the truth to Elijah. What she had in the jar and jug was not even enough to feed her and her son, and so she could not spare any bread for Elijah. She begins with the greeting, "your God lives," and concludes with the sad note, "eat and die." The words "living" and "dying" contrast the widow's feelings to the sojourner.

Elijah noticed her sadness and how she had reached the point of no hope, and so he encouraged her not to be afraid (17:13a). Then he commanded her to make a small loaf of bread with her remaining oil and flour, but first to share what she had made with the prophet and then to eat the rest with her son (17:13b). Then he comforted her saying that God will provide for all that she needs until the famine ends (17:14). The Lord had told Elijah that this widow would feed him, and so he trusted God to take care of both him and those who helped him. The life-threatening situation faced by the prophet and the widow's family was handled by God, who had directed Elijah to this widow in Zarephath. The prophet had trusted God and obeyed his command to travel to Zarephath. Obeying God's command is the only way to receive God's blessing. Elijah revealed God's command to the widow, saying, "this is what the LORD, the God of Israel says." In this way, she came to know Elijah's identity as a prophet and Yahweh as his God.

The Lord – not Elijah – would perform this miracle so that they would not lack flour and oil. But the widow's cooperation was necessary, and so Elijah asked her to make the bread for him first. Her obedience would lead to a blessing so that she would have a continuous supply of flour and oil. Human cooperation is often necessary for God to fulfill his purpose. One important shift in the narrative is diverting the focus from the power and authority of the kings and rulers to the poor and needy. God uses his servants as his agents to stand with those who are suffering. The widow of Zarephath bears witness to the way that God expresses his solidarity with his servants and the poor rather than Ahab and Jezebel. The widow's story represents the pain of all the widows and poor who are suffering from famine. God is concerned about all who are suffering and calls the prophetic church to work on their behalf.

The widow obeyed Elijah's words and made bread for him and so discovered that what God had spoken through the prophet was true, for it was happening in her kitchen (17:15). Although she experienced the miracle and blessing of food, the narrator does not mention anything about her conversion to Yahweh. However, she later recognized Elijah as a "man of God" and declared that the word of the Lord from his mouth was the "truth" (17:24), thereby implying her faith in Yahweh. She made this confession out of her personal experience of receiving Yahweh's blessing. As prophesied, "the jar of flour was not used up and the jug of oil did not run dry" (17:16).

17:17–24 Resurrection of the Widow's Son

We do not know how long Elijah stayed in the widow's house in Zarephath, but as long as he remained, their lives were sustained by the miracle of having enough flour and oil to feed them each day. The oral tradition among Hindus in Indian society tells a similar story about the *achayapattram*, a bowl in which food remained at the same level even after it was taken and given continuously to feed people at the sage's command. There is an echo between the story of Elijah and the widow and the story of God supplying daily manna to the Israelites in the wilderness (Exod 16:31; Deut 8:16; John 6:49).

Elijah faced another threat while staying with the widow, as her son fell ill and died (17:17). Naturally, the mother was upset and turned her reaction against the prophet, saying, "What do you have against me, man of God? Did you come to remind me of my sin and kill my son?" (17:18). Just as some parents today connect the death of their son or daughter to their sins, this widow related his son's death with her sins. The widow goes one step further and connects the death of her son to Elijah's presence because she knew that Elijah was a man of God, having seen the miraculous supply of flour and oil day after day.

A holy man's presence in a family can be both a blessing and a problem. His holiness sometimes makes the members of the family feel bad about their sins. Zacchaeus realized his sins after Jesus entered his house (Luke 19:1–10). The Roman centurion did not want Jesus to come to his house and heal his servant because he felt he was not worthy to receive Jesus (Luke 7:1–10).

When people feel worthless in front of a holy person, they often relate any happening to that person's presence. Elijah could have been upset with the widow's accusation; instead he asked for and received the body of the son and took him to the upper room where he was staying and laid the body on his bed (17:19). Then Elijah cried to the Lord for bringing this tragedy on the widow, saying, "Lord my God, have you brought tragedy even on this widow I am staying with, by causing her son to die?" (17:20). As an ordinary human, he is expressing his feelings of loss to God. Then he stretched himself out on the boy three times, while praying for his life (17:21). He knew that the boy was not unconscious or asleep. The word "stretched" (or "measured himself" in Hebrew) could mean standing near the body and stretching one of his hands towards the head and another hand towards the feet of the body, or it could mean falling on top of his body. Either way, his action was not meant to warm him up or breathe into his nostrils because the son was already dead. Rather, the action of stretching himself out three times symbolizes dying and rising up again. His cry, "Lord my God," is not a simple petition, but a challenge for God to raise him up. His request, "Let this boy's life return to him," conveys that the breath has gone out of the boy's body and needs to return to him so that he will live (17:21). This resurrection is only possible through the Lord, who is the creator and Lord of all that lives on the earth. The Lord answered his cry by returning the life to the boy (17:22). God alone has authority over life, death, and resurrection – not Baal.

The widow could have lost hope and started arranging the boy's funeral, but she obeyed the prophet and allowed him to take her son's body upstairs. But when she saw Elijah carrying down the living son and giving him to her saying, "Look, your son is alive!" (17:23), the widow said, "Now I know that you are a man of God and that the word of the Lord from your mouth is the truth" (17:24). She understands Elijah as a "man of God." And, she acknowledges Elijah as the messenger of the Lord God, who speaks only truth. A prophet's speeches are true or false based on the person's individual holiness, the fulfillment of the person's prophecy, and the power of the miracle or the risk taken to fight against injustice.

All religious communities in South Asia expect divine miracles, and they are particularly important for people in need. There are three miracles in the story of Elijah in this chapter: the prophet being fed daily by the ravens (17:5–6), the widow receiving a daily supply of flour and oil (17:14–16), and the resurrection of her son (17:17–20). Miracles occur because of the power of God, not the effort or power of his servants. Though God is all powerful, all problems cannot be solved through miracles. People should approach the true God in faith and prayer rather than seeking fortune tellers, magicians, gurus, or Babas. God can use medical treatment to heal people. In sum, God can do miracles in the lives of people. Although we cannot promise this to people, we can ask them to seek it. If it's his will, God will give them the needed miracles.

1 KINGS 18:1–46
ELIJAH'S CHALLENGE:
CHOOSE YAHWEH

The life-threatening situation of a prolonged drought finally comes to an end. Elijah gives a choice to the people: choose Yahweh or Baal. They can't worship both. Elijah sets up a power match to prove that only Yahweh is the living God and Baal doesn't hear, answer, or live!

This chapter has three sections: Elijah prepares to meet Ahab (18:1–16); Elijah meets and challenges Ahab (18:17–40); and Elijah makes it rain as a proof that Yahweh is God and Baal is not (18:41–46). Elijah's opposition to Ahab began with his oath that the rain would stop for three years (17:1), which brought about drought and severe famine in the land, and ended with the arrival of rain after a life-risking contest on Mount Carmel in order to prove that Yahweh alone could bring rain, not Baal (18:45).

18:1–16 ELIJAH PREPARES TO MEET AHAB

Once again, Elijah received the word of God to come out of his hiding and to face King Ahab in person and tell him that Yahweh would bring rain again (18:1). For the past three years, the king and the prophets of Baal had been trying to bring rain, but their efforts had been in vain. It was dangerous for Elijah to appear before the king since Ahab had been seeking the prophet's life. Nevertheless, Elijah did not question or resist God but obeyed his command and proceeded to meet the king (18:2).

In the meantime, the king had decided he could not keep waiting for rain, but he had to do something to find water and grass to keep his horses and mules alive, which he needed to protect the country from attacks and to transport goods for trade. So he called Obadiah, a reliable official in his palace, to help him survey all the springs and valleys to find grass for the horses (18:3–6). "Obadiah," whose name meant "servant of Yahweh," was faithful to the Lord, while being faithful to the king. As a devout believer of Yahweh, he had been protecting the prophets of Yahweh whom Jezebel had been trying to kill (18:4). While Obadiah was searching for water and grass for the king's horses in one direction, Ahab went searching in another direction, but he could not find anything (18:6). Ahab's personal visit to various regions would have made him see the serious consequences of the severe drought and to long for a solution.

As Elijah was traveling to the palace, he met Obadiah, who was searching for water and grass for the king (18:7). Obadiah recognized Elijah and bowed down to pay his respects, asking, "Is it really you, my lord Elijah?" This question reveals Obadiah's shock that Elijah had survived the famine. Elijah confirmed his identity and ordered Obadiah to tell Ahab that Elijah had come to meet him (18:8). He did not give Obadiah any other details about his purpose in wanting to meet the king. The phrase, "Elijah is here," appears three times in the narrative (18:8, 11, 14). This phrase implies the Lord protected him through the famine, and he is there to confront the king. He is not afraid of Ahab.

Obadiah fears death if he tells Elijah's words to the king (18:9). Ahab has been looking for Elijah in every nation – "there is not a nation or kingdom where my master has not sent someone to look for you" (18:10), and yet, now, Elijah is alive and is looking for Ahab. And Elijah is requesting Obadiah to say to the king "Elijah is here" (18:11). Obadiah is worried that if he goes and tells the king that Elijah has come to meet him, the spirit of the Lord will carry the prophet away to some unknown destination, and Obadiah will be liable for telling lies, cheating the king, and not capturing Elijah alive, but allowing him to escape (18:12). He then tells Elijah that Jezebel has been killing God's prophets, and he has been rescuing and hiding a hundred of them in two caves (18:13). So, why should Elijah bring him and the prophet's disaster by announcing his visit? (18:14).

But Elijah replied firmly that he wanted to present himself to Ahab, and he expected Obadiah to obey (18:15). In his reply, he uses the phrase, "As the LORD Almighty lives whom I serve," an oath formula that affirms his decision is true and confirmed (18:15). Elijah had a strong faith that Yahweh, the almighty God, had power over both Ahab and Jezebel. As servants of Baal, an idol of the Sidonians, they could not do anything against the servants of Yahweh, the living God of Israel. Obadiah's fear and worries were understandable, but Elijah had to obey the command and leading of his God at any cost. So, Obadiah reluctantly obeys Elijah and tells Ahab about Elijah's request for an audience (18:16a). Ahab listens and meets Elijah (16:16b).

18:17–40 ELIJAH MEETS AND CHALLENGES AHAB

Elijah challenges King Ahab in words (18:17–20) and action (18:21–40). The contest is two pronged between Yahweh and Baal at a religious level and between the political authority of the king and queen and the prophetic authority of Elijah at another level.

18:17–20 Elijah Challenges Ahab in Words

The moment that Ahab met Elijah, his anger came out in his words, "Is that you, you troubler of Israel?" (18:17). The way Obadiah addressed Elijah as "my lord," holding him in high respect, contrasts significantly with the way Ahab addressed Elijah as "troubler of Israel" in a derogatory sense. Eljiah was troubling Israel by creating both social and political problems for the king. The agrarian society was suffering without rain and harvest, and the famine was causing both the people and animals to starve to death. The worship of Baal, the rain and thunder god, had failed signifying the failure of the religion that was promoted by the political rule. Elijah denied Ahab's charges and reversed the critique to the king and his family (18:18). The prophet held Ahab accountable for bringing trouble to Israel for two main reasons. First, Ahab led the people of Israel to abandon the Lord's command to worship him alone. Second, he and Jezebel led the people to follow Baal and to worship idols and offer sacrifices, just as Ahab's ancestors had done.

After rejecting the king's accusation, Elijah called for a contest to prove that the king was the real troubler of the nation. He challenged Ahab to summon two groups of people to be part of this contest. First, he wanted Ahab to summon the people from all over Israel, referring to the key leaders representing the families, tribes, and the court (18:19a). He wanted the public to bear witness to the contest so that they would repent and return to the Lord after seeing the result. Second, he wanted Ahab to summon four hundred and fifty prophets of Baal and four hundred prophets of Asherah to be participants in the contest (18:19b). The phrase, "who eat at Jezebel's table," refers to the prophets whose financial and physical needs were supported by the treasury of her government. Ahab agreed to this contest because he may have wanted to solve the problem of the prolonged drought and famine and use this opportunity to kill Elijah if he failed in the contest. So, Ahab sent word throughout Israel and gathered the prophets and people on Mount Carmel (18:20).

18:21–40 Elijah Challenges Ahab in Action

Elijah was confident that he could prove that the Lord was the true God, who alone could bring rain. Thus he challenged the people who gathered on Mount Carmel, just as David had challenged the giant Goliath. Pronouncing the theme of the contest, he asked, "How long will you waver between two opinions? If the LORD is God, follow him; but if Baal is God, follow him" (18:21a). The word "waver" in Elijah's question can be better translated by the word "limping" (Heb. *phasah*). According to the oral tradition even today, it is said that the prophets of Baal kept one foot on the upper step and another foot on the lower step of the altar and danced around (18:26).[1] To Elijah, it may have looked as if the prophets of Baal were limping as they called the name of Baal and dancing around the steps of the altar in this way. Thus he challenged the Israelites to stop wavering ("limping") between Yahweh and Baal. His prophetic challenge to the nation is to choose either Yahweh or Baal because worshiping both is wrong in the sight of the Lord. Elijah was asking the people and the king to put an end to syncretism. The time has come for the people to stop their evil ways. Surprisingly, the people were silent after they heard these challenging words from Elijah (18:21b). They may have been afraid of responding in the presence of the prophets of Baal and Asherah, or they may have been wondering what would happen at the end of the contest and wanted to wait to respond until they witnessed the result. Their silence mirrors the silence of Baal, who has kept silent even though they have been calling on him for three years for rain. Just as Baal was not responding to his prophets, the people of Israel were not responding to Elijah's call for them to follow Yahweh.

After witnessing the people's silence, Elijah described his situation as a minority witness for Yahweh amidst hundreds of prophets of Baal (18:22). This description is reminiscent of David standing alone in front of Goliath and the army of the Philistines. In fact, Elijah was not the only prophet of Yahweh remaining in Israel, as Obadiah had hidden a hundred prophets of Yahweh. However, only Elijah was standing boldly in front of the king and prophets of Baal, risking his life because he knew the God in whom he believed. Jezebel had threatened other true prophets and was also waiting for a chance to kill Elijah. This confrontation is not only between Yahweh and Baal, but also between the prophets of Yahweh and the prophets of Baal, as well as between Elijah and the king. Throughout history, we can notice how God raises a single person

---

1. This was said by a Tourist Guide continuing the oral tradition.

with vision, power, and strength to confront a majority who are committing injustices against other people, who are usually minorities.[2]

Moving forward with the contest, Elijah established the procedures by asking the people to bring two bulls, choose one for themselves, cut it into pieces, and place it on the wood as a sacrifice without setting fire to it; he would do the same with the other bull (18:23a). The deciding factor for success in this contest was that "the god who answers by fire" was the true God (18:24). Elijah chose this method of contest because often Baal was depicted as a bull and he was believed to be the god of lightning and thunder. The people believed that he had the power to send lightning to ignite a fire on the sacrificed animal. Elijah wanted to challenge their belief and practice to bring forth rain. Some Indians in villages still offer sacrifices to please gods and goddesses so that they will send rain. In some other places, priests and people burn the effigy of an evil person, sending the smoke to the sky in order to eliminate the one who is blocking the rain and clear the way for the sky to pour down rain.[3] Elijah wanted to teach the people about Baal's failure so that they would follow Yahweh alone. The crowd responded by saying, "What you say is good" (18:24b).

When the actual contest began, Elijah invited the prophets of Baal to choose the first bull and prepare it for the contest, leaving the second bull for Elijah to prepare (18:25a). In this way, Elijah carefully avoided any criticism that he had chosen a bull that would somehow ensure his success. Next, he allowed the prophets of Baal to call on their god first, and he gave them many long hours to prove their god because he knew that calling on Baal would not bring any answer (18:25b). In this way, Elijah avoided another criticism that the prophets of Baal had not been given sufficient time. So they called on the name of Baal from morning until the evening, saying, "Baal, answer us" (18:26), while shouting to Baal more and more, dancing around the altar to please Baal, using ecstasy, prophesying, and slashing themselves with swords and spears until the blood flowed from their bodies, according to their custom (18:26–29a). Elijah mocked them and asked them to shout louder to wake up Baal (18:27). Even the scorching sunlight at midday did not bring fire on the sacrifice. Eventually, their time ran out, and this part of the scene closes with

---

2. Moses stood against the power of Pharaoh in ancient history. More recently, Nelson Mandela and Martin Luther King Jr., stood against the racial discrimination of the minority and majority rulers in South Africa and the U.S. respectively.
3. See https://economictimes.indiatimes.com, "Dussehra: Ravana effigies burnt in Delhi to mark win of good over evil," accessed on October 25, 2020, 1.

the note, "But there was no response, no one answered, no one paid attention" (18:29b). These three phrases confirm the failure of Baal.

When Elijah's turn came, he took every precaution to avoid criticism from the defeated party by making meticulous preparations (18:30–35). First, Elijah called all the people to assemble before him in order to witness his actions (18:30). Second, he rebuilt the altar of the Lord, which had been established on Mount Carmel before the division of the kingdom of Israel (18:31). Because the prophets of Baal had built another altar for their god, the altar of Yahweh had been abandoned and was in ruin. To rebuild the altar, Elijah selected twelve stones, one for each of the tribes descended from Jacob, as a way of reclaiming their historical heritage and remembering the covenant that all the tribes had made earlier to follow Yahweh alone, according to the Lord's instructions through Joshua (Josh 4:1–9; 24:19–28).[4] While rebuilding the altar, Elijah recalled the words of the Lord to Jacob, "Your name shall be Israel" (1 Kgs 18:31). He wanted to remind them of their beginning as descendants of Jacob and unite them under one banner (the name of Israel), even though they are currently living in a divided monarchy. Elijah's third preparation was to dig a large trench (three hundred square meters) around the altar, large enough to hold two *seahs* ("measures") of seed, which was roughly fifteen liters (18:32).[5] Fourth, Elijah arranged the wood on the altar, cut the bull in pieces, and laid it on the wood, as a priest would do at the time of sacrificing animals (18:33a). Fifth, he asked the people standing with him to fill four large jars with water and pour the water on the offering and also on the wood (18:33b). He asked them to repeat this action two more times until the water ran down around the altar and filled the trench (18:34–35). Elijah wanted to involve the people in bringing water because he believed that the people should join hands to prove that Yahweh was their Lord. By this time, everyone watching the event would know that the animal and the wood were completely soaked with water and could not be easily burned with fire. Elijah followed this procedure to guard against any accusations of fraud or criticism that he had used magic. He wanted everything to be foolproof to demonstrate that only the mighty

---

4. Hens-Piazza, *1–2 Kings*, 179.
5. Wiseman, *1 and 2 Kings*, 182. In light of the famine and lack of rain, one question that rises is, how did they get that much water? The narrator does not answer these questions. One possibility is that there was a small stream of water springing from the rock of Mount Carmel. Some shepherds use water from natural springs on the mountains even today. Animals that roam on the mountains know where to find these pools of water between the rocks, which flow from natural springs.

fire of the Almighty God could burn up the sacrifice. Finally, when all the preparations were finished, Elijah stepped forward and prayed (18:36–37).

Elijah's prayer was simple and genuine and revealed his strong faith in the Lord. His prayer had two clear purposes. First, he wanted the Lord to prove himself as powerful so that the people would know that Yahweh was the God of Israel, not Baal (18:36). Second, he wanted to turn the hearts of the people back to Yahweh, which could only be done by the power of the Lord and not his human effort (18:37). In calling on God, Elijah used the phrase, "the God of Abraham, Isaac and Israel." This phrase also implies Elijah's expectation that God would act now in this contest, just as the Lord had acted in the history of Abraham, Isaac, and Jacob. In calling on God, Elijah expressed his role as the servant of Yahweh. He was not engaging in this contest on his own, but according to the command of Yahweh (18:36). The phrase, "answer me," is a formula for petitions that plead with the Lord in faith (Pss 4:1; 20:1; 27:7; 81:7; 91:15). The word "answer" is repeated four times in chapter 18 (vv. 21, 26, 29, 37) and is an important motif in this story. We can notice a contrast between Elijah asking God to answer him (18:37) and the prophets of Baal saying, "Answer us" (18:26). There is also a contrast between the people not answering Elijah when he called them to choose between Yahweh and Baal (18:21) and Baal not answering the prophets (18:29). Elijah does not shout, or dance around the altar, or cut his body with swords or lances. We might imagine him standing in front of the altar and lifting up his hands, as Jews continue to do today when they pray to the Lord.

As Elijah was praying, the fire of the Lord came down on the altar and burnt up the sacrifice, wood, stones, dust, and even licked up the water in the trench (18:38). The imagery of a consuming fire from above is also used to describe the covenant event between Moses and Yahweh on the top of Mount Sinai (Exod 24:17). The people who witnessed this event must have felt the heat of the powerful fire because the text says that they immediately fell prostrate and confessed, "The LORD – he is God! The LORD – he is God!" (1 Kgs 18:39). This acknowledgment of Yahweh as their God and not Baal signifies their repentance. Having risked his own life, Elijah fulfilled the purpose of the contest on Mount Carmel.

In the culmination of the contest, Elijah ordered the people who were around him to seize the prophets of Baal for misleading the nation and causing the land and people to suffer drought and famine (18:40a). Then Elijah brought the prophets of Baal down to the Kishon Valley and killed them (18:40b). This action fulfilled the Deuteronomic law, whereby "A prophet who presumes to speak in my name anything I have not commanded, or a prophet who speaks in the name of other gods, is to be put to death" (Deut 18:20). What began at the top of the mountain ended in the valley, sending a warning signal to Ahab, Jezebel, and the rest of the Israelites to abandon Baal and Asherah and follow Yahweh alone.

18:41–46 ELIJAH MAKES IT RAIN

After proving who the true God is, Elijah told Ahab that a heavy rain was coming (1 Kgs 18:41). Elijah knew that the miracle of the fire consuming the sacrifices, stones, and water was not enough. Yahweh had to send rain and put an end to the three-year drought and famine in order to prove that he alone had power over nature. Without rain, the powerful victory at the contest on Mount Carmel would be in vain. So Elijah returned to the top of Mount Carmel to watch for the cloud that would bring rain (18:41). There he "bent down to the ground and put his face between his knees" (18:42), which conveys his humble posture, as he prayed for rain. As a true prophet, Elijah pleaded with the Lord to send rain so that the nation could have water and the land would be blessed. His intercession continued while he sent his servant to look for a raincloud. This event repeated seven times. Finally, the servant reported that he saw a small cloud rising from the sea (18:44a). Elijah did not want to leave Mount Carmel until the Lord had answered his prayer for rain so that the nation would know that Yahweh was the Lord and God of Israel. When Elijah saw the sky grow black with clouds and blowing winds, he sent his assistant to urge the king to return to Jezreel before the heavy rain stopped his chariots from being able to reach the palace (18:44b). The earlier event of Elijah running away from Ahab after proclaiming God's word about the drought (17:1–4) is reversed here at the end, when Elijah told Ahab to flee to Jezreel to avoid the coming rain (18:44). In the meantime, "the sky grew black with clouds, the wind rose, a heavy rain started falling and Ahab rode off to Jezreel" (18:45). God's power came over Elijah and tucking his cloak into his belt, he outran Ahab (18:46). This story recounts the tremendous achievements of Elijah through the power of God because of his obedience to the word of God and his desire to seek the glory of the Lord.

1 KINGS 19:1-21
ELIJAH'S SETBACK AND REBOUND

Following a great victory on Mount Carmel, Elijah had a setback – he heard Jezebel's vow to take his life and went into hiding. But the Lord gave him the needed rest, reassured him, and commissioned him in a new mission. 1 Kings 19 recounts Elijah's setback (19:1–4), God refreshing him with angels and his presence (19:5–14), and Elijah's rebound from fear and depression to a new challenge (19:15–21). There are a number of parallels between Elijah and Moses and the historical events of the present and past.

19:1-4 ELIJAH'S SETBACK

After Ahab arrived in Jezreel, he told his wife Jezebel everything that Elijah had done on Mount Carmel, including his slaughter of the prophets of Baal in the valley (19:1). Upon hearing the details of this event, Jezebel became very angry. Rather than repenting and turning to Yahweh, she decided to take vengeance on Elijah and kill him. She uses an oath formula, "May the gods deal with me, be it ever so severely," in the name of her gods (19:2a). She set a time limit of twenty-four hours to kill Elijah (19:2b). She expressed her vengeance as life for life, and there was no compromise on this decision. She sent her death verdict on Elijah through a messenger (19:2). Instead of abandoning Baalism and following Yahweh after witnessing Yahweh's power in the contest on top of Mount Carmel and after seeing the long-awaited rain pouring out of the sky, they planned to take Elijah's life. Ahab, at least, should have prevented Jezebel from seeking to kill Elijah, since the prophet had spared his life on top of Mount Carmel and sent him back to the palace alive.

It is natural for humans to be afraid of those who have absolute power and authority to kill them. After hearing about Jezebel's oath of vengeance and death verdict, Elijah was afraid and ran for his life across the southern border of northern Israel (19:3a). When he reached Beersheba in the kingdom of Judah, he left his servant there (19:3b). Elijah walked alone for another day until he found a broom bush to sit under, where he prayed to the Lord (19:4). Earlier, he wanted to live for the Lord and fulfill his mission according to the word of the Lord, but now he wanted to die. Elijah did not want to be killed by Jezebel, but to have the Lord take his life from him. He expressed his frustration, saying, "I have had enough, LORD" and "Take my life" (19:4). He was experiencing discouragement about his life and ministry, comparing himself with his ancestors, particularly the prophets of God in the past. The words, "I am no better than my ancestors," do not refer to his failure or disobedience. Rather, they are meant to express his upcoming death that everyone, including prophets and kings, faced.

19:5–14 GOD REFRESHES ELIJAH

When frustration and discouragement encircle the life of a servant of God, he or she often becomes inactive, passive, and goes to sleep without knowing what to do. In this state, Elijah went to sleep under the broom bush (19:5a).

God acted again to encourage Elijah. The angel of the Lord came and touched Elijah and said, "Get up and eat" (19:5b). Elijah woke up and saw some bread that had been baked over hot coals and a jar of water placed beside his head, but he could not see anyone standing there (19:6). Physically exhausted after walking such a long distance, he ate and drank, but he was still too psychologically exhausted to pray and seek God's guidance, and so he went to sleep again. Once again, the angel of the Lord came, touched him, and told him to eat and drink. This time, Elijah was more alert, and recognizing that the provision was from God, he listened to the words of the angel, who told him to walk a long distance again (19:7). Obeying the words of the angel, he ate and drank and then travelled for forty days and forty nights until he reached Horeb, the mountain of God (19:8). The estimated distance between Beersheba and Horeb is four hundred kilometers.[1] To cover this distance, Elijah would have had to walk ten kilometers a day. Horeb is called "the mountain of God" because it is where the Lord revealed himself to Moses and the people of Israel and made a covenant with them (Exod 19–23). A reader can recollect a parallel with Moses, who stayed on Mount Horeb in the Sinai region for forty days and forty nights without eating any food in order to meet God (Exod 3:1–5; Deut 9:8–10).[2]

While Elijah was running away from Jezebel, he was also running towards God and seeking God's protection for his life. Once Elijah reached Mount Horeb, he found a cave and stayed there (19:9a). Then the Lord questioned him for coming to Horeb, saying, "What are you doing here Elijah?" (19:9b). With this question, God was rebuking Elijah for his impatience and for not

---

1. Wiseman, *1 and 2 Kings*, 184.
2. It was a Jewish custom to fast for forty days, as we noticed in the life of Jesus (Matt 4:1–2).

seeking God's guidance before fleeing to northern Israel, but God was not rejecting him. Elijah's frustrated reply reveals his reason for asking the Lord to take away his life (19:10). First, he said that his spirit, mind, and soul were filled with enthusiasm and zeal for the Lord, similar to David's love and commitment for the Lord. Second, he complained to the Lord that the people of Israel, including the rulers, had rejected his covenant and followed after other gods and goddesses. Third, the people of Israel had "torn down" the altars of the Lord, thereby destroying the cultic places of Yahweh and abandoning their worship and sacrifices to the Lord. Fourth, the people of Israel had killed the prophets of the Lord (19:10). Finally, Elijah poured out his heart to the Lord, expressing his precarious situation at the hands of the ruthless followers of Baal (19:11).

But Elijah's ministry was not over, and he still had some more work to complete, and so the Lord asked him to come out of his cave and stand on the mountain to experience the presence of the Lord as he passed by Elijah. Then the Lord revealed himself to Elijah (19:11–13). First, a powerful and great wind blew, shaking and tearing the rock and shattering it into pieces. This signaled that the Lord was coming down (19:11–12). Next an earthquake came and shook the rocks of the mountain. The earthquake was followed by fire (19:12). God used the wind, earthquake, and fire to reveal himself, as in the stories of Abraham (Gen 15:12, a thick and dreadful darkness; 15:17, a smoking fire pot with a blazing torch) and Moses (Exod 3:2; 19:16). But the Lord was not in the wind, earthquake, or fire, and Elijah did not hear any words of the Lord. Lastly, there came a gentle whisper. Hearing this whisper, Elijah was afraid and wrapped his cloak around his face and stood in the entrance to the cave (19:13). Moses had a similar experience, but the Lord covered his face so that he could not see God (Exod 19:3–25; 33:20–23). In the gentle whisper, Elijah heard the same question, "What are you doing here Elijah?" (19:13). Elijah replied with the exact same answer (19:14), indicating his lament about the unchanging situation of Israel. His lament is also self-focused, expressing his frustration and fear rather than asking God to give him new vision and experiences to carry on the ministry. When we are filled with frustration about our ministry situations, we need to reassess our theology to come out of our fear and depression.[3]

---

3. House, *1, 2 Kings: An Exegetical and Theological Exposition of Holy Scripture*, 224.

19:15–21 ELIJAH'S REBOUND WITH A COMMISSION

Then the Lord spoke directly to Elijah on the mountain of Horeb and told him to return to the desert of Damascus in Syria (19:16). Elijah ran to the south in despair, into the desert of Beersheba, and now this action was reversed as God told him to go north into the desert of Damascus with a new mission. His experience at Horeb was a turning point, drawing him out of his depression so that he could continue the ministry of the Lord, which was to raise up new successors for the kingdom of Aram and Israel, as well as a new prophet to continue his ministry. God told Elijah the specific names of the people that he was to anoint (19:15–17). "Anointing" suggests an authorization from God that a certain person has been selected for a particular task. Elijah was to anoint Hazael to be king over Syria and to anoint Jehu, the commander of the army, to be king over northern Israel in Ahab's place. These instructions reveal that Yahweh's sovereignty was not limited to Israel. And God can use any kings to chastise and rebuke his people who turned to idolatry. This instruction imparts the rest of the mission to Hazael, Jehu, and Elisha so that Yahweh will have the final victory over the worship of Baal in Israel. Elijah's role is not to complete this task himself, but to anoint these three people to complete it.[4] Along with these leaders, the Lord had also preserved seven thousand people in Israel – "all whose knees have not bowed down to Baal and whose mouths have not kissed him" (19:18).

As we read the rest of the chapters in 1 and 2 Kings, we will notice the fulfillment of this purpose in anointing these three leaders. The theological implication of anointing these leaders is to fulfill the prophecy against the house of Jeroboam (1 Kgs 14:10) and later against the house of Ahab (1 Kgs 21:20–24; 2 Kgs 9:34–37; 10:1–29; 2 Chr 18:33–34). Elijah only slaughtered the prophets of Baal, not the people, priests, and rulers in the land who were still worshiping Baal and working against the prophets of Yahweh. This could only be done by raising up a new force of kings and their armies. To carry on the prophetic ministry, the Lord told Elijah to anoint Elisha, the son of Shaphat from Abel Meholath, as his successor (19:19). Shaphat may have been a rich land owner who had cattle and oxen to plough his land. Abel Meholath was in the valley of the river Jordan, south of Beth-Shan,[5] and so Elijah had to take a detour on his way through Beth-Shan to meet Elisha in his village.

---

4. Provan, *1 and 2 Kings*, 146–147.
5. Wiseman, *1 and 2 Kings*, 186.

There are several theological implications that arise from this event. First, God made it clear to Elijah that he was not silent, and he would act against the idolaters. All the kings and prophets were under his sovereign authority and could not continue worshiping Baal in Israel. He would bring them to account by anointing these three agents. Second, the human rulers could not go on persecuting the followers of Yahweh. God would interfere and bring their persecution to an end. Third, there would be always a few remnants who followed the Lord truly, even in difficult situations of persecution. God told Elijah that he was not the only faithful follower of Yahweh remaining in Israel. There were still seven thousand people who were faithful followers of Yahweh (19:18), along with a hundred prophets who had been protected by Obadiah (18:4). True followers would be always a minority, but Elijah was in good company.

After receiving God's encouragement, plan, and instructions, Elijah traveled from Horeb to Damascus. On his way, he saw Elisha, whom the Lord had described, ploughing his land, using the twelfth pair of oxen along with others. Elijah went near to Elisha and threw his cloak around him (19:19). The name "Elisha" means "God is salvation," reminding the people of Israel that God is their salvation, not Baal. The cloak refers to a garment, possibly made out of sheep's skin that one used to wrap around the body for protection from the weather. Throwing it on Elisha is a symbolic action of calling or adopting him or transferring Elijah's authority onto Elisha to continue the task that God had given to Elijah. Elisha ran after Elijah, but asked if he could go and kiss his parents before following him. "To kiss" here means to say "goodbye" or "farewell" (19:20). Elijah's response – "What have I done to you?" – does not convey rebuke or displeasure, but implies that Elijah is giving Elisha permission to say goodbye to his parents. Nevertheless, Elisha should not forget the action of the cloak being thrown on him and should follow Elijah without much delay.

Elisha left Elijah and went to his house and arranged a farewell meal with his family. His actions deserve our attention (19:21). First, he slaughtered the oxen he had used in ploughing to prepare the meal. Second, he used the yoke of his oxen, broke it, and burnt it for cooking the meal. Third, he gathered all the people in his family and shared the meal with them. This action of slaughtering his own animals and burning the yoke to prepare a feast conveys Elisha's intention to transfer his work to another family member. Elisha understood that he had been called to serve the Lord hereafter. As a symbolic expression of breaking his ties with his profession of ploughing the land, as well as his ties to his family and friends, he made it clear that he was accepting the call of God and changing his vocation to serve the Lord. This scene is similar to the fishermen of Galilee, who leave their nets and boats and follow Jesus at his command. It is always a challenge to break away from our old life, leaving behind our possessions and family, in order to enter into a new vocation to serve the Lord Jesus Christ. It is good to remember that no one can serve two masters (Matt 6:24a). Elisha could not keep his livelihood of ploughing while also following Elijah. So he left everything and followed Elijah and became his servant. It may take time for some people to break away from an old profession and possessions as Elisha did and to commit fully to the service of God, but we cannot hold both old and new assignments when the Lord calls us to full-time ministry. We have to discern the steps and timing according to the call and guidance of the Lord. Though Elijah had left his servant at Beersheba on his way to Horeb, God now gave him a new servant, Elisha, on his way to Damascus. Elijah would train Elisha as a prophet so that he could succeed Elijah, in time, to complete the particular task that God had ordained for Elisha.

1 KINGS 20:1–43
AHAB'S VICTORIES AND ACCOUNTABILITY

The story of Elijah is disrupted with an account of two attacks on northern Israel from Ben-Hadad, the king of neighboring Aram, Ahab's victory in both wars, and Ahab's accountability to the Lord who granted the victories (20:1–43). As such, this chapter has three sections: Ahab's defeat of Ben-Hadad in the war at Samaria (20:1–21), Ahab's defeat of Ben-Hadad in the war at Aphek (20:22–34), and Ahab's condemnation by the Lord by refusing to obey God (20:35–43).

20:1–21 THE WAR AT SAMARIA

Ben-Hadad, which means "son of the god Hadad," is a continuation of the royal title for the king of Aram (otherwise known as Syria). Asa, the king of Judah, made a treaty with Ben-Hadad by paying him silver and gold from his treasuries in exchange for Ben-Hadad's agreement that he would not help Baasha, the king of Israel, attack the southern kingdom (1 Kgs 15:16–22). But now, he musters war against Israel.

20:1–12 Ben-Hadad Attacks Israel

During the period of Ahab, Ben-Hadad became aggressive and gathered all his forces to attack the northern kingdom. He was also accompanied by thirty-two other kings, who might have been chieftains of various tribes paying tribute to him (20:1). After besieging the capital city of Samaria, he sent his messengers with a series of requests that were aimed at provoking Ahab either to fight against him or surrender (20:2). He sent a messenger saying, "Your silver and gold are mine, and the best of your wives and children are mine" (20:3). Ben-Hadad not only wanted the wealth but also he wanted to humiliate Ahab by taking his wives and children. Ahab agreed to give all of these to Ben-Hadad, addressing him as "lord," thereby accepting a subordinate position to the king of Aram (20:4). But Ben-Hadad was not satisfied with Ahab's reply.

Ben-Hadad sent his messengers a second time to Ahab, informing him that a raid would be carried out by the officials of Aram, that Ahab's palace would be searched thoroughly, and that all the valuables would be seized and carried away (20:5–6). Ahab did not want Ben-Hadad to enter his palace, and so he called the elders of Israel to consult with him (20:7). Ahab said, "See how this man is looking for trouble!" In Hebrew, Ahab said *ra'ah*, which meant "evil." Ahab is using the word "evil" (*ra'ah*) to describe Ben-Hadad as someone who is deliberately creating trouble. The elders of Israel advised Ahab to refuse the demands of the king of Aram (20:8). Once again, Ahab humbled himself, identifying himself as a "servant" and addressing the king of Aram as "lord," and said that he would agree to the first demand but not the second demand (20:9).

In the third round of confrontation, the king of Aram vowed to attack Samaria (20:10). His words, "May the gods deal with me, be it ever so severely," are a formula for an oath or vow taken in the name of his gods. This text echoes a similar vow taken by Jezebel in the name of her gods against Elijah (19:2). In Ben-Hadad's vow, he asked his gods to take severe action on him if he failed to succeed in his attack. The words of his oath reveal his anger and willingness to be punished by his gods if he returns without achieving his purpose against Israel. The phrase in the oath, "if enough dust remains in Samaria to give each of my men a handful," is a roaring boast that Samaria will be completely destroyed into dust, and each warrior in the army can have only a handful of dust. He is saying that nothing will be left in Samaria to threaten Ahab into surrendering to his conditions. Upon hearing this boast, Ahab replied with a proverb: "One who puts on his armor should not boast like one who takes it off" (20:11). The Hebrew verb for "arming and disarming" here literally refers to "putting on one's girdle in the morning and removing it at night,"[1] an idiomatic expression that means "preparing for war is one thing and winning it is another."[2] Put differently, anyone can boast or roar like a lion with an offensive voice before the war, but he needs to prove it with victory. In ancient India, some tribal leaders would not remove their swords or daggers unless they were sure of being able to kill their enemies. For if they failed to stain their swords with the blood of the enemy, it was considered to be shameful to return it to the sheath. So if a leader had not killed an enemy, he would make a cut on his own hand so that there would be bloodstains on the sword, and only then would he put it back into the sheath. Ben-Hadad

---

1. Gray, *I and II Kings: A Commentary*, 423.
2. Wiseman, *1 and 2 Kings*, 188.

heard Ahab's message while he was drinking in his tent, and then he ordered his army to prepare to attack (20:12).

20:13–21 Ahab Defeats Ben-Hadad

As Ben-Hadad and his allies prepared to attack Samaria, an unnamed prophet came with a message for King Ahab. This prophet informed Ahab that the Lord would give Ben-Hadad's vast army into Ahab's hands. The purpose of this defeat was that Ahab would know that Yahweh was the Lord and that the victory was from Yahweh (20:13). The prophet gave Ahab the instructions of the Lord regarding the timing, approach, and tactics of war against Ben-Hadad. Ahab did not need to muster all the people for this war. Instead, he should only select 232 junior commanding officers from within each district of northern Israel who would fight and win the war for Ahab (20:14). After them, seven thousand Israelites would follow (20:15). The strategy of sending the junior commanders to lead the Israelites would give the impression to Ben-Hadad's army that a small group was approaching to negotiate peace. The timing of the advance towards Ben-Hadad's army should be at noon because the enemy would be eating and drinking in their tents (20:12, 16). When Ben-Hadad was informed that the commanders were coming towards him (20:17), he ordered his men to capture them alive, whether they had come for peace or war (20:18). But the Israelites struck down their opponents, pursuing and killing them as Ben-Hadad escaped on horseback, accompanied by some chariots (20:19–21).

20:22–34 THE WAR AT APHEK

Then the unnamed prophet came to King Ahab a second time and instructed him to strengthen his army and establish a strong base because Ben-Hadad would return to attack Israel (20:22). The prophet does not identify the location of the next war, but he says that that it will take place during the "turn of the year," referring to the spring season. The prophet warned Ahab not to have confidence in his army but to obey all the words of God and to start preparing and strengthening his military positions throughout the country.

As predicted by the prophet, the king of Aram could not accept his previous defeat and started planning to attack Israel again. His "servants" – who may be court officials, prophets of his religion, or military commanders – advised him to fight this war on the plains because Israel's God was the God of the hills (20:23). The gods of the Arameans have power over the plains. The Arameans believed that they could hope for victory if the war was set on the plains. They did not understand that Yahweh, the God of Israel, can fight against any army at any place and at any time on behalf of those who believe, worship, and obey him. The servants advise Ben-Hadad to remove all the kings who accompanied him in the previous war and replace them with other officers (20:24). The servants also advise the king to make his military stronger by raising more men for the army and acquiring more horses and chariots to replace the losses from the previous war at Samaria (20:25). Ben-Hadad agrees to their advice, expecting a victory in the war on the plains.

Just as the unnamed prophet told Ahab, Ben-Hadad mustered the Arameans and went to war against Israel at the "turn of the year" in a place called "Aphek" (20:26). This word literally means "a source of water," referring to a fertile plain region east of the Sea of Galilee at the confluence of the Yarmuk and Jordan rivers. This location gave the advantage to the Arameans because it was located *en route* to Israel from Damascus. As the Israelites set up camp opposite to the Aram army, the narrator draws a comparative picture saying that King Aram's army covered the entire countryside whereas the Israelite army looked like two small flocks of goats standing on the fertile plains (20:27). This picture confirms that the outcome of the forthcoming battle was not determined by the strength or weakness of the army, but by the power of the Lord. In a similar case, Gideon was asked to reduce the number of those fighting against the Midianites to three hundred (Judg 7:4–7). Zerubbabel was also told that the power of the Lord was more important than the number of men (Zech 4:6).

Knowing the compromised situation of the Israelite army, the unnamed prophet came to Ahab a third time to communicate the word of God (20:28). God reveals to Ahab what Ben-Hadad had discussed with his elders about the God of Israel being a God of the hills and their gods being gods of the valleys. The God of Israel wants to challenge this religious worldview by defeating the Aramean army in a battle on the plains. Once again, the battle is not Ahab's but Yahweh's, and the main purpose is so that Ahab and Israel will know that Yahweh is the Lord (20:28). According to the word of the Lord, Ahab's army defeated Ben-Hadad's army at the plains of Aphek, killing a hundred thousand Arameans, though Ben-Hadad escaped and hid himself in the city of Aphek (20:29). The remaining soldiers who escaped also hid themselves in the city of Aphek, where the wall collapsed and killed twenty-seven thousand (20:30). The encounter between Yahweh and Baal on Mount Carmel (1 Kings 18) and the encounter between the nations of Israel and Aram (1 Kings 20) show Yahweh is victorious over other gods and nations.

"Yahweh is the Lord" (20:13, 28) or "I am the Lord," appears in Exodus in connection with the liberation of the Israelites from the bondage of Pharaoh (Exod 6:6–7). Originally, this statement belongs to the Exodus tradition, indicating that both the Egyptians and the Israelites will know that Yahweh is the Lord above all other powers and authorities. Later, the statement appears in the context of "holy war." There is no other God more powerful than Yahweh, the sovereign Lord of the universe, who is over all powers on earth. The kings and people of Israel should never boast about winning a war due to their strength or tactics, because it is Yahweh who fights for them and gives victory. Yahweh lays down the conditions of war and how the Israelites should deal with the defeated enemies and their possessions and land. When the Israelites see the power of God giving them victory over their enemies, they will be reminded to worship and follow Yahweh alone. Unlike the nations who believe that the power of their deities is determined by a particular location or function, Yahweh alone is global and almighty. The key assertion is "I am Yahweh" or "Yahweh is the Lord."[3] The Lord fought the battle and gave victory to Ahab.

After experiencing defeat at the plains, the servants of Ben-Hadad were afraid and wanted to stop the advancement of Ahab's army into their country. Desperate to save their lives and the life of their king, they came to Ahab wearing sackcloth around their waists and ropes around their heads (20:31–32). Wearing sackcloth communicates their posture of mourning and seeking penitence. The "ropes" could indicate the readiness of the defeated king (Ben-Hadad) to be the porter or servant of Ahab.[4] In railway stations in India, porters wear red headbands (a piece of red cloth tied around the head) and red shirts so that passengers will be able to identify them easily when they need help carrying their luggage. The "ropes" could also refer to a soldier wearing a bandage over his bleeding wounds.[5] Dressed in this way, the servants begged Ahab to extend mercy to their king (20:31–32). The Hebrew word for "merciful" (*hesed*) is connected with the covenantal relationship with Yahweh and usually means "steadfast love" or "lovingkindness" (20:31). The servants of Ben-Hadad use this word to plead with Ahab to spare the life of their king. The picture of the king boasting is reversed by this picture of his servants begging Ahab to show kindness to Ben-Hadad. While Ahab called Ben-Hadad "lord"

---

3. R. P. Gordon, "War," in *NBD*, 1240–1242; Gerhard von Rad, *Old Testament Theology*, vol. 1 (London: SCM Press, 1975), 17, 307.
4. Gray, *I and II Kings: A Commentary*, 429.
5. Wiseman, *1 and 2 Kings*, 192.

earlier (20:4), now the officials of Ben-Hadad call their own king the "servant" of Ahab (20:32). Appropriate words can have the power to change the hearts of rulers, and Ahab was taken by the words and actions of these officials and showed mercy to Ben-Hadad. He even went one step further by calling Ben-Hadad his "brother" and expressing surprise that he was still alive (20:32b). Noticing Ahab's cordial tone, the officials cleverly took it as a good sign to reiterate the old friendship between Israel and Syria (20:33a). Ahab ordered them to bring Ben-Hadad to him. They brought him into his chariot where they negotiated a peace treaty (20:33b).

The negotiations included that Ben-Hadad would return to Ahab all the cities that his father had captured (20:34a; see 1 Kgs 15:20). Moreover, Ahab would set up a market area in Damascus for trade, just as his father had done in Samaria. Ben-Hadad agreed to the treaty and Ahab set him free (20:34b).

Acknowledging the mistakes and expressing humility are needed today for leaders. Christians can learn to forgive those who humble themselves before them and ask for pardon without taking advantage. Many religions teach forgiveness and acceptance of others as brothers and sisters. It is not something new in the OT. David forgave Saul but did not take the action of killing Saul. Though showing love and pardon is part of human nature, people in general want to take vengeance. Ahab is showing forgiveness in the context of war and defeating enemies.

20:35–43 AHAB'S CONDEMNATION

Ahab shouldn't have let Ben-Hadad go. An unnamed prophet of the Lord vividly illustrates this in this section.

This unnamed prophet was "one of the company of the prophets," who received a word of God (20:35a). The phrase, "the company of the prophets," refers to the prophets who worked as an organized guild under a senior prophet and regarded him as a father. The prophet who came to Ahab three times may have been one prophet or three different prophets, but they all belonged to a company of prophets in Israel.[6] That unnamed prophet asked another prophet in his company to strike him with a weapon (20:35b). But the other prophet refused to strike his fellow prophet (20:35b). That act was an act of disobedience to the word of the Lord. So the unnamed prophet prophesied that the one who disobeyed God's word would be killed by a lion; it happened as he prophesied (20:36). This incident reminds us of the prophet who disobeyed

---

6. Some scholars suggest this prophet could be Micaiah. See Wiseman, *1 and 2 Kings*, 192.

God's instruction when he came to deliver a prophetic word to Jeroboam and was also killed by a lion on his way home (13:20–25).

After this incident, the prophet called another prophet in his company to strike him, and this prophet obeyed (20:37). The wounded prophet covered his head with a headband, disguised himself as a wounded soldier, and went to meet Ahab on the road (20:38). As he was waiting, he saw the king and made a complaint, using a parable known as a "judicial parable." The wounded soldier-prophet said that while he was in the middle of the battle, a captive was handed over to him to guard with the condition that he would not lose him. If he let the captive go free, then his own life would be accountable or else he had to pay a penalty of a talent of silver (20:39–40). But the captive escaped and ran away while the soldier was busy with other work. Any reader of this parable would assume that the soldier was seeking help from the king so that he would not be punished for his carelessness and failure to fulfill the condition. In fact, the prophet wanted to provoke the king to uphold the condition and punishment. As expected, the king replied, "That is your sentence . . . You have pronounced it yourself" (20:40). When the prophet received this answer, he removed his headband to reveal himself (20:41). Ahab recognized him as one of the prophets, and then the prophet pronounced the same judgment on the king, using the messenger formula, "This is what the LORD says" (20:42a). Ahab had let Ben-Hadad go free, which was against God's plan. "Therefore it is your life for his life, your people for his people" (10:42b). His lenience toward Ben-Hadad and Aram would one day result in his defeat and the captivity of the people of Israel. Hearing this judgment, the king of Israel went to his palace in Samaria "sullen and angry" (20:43). Ahab understood that his fate was sealed because of his disobedience and for forgetting the claim, "Yahweh is the LORD."

1 KINGS 21:1-29
AHAB'S INJUSTICE TO NABOTH

Vineyards, vegetable gardens, and paddy fields are precious to farmers in any society. Today, viniculturists cultivate large vineyards and devote great care and effort to tending the vines because they can earn a good income from winemaking. In ancient Israel, vineyards supplied fruit and wine for the families of farmers. The story of Naboth's vineyard is a classic example of the strong bond that exists between a farmer and his land because the land is his inheritance that cannot be sold or exchanged (Lev 25:23–24; 1 Kgs 21:3).

Elijah reappears in this story to confront King Ahab. Once again, a reader can notice the polarization between the king, who represents the power and authority of the political institution and the ruling class, and the prophets of Yahweh who represent the religious institution and raise the voice of God's justice for the poor and needy. This chapter has two sections: Ahab's desire for Naboth's vineyard along with Jezebel's plot to get the vineyard (21:1–16) and God's proclamation of justice through Elijah (21:17–29).

21:1-16 AHAB, NABOTH, AND JEZEBEL

Although a wealthy king, Ahab desires the vineyard of his neighbor, Naboth. When he couldn't receive it, he sulks. Seeing his dejection, his wife Jezebel acts on his behalf and kills Naboth. These events seems like a movie from Bollywood, and yet, they reflect the moral decay of a king who would stoop low to take the possession of a simple person. The incidents of this chapter can be divided into three scenes: the pettiness of the king (21:1–4), a pouty king being soothed by his cunning wife (21:5–7), and the ruthless actions taken by the king's wife to get what she wants, regardless of the cost (21:8–16).

21:1-4 Ahab Approaches Naboth

Sometime later, Ahab gets involved in a dispute with his neighbor about a vineyard near his palace, which he wants to buy and convert into a vegetable garden (21:1–2). The vineyard belonged to Naboth, the Jezreelite. Ahab approached Naboth and asked him to sell the vineyard either in exchange for another vineyard in a different location or for a good sum of money. The king's offer was fair; he was not trying to exploit the peasant to get the vineyard for a cheaper price. However, Naboth did not want to exchange or sell the vineyard because it was an inheritance from his ancestors. The inheritance system in Israel has a long history and a theology behind it. First, the Israelites were given land when they settled in Canaan. Each family was given land to cultivate (Josh 13–19; Num 26:52–56). Second, cultivating the land gave them work and sustained them. If they lost the land for some reason or sold it for money, they would lose their livelihood. Those who lost their livelihood could easily become laborers or bonded slaves to a landlord for many generations. Thus the Lord had declared a rule that inherited land could not be sold in Israel (Lev 25:23–24). This sociological reason was strengthened by a theological reason, which is that the Lord is the creator and owner of the land, and God is allowing the Israelites to be tenants on his land so that they can cultivate it and support themselves.[1] No human being can own or sell land that belongs to God. If the land is ever mortgaged, it must be returned to the original owner on the fiftieth year of Jubilee (Lev 25:23–25). Third, in some ancient societies, those who owned the family inheritance in a village received citizenship in the country.

Naboth did not want his land to be sold or exchanged for any purpose (1 Kgs 21:3). Though the focus of the narrative is on the land as a family inheritance, the vineyard is an important symbol and a part of the Israelite identity. Throughout the biblical narrative, Israel is portrayed as a vineyard that is tended by the Lord, and so the grapevine is highly regarded by the prophets (Isa 5:1–4; Hos 10:1), the psalmist (Ps 80:8–14; Song 1:6; 2:15), and Jesus (John 15:1). The Israelites needed to tend vegetable gardens after their settlement in Canaan, but they would always remember the stories about their hard labor of sowing and irrigating the gardens in Egypt as slaves in contrast to trusting God to send rain to water the plants in the Promised Land (Deut 11:10–11).[2] Having one's inheritance passed from one generation to the next reminded the Israelites of their long history of the land as a gift from God, the land as their sociological sustenance and livelihood, the land as their right to citizenship and participation in the life and leadership of the community, and the land as the recipient of Yahweh's provision and care. Regardless, Naboth refused to trade the vineyard or sell it to the king.

---

1. J. B. Jeyaraj, "Jubilee and Society: Reflections," in *Evangelical Review of Theology*, vol. 25:4 (2001): 337–349 and revised and reprinted as "Jubilee and Mission," Missiology for the 21st Century: South Asian Perspective, ed. R. E. Hedlund (Delhi: SPCK, 2004), 43–52.
2. Hens-Piazza, *1–2 Kings*, 206.

Naboth's reply to Ahab, "The Lord forbid" (21:3) means he cannot violate the age-old law and regulations of the inheritance system in Israel, and the Lord forbids him to do so. He expresses his fear of God and respect for the law by using the name of the Lord in his oath (21:3). Ahab did not expect this refusal from Naboth. He had assumed that a citizen of his country would respect the request of the king and cooperate with an offer from a higher authority. Naboth's firm stand based on the religious law of the land goes against the political power of the king. Ahab returned to the palace angry and resentful (21:4), just as he did after being criticized by the unnamed prophet at the end of the previous chapter (20:43).

21:5–7 Jezebel Intervenes

When Jezebel noticed that Ahab was refusing to eat, she asked the reason for his sadness (21:5). Ahab explained the reason for his sorrow (21:6), but he did not include Naboth's explanation about the law of inheritance in Israel and how he could not violate the principles of the Lord. Jezebel was a Phoenician worshiper of Baal, and so she would not have respected the Israelite law of inheritance. Based on the custom of her country, she felt that the king should be respected and obeyed whenever he demanded something from the public. Her words, "Is this how you act as king over Israel?" (21:7), indicate that she believes that the king is above the tradition of Israel and should use his power to get anything he wants. Since he had failed to exercise his political power and authority as king, she assured him that she would get the vineyard for him. In terms of intertextuality, we can contrast her response to the king, "I will give you the vineyard of Naboth" (21:7 ESV), with Naboth's response to the king, "I will not give you the inheritance" (21:4 ESV). Because she does not care about the law of inheritance in Israel, she asserts her authority over the commandments of Yahweh. Ahab did not prevent Jezebel from acting to get the vineyard from Naboth.

21:8–16 Jezebel's Cunning Plot

In the next scene, Jezebel takes the law and authority into her own hands by acting in the name of the king (21:8–16). She wrote letters in Ahab's name, sealed them with the royal seal, and sent them to the elders and nobles of Jezreel (21:8).

In the letters, she outlined her plot. First, she asked the elders and nobles to declare a day of fasting, implying that a great sin had happened in the country, and to arrange a trial and make Naboth sit in a prominent place among the people (21:9). In ancient Israel, when a day of fasting was declared, the people would pray to ask God to forgive their sins or to help them win a war. This spiritual exercise was declared in times of emergency so that people would cooperate and accept any corporate decision that was made after the day of prayer and fasting. By placing Naboth in a prominent place, he was being targeted without his knowledge. Second, Jezebel would seek the death of Naboth (21:10).

Jezebel must have known the Deuteronomic law that punished with death anyone who worshiped other gods (Deut 13:10–15; 17:5–7), and the law required a minimum of two witnesses to accuse someone of apostasy. Thus Jezebel asked the elders and nobles to seat two scoundrels across from Naboth and to have them accuse him falsely of cursing God and the king. Jezebel manipulated the law to ensure that these scoundrels would accuse Naboth so that he would face the death sentence. Cursing God happens when a person worships Baal, joins the religion of Baalism, and speaks against Yahweh. Naboth did not do any of these things, but he used the name of God to make an oath to Ahab that he would not sell his vineyard. Cursing the king involves speaking against the king or committing an act of political treason, which also carried a death sentence. Jezebel interpreted Naboth's refusal in the name of God as a curse of both God and the king. In arranging these false accusations, the elders and nobles were collaborators. They knew very well that they were doing injustice to a righteous man who was upholding the law of God. They, too, were guilty of killing Naboth by perverting justice. As a punishment, Jezebel asked the elders and nobles to stone Naboth to death, according to the law in Israel (21:10b). The elders and nobles followed Jezebel's orders (21:11–13). When they had stoned and killed Naboth, they informed Jezebel of their actions (21:14).

Even after killing Naboth, the king could not legally take his vineyard because the law of inheritance would transfer the ownership of his land to his sons or the next of kin in his family (Num 27:1–11; 36:1–7). According to the ancient social order, property and inheritance could not be changed unless God made changes in Israel. However, when Jezebel informed the king about Naboth's death, she told him to take possession of the vineyard (21:15–16a). Since Ahab had no right to the land after Naboth's death, she was telling him to steal it. Ahab followed her advice and took Naboth's vineyard (21:16b).

In Jezebel's plot, she committed multiple crimes: she manipulated the office of the king by writing false letters and using the royal seal; she set up false witnesses; she committed murder and theft; she broke the covenantal law of the Israelites. The ownership of the land is an important theological and ethical issue in ancient Israel. The inheritance law is based on a theological principle that can still be a lesson for us today. The development of civilization has led most people living today to sell and buy land. Nevertheless, Naboth's firm stand to keep the land within his family for his descendants to work and sustain themselves can challenge us.

In South Asia and Southeast Asia, many peasants have lost their land and become poor laborers under landlords. The rich have become richer, and the poor have become poorer. Most of the landless people who were uprooted from their villages have migrated to cities and towns and now live on the sides of roads. The landless poor are vulnerable and often become exploited sexually or become bonded laborers of real estate owners. In response to this situation, Vinobave, an ardent follower of Mahatma Gandhi, created the *Bhoodan* movement. In this movement, landlords are asked to donate some of their land to landless families so that they can sustain themselves. Unless the governments in Asian countries bring radical reform to the land tenure system by limiting land holdings and redistributing land to landless peasants, we will see only poverty and violence on the streets.[3]

21:17-29 GOD PROCLAIMS HIS JUSTICE

Both Ahab and Jezebel misused their authority and power to kill a man who had claimed his right to keep his ancestor's property. They were ruthless against anyone who questioned them or the prophets who pointed out their crimes. This story highlights the importance of developing a responsible and ethical theology of administration and power. Ahab and Jezebel misused their administrative power and political authority without fearing God or people. Those who accumulate power, wealth, and money often think they can interpret the law to their advantage. Yet good governance must be based on the principles, character, and values of God. The word of the Lord spoken against Ahab and Jezebel reveals God's anger against those who misuse their power. God stands on the side of the poor and exploited – not with those who pervert justice (Exod 2:24–25; 22:21–24).

After bearing witness to Ahab and Jezebel's atrocity, God sent Elijah to proclaim God's punishment on Ahab. The word of the Lord came to Elijah

---

3. J. B. Jeyaraj, "Siding with the Landless: Important Mission Ahead," AD 2000 and Beyond: A Mission Agenda, eds. Vinay Samuel and Chris Sugden (Oxford: Regnum Books, 1991), 97–111.

to meet Ahab as he was taking possession of Naboth's vineyard (1 Kgs 21:17). The message communicates both accusation and punishment in the style of a prophetic judgment; Elijah was the man to do it (21:18). The accusation is expressed in a rhetorical style, asking if Ahab has "murdered" Naboth and "grabbed" his property (21:19a). This rhetorical question is followed by a messenger formula, using "This is what the Lord says" to proclaim a clear verdict of the death sentence. Ahab will be put to death in the place where the dogs licked up Naboth's blood, indicating that he will die a cruel death, and no one will save his body from the dogs. Such a death was regarded as an insult and humiliation (21:19b).

Ahab's response to Elijah, "So you have found me, my enemy!" (21:20a) conveys two assumptions. First, Ahab assumes that no one knows about his crime, and yet Elijah has discovered it. This shocks Ahab, because Jezebel had conceived her plot secretly through the proper arrangement, but now Elijah is bringing it into the light. Second, Ahab immediately assumes that Elijah is his "enemy." Earlier, in 1 Kings 18:17, he referred to him as a "troubler." By calling Elijah his enemy rather than "troubler of Israel," the king is emphasizing the mounting tension between the political institution and the religious institution. The king doesn't have the freedom to do whatever he wants and live in peace because the prophet keeps coming and pointing it out. Elijah's bold reply, "I have found you," is similar to a police officer saying, "I found out the murderer." After making this declaration, Elijah says that Ahab has sold himself to do evil in the eyes of God (21:20b). The Hebrew word for selling in this context gives us a pictorial view of transferring one's right completely. The irony of the word, "selling," flashes back to the way Ahab sold himself to evil by taking what Naboth would not sell, both in terms of his life and his land. Instead of committing himself to uphold the law of God by honoring the law of inheritance and administering justice as his duty, he has become a slave to sin.

In verses 21–26, Elijah pronounces God's punishment on Ahab. The Lord will punish Ahab and his family – just as he punished the families of Jeroboam and Baasha, the son of Ahijah – because Ahab caused Israel to abandon Yahweh and worship Baal (21:21–22). This sin is idolatry – following idols just as the Amorites worshiped gods and goddesses.

Then the Lord testified against Jezebel: "Dogs will devour Jezebel by the wall of Jezreel" (21:23). Just as dogs ate those who died in the city and birds (vultures) ate those who died in the country, the dogs in the city would devour the flesh of Jezebel (21:24). All these were because Ahab did evil in the eyes of the Lord and did more evil than any of his ancestors (21:25). He loved idols and gods of other nations, for which the Lord punished him (21:26). Ahab's vilest action was that he worshiped idols and promoted the fertility cult in Israel by supporting the worship of Baal and establishing shrines in the hills and valleys. His wife, Jezebel, pressured him to do this evil by urging him to promote the cult of Baal, which led the nation to worship idols, and also by killing the prophets of Yahweh. Both of them aroused the anger of the Lord, and so both will be punished. God will not only punish Ahab and Jezebel, but he will wipe out every male in his household, both descendants and slaves. This means there will not be any male from the nucleus or extended family of Ahab because they will be killed in the near future.

Ahab reacts to Elijah's prophetic judgment by tearing his royal clothes, wearing sackcloth, and fasting (21:27). In ancient Israel, the symbolic actions of wearing sackcloth, sprinkling ashes on one's head, and fasting showed repentance and humility before the Lord. Ahab went around wearing sackcloth rather than his royal clothes so that people in the palace and court would see a change in him.

Ahab's action of humbling himself pleased the Lord, and so he asked Elijah to communicate a message of grace to Ahab (21:28). The Lord accepted Ahab's repentance and altered his punishment so that the total annihilation would not happen during his lifetime, but in the days of his sons (21:29). This does not mean that Ahab and Jezebel will not be punished for their atrocities, as we will see in the following chapters.

1 KINGS 22:1–53

DEFEAT AND DEATH OF AHAB

What happened to the prophecies against Ahab? Did they become invalid? Were they unfulfilled? At the end of chapter 21, a reader would naturally raise these questions. But the story of Ahab is not yet over, 1 Kings 22 connects back to the prophecies made against Ahab in 1 Kings 20–21. There are three major divisions in this chapter: the consultations between Ahab and Jehoshaphat (22:1–28); the killing of Ahab in battle and the fulfillment of the prophecies against him (22:29–40); and, an account of the new rulers of Judah and northern Israel (22:41–53).

22:1–28 AHAB, JEHOSHAPHAT, AND MICAIAH

Once again, the reader of this section can notice a tension between the political and the religious authorities in the northern kingdom of Israel. This section has three sub-units: an alliance between Ahab and Jehoshaphat to go to war against Ben-Hadad (22:1–12), the vision and prophecy of Micaiah (22:13–23), and the death of Ahab (22:24–28).

22:1–12 Ahab and Jehoshaphat

There was peace between Israel and Aram for three years (22:1). In the third year, a meeting occurred between the southern king, Jehoshaphat, and the king of Israel, Ahab (22:2). They both agreed to fight for Ramoth-Gilead (22:3–4). Ahab wanted to recover Ramoth-Gilead, a town that had previously belonged to Israel and was situated along the border of Aram, from the hands of Ben-Hadad. Jehoshaphat agreed to this assimilation.

Jehoshaphat's words, "I am as you are, my people as your people, my horses as yourselves" (22:4), indicate his willingness and cooperation. He and Ahab are of the same mind in wanting to recover the town for Israel. His people in Judah and the people in northern Israel are one people of the same God, though they are living in two nations, and they need to support each other in need. His army of chariots and horses is ready to participate in the war. All three of these aspects convey that the king, his people, and his military are committed to making an alliance for this war against Aram. However, before proceeding, he asked Ahab to seek the counsel or guidance of the Lord (22:5), which was a customary practice before waging a battle in Israel (Deut 20:1–4). He wanted to know whether the God of Israel would agree and go with their armies to grant victory, or not.

So Ahab brought together four hundred prophets and asked them to determine the omen for going to war (22:6a). All of them assured Ahab of victory in retaking Ramoth-Gilead (22:6b). Jehoshaphat, a true worshiper of Yahweh, was suspicious that all the prophets gave the same answer in unison, and so he asked Ahab to get a second opinion from another prophet (22:7). While Ahab was seeking the omen to agree with his own ambition, Jehoshaphat was seeking God's will. Ahab's reply reveals that he knew that Micaiah, the son of Imlah, was a true prophet of Yahweh. However, Ahab had deliberately not called Micaiah because of the bad prophecies that this prophet of the Lord had delivered against him in the past (22:8a). But Jehoshaphat insisted on hearing from a prophet of the Lord (22:8b), and so Ahab called for Micaiah (22:9). This consultation with the prophets took place as Ahab and Jehoshaphat were sitting in their royal robes at the threshing floor outside the entrance of Samaria (22:10). Usually, the city gate is where elders of the community listen to complaints and pronounce justice. Before Micaiah arrived, Zedekiah, the son of Kenaanah (not king Zedekiah of a later period), performed a symbolic action as the leader of all the prophets by making iron horns and putting them on his head. Animals use their horns to defend or drive back or attack other animals. Wearing these irons horns, Zedekiah declared that Ahab would pierce the Arameans just as horns destroy an attacking animal (22:11). All the other prophets joined with Zedekiah and gave the same response (22:12).

22:13–23 Micaiah's Vision and Prophecy

The messenger who summoned Micaiah said to him, "Look, the other prophets without exception are predicting success for the king. Let your word agree with theirs, and speak favorably" (22:13). But Micaiah told the messenger that he could not tell lies but could only say what the Lord wanted him to tell the king (22:14). His reply reveals his honesty to God and his courage in accepting the king's call and being willing to tell the truth alone. When Ahab asked Micaiah if Israel should go to war against Ben-Hadad for Ramoth-Gilead, the prophet replied, "Attack and be victorious . . . for the LORD will give it into the king's hand" (22:15).

Ahab realized that this might not be in his favor and said, "How many times must I make you swear to tell me nothing but the truth in the name of the LORD?" (22:16). To which, Micaiah declared the message in two parts.

First, he revealed a vision that the Lord had shown him about the sheep who were scattered on the hills without a shepherd. The Lord had also given Micaiah the interpretation for the vision, which compared the sheep to Israel and the shepherd to the king (22:17). This imagery indicated that the king, the shepherd, would be killed in the battle, and the Israelites would be like sheep scattered on the battlefield.

The idiom, "each one goes home in peace," means to return home without success. Ahab understood this point and became angry. Turning to Jehoshaphat, Ahab accused Micaiah of only communicating bad prophetic messages to him (22:18). This scene remains an important challenge for Christians and ministers today, as it is important for leaders not only to communicate their vision, but also to seek an interpretation from the Lord. Many church communities have been misled when preachers interpret their own visions without confirming them in the light of biblical teachings and prayerful revelations from the Lord.

In the second part of the message, Micaiah responded to Ahab's reaction of anger (22:19). The word "therefore" indicates that the prophet had to defend himself from the king's accusation, and so he was forced to interpret the vision the Lord had given to him about the shepherd and the sheep. He said that all the prophets were giving the same answer to please the king because of the lying spirit that had been sent into them (22:19). Micaiah explained that the Lord had permitted this lying spirit to speak through the mouths of all the prophets. The phrase, "I saw the LORD sitting on his throne with all the multitudes of heaven," contrasts with the kings, who are sitting in their royal robes on the throne at the city gate. In the vision, Micaiah could see what was going on in the heavenly counsel to fulfill the prophecies of the earlier prophets against Ahab. The Lord was asking the heavenly host for a volunteer to entice Ahab to go for war and so be killed in the battle (22:20). One of the spirits came forward and offered to entice Ahab by being a lying spirit in the mouths of all his prophets so that they would give the same prophecy in favor of going for war (22:21–22). Because Ahab would only believe his own prophets, the Lord sent the lying spirit to give a false prophecy through the prophets. Micaiah revealed this secret and told Ahab about the Lord's decision to bring disaster for the king (1 Kgs 22:23).

Very few servants of God in ancient Israel had the privilege of seeing a vision given by the Lord. Isaiah saw the vision of the Lord with the heavenly host and heard the judgment on the Israelites (Isa 6:1–13). Job's case came to the counsel of the Lord, and Satan was permitted to persecute him, but not to put him to death (Job 1:6–12). Today, people raise ethical questions about God himself giving Satan permission to test Job or asking a lying spirit to mislead Ahab and his army. Some mysteries cannot be explained or solved by us today, and so we can accept this limited information and trust that it was for God's particular purpose or plan rather than adding our own assumptions and interpretations.

22:24–28 Micaiah's Humiliation and Punishment

Ahab should have changed his mind after hearing from Micaiah that the prophecy of all the prophets was false because of the lying spirit that had been sent into them. But Ahab was not willing to accept the true prophet's vision and interpretation or the message sent to him by the Lord. So, Zedekiah, the lead prophet who had made the iron horns, slapped Micaiah (the false prophet) on the face in front of the king and all the others who were assembled there (22:24). This scene is similar to when Pashhur slapped Jeremiah (Jer 20:1–6). True prophets often have to face humiliation for telling the truth of the Lord. Second, Zedekiah challenged Micaiah by asking about the lying spirit that had been sent by the Lord. How could both he and Micaiah speak in the name of Yahweh? Who was telling the true prophecy? Micaiah did not answer him or argue with him. Everyone would have to wait for the result of the prophecy to discern the truth, but Zedekiah would flee for his life and hide himself in an inner chamber (22:25). Third, Ahab ordered his officials to arrest Micaiah and send him to Amon, the ruler of the city, and Joash, the king's son, who should put him in prison and give him only bread and water until Ahab returned from battle (22:26–27). If Ahab came back with victory, then Micaiah was a liar and could be punished with death.

Micaiah was certain that Ahab would not return with victory but would die in the battlefield, and so he boldly challenged Ahab, saying that if Ahab returned safely from the battlefield, then Micaiah was willing to accept that the Lord did not speak through him (22:28). This scene raises an important theological and practical issue, which is that religious leaders and administrators need to have a discerning spirit. Waging war is not a pleasure game but costs the lives of people and the economy of a nation. All leaders should seek God's will. If God sends a word through a prophet, the leader should obey the word, even if it is not pleasing. When a true prophet proclaims the word of God, he or she should believe that the Lord will fulfill the word he has spoken – even if the prophet has to risk his or her life. Micaiah proves that he believes the word of the Lord by asking the people to record his words and to wait for their fulfillment (22:28).

22:29–40 DEATH OF AHAB

The second part of the story narrates Ahab's defeat in battle, his death, and burial. Though Ahab knew the true prophecy from the Lord, he went up to war with Jehoshaphat. Ahab was afraid because of Micaiah's prophecy against him, and so he decided to disguise himself so that Micaiah's prophecy would be diverted (22:29–30). Ahab sent Jehoshaphat to battle in his royal robe to divert the attention of his enemies away from himself and to make Jehoshaphat their target (22:31). Jehoshaphat did not suspect Ahab and agreed to wear his royal robe.

When the battle for Ramoth-Gilead began, the king of Aram instructed his army and chariot commanders to identify Ahab and target him alone (22:31). Because Jehoshaphat was wearing Ahab's royal robe, he was mistaken for the king of Israel, and so the chariot commanders surrounded him (22:32). But Jehoshaphat cried out, revealing his identity, and the chariot commanders went looking for Ahab (22:33). Then a soldier drew his bow and shot an arrow that hit Ahab between his breastplate and armor, piercing his body (22:34a). Ahab asked his chariot commander to take him out of the battlefield, but the battle was severe, with the Arameans surrounding Ahab's army, and so he could not leave to return home (22:34b). The blood from Ahab's wound ran onto the floor of the chariot, and he died on the battlefield (22:35). The narrative announces Israel's defeat with the usual formula, "Every man to his town. Everyone to his land!" (22:36). King Ahab died and they buried him (22:37).

After the battle, the army washed the bloodstains off the chariots by a pool in Samaria that was ten meters long and five meters wide, where the prostitutes bathed (22:38).[1] The dogs licked his blood as prophesied (22:38b). This verse indicates Ahab's humiliation and the fulfillment of Elijah's earlier prophecy (21:19). Once again, the theme of prophecy and fulfillment are fulfilled, which is emphasized in the words, "as the word of the LORD has declared" (22:38). Though the Lord had given Ahab a grace period because of his humility, Ahab did not respect the word of God as it was revealed to him through Micaiah, but rather persecuted the prophet for telling the truth (22:39). Ahab's end is summarized by the usual formula, with the narrator mentioning his burial, the period of his reign, his achievements of building

---

1. Wiseman, *1 and 2 Kings*, 202.

a palace in Samaria and decorating it with ivory and also fortifying cities to provide security for Israel, a reference for obtaining further information in the annals of the kings, and concluding with a note that his son, Ahaziah, succeeded him to the throne (22:39–40).

22:41–53 A NEW REIGN

Chapter 22 began by introducing Jehoshaphat without providing any details about his background. He was one of the kings in the southern kingdom. In this final section of the chapter, we learn that he was a son of Asa, and his mother's name was Azubah (22:41). He came to the throne when he was thirty-five years old, and he reigned in Jerusalem for twenty-five years (22:42). The narrator makes two important comments about Jehoshaphat. First, he followed Yahweh and did what was right in his eyes (22:43), just as his father had done (15:9–15). But, he did not remove the high places, and so people continued to offer sacrifices and burn incense at local shrines that had been erected for Yahweh. Those who worshiped in these shrines tried to worship both Yahweh and other deities, meaning that the Israelites in Judah were still not following Yahweh alone. Second, the narrator says that Jehoshaphat kept peace with the king of Israel, avoiding unnecessary civil war between the northern and southern kingdom (22:44).

Jehoshaphat's other achievements include eradicating the male shrine prostitutes (22:46) and building a fleet of ships for trade to bring wealth to Judah, just as Solomon had done (22:48). In the meantime, there was no king in Edom to oppose Israel (22:47). Jehoshaphat was wise for refusing the request of Ahaziah, the son of King Ahab in the northern kingdom, to employ Ahaziah's men to sail with Jehoshophat's men (22:48). The reason is not clear in the text, but it may be because of Ahaziah's evil ways or because of Jehoshophat's bad experience when he joined with Ahab in the battle for Ramoth-Gilead (22:49). Soon thereafter, Jehoshaphat rested with his ancestors and was buried in the city of David (22:50a). Jehoram, his son, succeeded him as the king (22:50b).

22:51–53 Ahaziah, King of Northern Israel

In the northern kingdom, after the death of Ahab, his son, Ahaziah, ruled (22:51a). Ahaziah only reigned over Israel for two years (22:51b). Like his father and mother, he did evil in the eyes of the Lord by worshiping Baal, and he aroused the anger of the Lord (22:52–53). He served Baal and worshiped Baal instead of Yahweh God of Israel. Thus, he raised the anger of the Lord (22:53).

This concluded the first book of kings – although they were called and installed in the ministry of serving God's people as kings, they served their own interest and didn't honor God as God. As a result, God kept bringing enemies against them and defeating them in wars. When they cried to him for help, however, he came and delivered them because of his covenant with their father David. Israel survived because of God's faithfulness to David.

We learn from this that it is not by our faithfulness that we survive, but by God's faithfulness. His loving kindness (*hesed*) preserves us eternally.

2 KINGS

2 KINGS 1:1–18

ELIJAH CONDEMNS AHAZIAH

1 Kings narrated the stories of King Solomon and the kings of the divided monarchy up to Ahab, the king of the northern kingdom. 2 Kings continues the stories of the kings, starting with Ahaziah, the son of Ahab. When Ahab died, his son Ahaziah succeeded him (1 Kgs 22:40). His kingdom's capital was in Samaria, and his rule started in the seventeenth year of Jehoshaphat king of Judah (22:51). Ahaziah reigned over Israel for only two years (22:51). 2 Kings begins with his story, emphasizing Elijah's ministry.

2 Kings chapter 1 has four sections: Ahaziah's injury (1:1–2), Elijah's prophecy (1:3–8), Elijah's unwillingness to meet Ahaziah (1:9–15), and Ahaziah's death (1:16–18). The literary style is in the form of dialogues, either between the king and his captains, the Lord and Elijah, or the king and the prophet.

1:1–2 AHAZIAH'S INJURY

With Ahab's death, Moab, a territory controlled by the northern kingdom, started rebelling against Israel (1:1). Israel's threats were coming from outside its borders. Internally, Ahaziah was suffering a significant injury; he "had fallen through the lattice of his upper room" and had injured himself (1:2a). His palace was in Samaria. Instead of asking God for healing, Ahaziah went to messengers saying, "Go and consult Baal-Zebub, the god of Ekron" (1:2b). Ekron was one of the city-states situated on the northern side of the Philistine territory, closer to the border of Judah. Baal-Zebub (meaning "Lord of Flies") was the deity of Ekron. Among the Philistines, Baal was known with some variants, such as Baal-Poer and Baal-Zebul just as the Indian god Ganesh is known by various names: Vinayakar, Pillaiyar and Elephant face god (*Yanai Muthathon*).

Ahaziah sent his messengers to Ekron believing that Baal-Zebub had the power to reveal the nature of his illness and to tell him whether or not he would recover. Ahaziah's belief in Baal indicates his attachment with the fertility cult rather than his faith in Yahweh, who alone had the power to heal him. Ahaziah's action of consulting a god in the context of sickness contrasts Jeroboam's action of seeking a word from the Lord when his son was sick (1 Kgs

14:1–4). This difference implies the gradual deterioration of the religion of the kings. Ahaziah's attitude and action was not pleasing and acceptable to the God of Israel.

1:3–8 ELIJAH'S PROPHECY

Yahweh took a parallel action to Ahaziah by sending his own messenger to the prophet Elijah, instructing him to convey a strong message to the king.[1] The messenger instructed Elijah to confront the messengers of Ahaziah on their way to Ekron and ask, "Is it because there is no God in Israel that you are going off to consult Baal-Zebub, the god of Ekron?" (1:3). This rhetorical question challenged the messengers to seek Yahweh, who alone could reveal the need of the king and heal him. Yahweh's accusation was followed by Ahaziah's punishment: the king would not get up from his bed, but would certainly die because he neglected the God of Israel and went after Baal (1:4).

After receiving the message from Elijah, the messengers returned to the king. The king was surprised by their quick return and asked them for a reason (1:5). They reported what Elijah had told them (1:6). Ahaziah asked about the identity of the prophet and was told he was wearing a garment of hair and a leather belt around his waist. From this description, Ahaziah knew that the message had come from Elijah (1:7–8).

1:9–15 ELIJAH UNWILLING TO MEET AHAZIAH

So the king sent a captain with fifty soldiers to force Elijah to come to him (1:9a). Elijah was sitting on the top of the hill when the soldiers arrived. They addressed him as "man of God," meaning prophet of the Lord, and ordered him to come down from the hill to meet the king (1:9b). Because Elijah did not receive a word from the Lord telling him to go with the soldiers, he didn't obey them. Instead, he twisted their address, "man of God" (*'ish Elohim*) into "fire of God" (*'esh Elohim*). This wordplay echoes the previous contest between Yahweh and Baal on Mount Carmel (18:38) and communicates that Yahweh alone has power over fire and nature, and Baal doesn't. Ahaziah should have known this and send his messengers to Elijah and Yahweh, not Baal-Zebub. Elijah is a true prophet and whatever he says will happen, according to the word of the Lord. Just as he prophesied, fire came from heaven and consumed the captain and his fifty soldiers (1:10).

---

1. NIV uses the word "angel" in verses 3 and 15 but most likely, it is a "messenger," the common meaning of the Hebrew word, *mal'akh*.

After the first captain and his fifty soldiers were consumed by fire, the king sent another captain with another batch of fifty men to make Elijah come down to him. Again, the fire of God came down and destroyed them (1:11–12). Then Ahaziah sent a third captain with another batch of fifty men, but this captain humbly pleaded with Elijah to spare him and his men (1:13). His words and humility can be contrasted with the previous two captains, who used their power and authority to command Elijah to come down. Ahaziah doesn't show such humility; instead, he wants to forcefully bring Elijah to his chamber and Elijah to bring him healing.

This story has contrasts and comparison with the incident on Mount Carmel (1 Kgs 18:20–39). Both the incidents take place on a mountain within Elijah's ministry range. In both cases, fire fell from above. In contrast, Baal was represented by 450 prophets on Mount Carmel, but Ahaziah's messengers were sent to present his case to Baal-Zebub, the god of Ekron. Whereas the fire burnt the sacrifice on Mount Carmel, in this story, the fire burnt Ahaziah's soldiers and captains. On Mount Carmel, the fire proved that Yahweh was the only true God who had authority over nature and people, not Baal. But on the hill, the fire that consumed Ahaziah's soldiers and captains proved that Elijah was a man of God and his message from God for Ahaziah would be true. Elijah was not interested in killing people but wanted to convince Ahaziah's men to tell the king that whatever Elijah said would happen. After hearing this report from his men, Ahaziah should have repented for consulting Baal of Ekron and his evil ways (1 Kgs 22:52). On Mount Carmel, Elijah brought the prophets into the Kishon Valley and slaughtered them there (1 Kgs 18:40). In this story, however, Elijah refused to come down from the top of the hill when the king's captain ordered him to do so.

All through these stories, there is a wordplay in the phrases, "go up" (2 Kgs 1:3, 4, 6, 7, 9, 13) and "come down" (1:3, 10, 11, 12, 14, 15, 16). Ahaziah went up to his bed due to sickness, and Elijah went up to meet the messengers of the king (1:3). Elijah went up the hill, and the captains of the king went up to meet Elijah (1:9). When Elijah repeatedly said that he would not come down the hill, the king at the same time could not come down from his bed (1:4, 16). Elijah's actions symbolically communicate the message of the Lord to the king, which is that Ahaziah will not "come down" from his sickbed, but will die (1:4).

At the end of Elijah's encounter with the third captain and his soldiers, a messenger (or angel) of the Lord came and told old Elijah to go and visit the king and not be afraid (1:15a). Elijah obeyed God and went to see the king (1:15b).

1:16–18 DEATH OF AHAZIAH

When Elijah met Ahaziah, he repeated the same message from the Lord, accused the king of seeking Baal-Zebub to predict the outcome of his illness, and pronounced God's punishment (1:16). As Elijah pronounced God's judgment, King Ahaziah died (1:17). The prophetic ministry in ancient Israel was unique: what was prophesied would come true. The Lord used the prophets to receive and communicate his word, and his true prophets were careful to speak on God's behalf without adding their own views or opinions.

The chapter concludes with the note that Joram (Heb. *Jehoram*) succeeded Ahaziah to the throne (1:17). Joram was the son of Ahab (3:1). He succeeded Ahaziah because Ahaziah did not have a son (1:17). The usual formula directs readers to the annals of the kings for more details about the reign of Ahaziah (1:18).

2 KINGS 2:1-25
TRANSITION FROM ELIJAH TO ELISHA

According to the leading of the Lord, Elijah called Elisha to be his disciple (1 Kgs 19:19–21). Elisha obeyed and followed him. He was loyal to his master and refused to leave Elijah until the end of his life. They travelled to Gilgal, Bethel, and Jericho, and then crossed the Jordan River. On the other side of the Jordan, Elijah was carried up to heaven by a whirlwind and Elisha retreated to Mount Carmel with greater power than that of Elijah.

2 Kings 2 narrates these events. This chapter has two sections: the end of Elijah's ministry (2 Kgs 2:1–12) and the beginning of Elisha's ministry (2 Kgs 2:13–25).

2:1-12 END OF ELIJAH'S MINISTRY

Elijah knew that he was about to be taken up to heaven in a whirlwind (2:1). Knowing that his ministry was coming to an end, he asked Elisha to stay back while he went to Bethel (2:2). But Elisha refused and vowed in the name of the Lord that he would not leave his master until his departure. Since Elisha vowed in the name of the Lord, Elijah allowed him to accompany him to Bethel.

At Bethel, a company of prophets met Elisha and asked if he knew about God's plan to take up Elijah on that day. Elisha replied that he knew God's plan, which may explain his reason for not wanting to leave his master, and asked them to be quiet (2:3).

Elijah then asked Elisha to remain in Bethel while he traveled to Jericho (2:4a). Again Elisha refused (2:4b). Again, a company of prophets met Elijah and questioned Elisha (2:5). After visiting Jericho, the Lord led Elijah to the Jordan (2:6a). Again, Elisha refused to stay in Jericho, but continued to follow Elijah (2:6b). Fifty prophets from Jericho followed Elijah and Elisha until they came to the riverbank (2:7). At the edge of the Jordan, Elijah rolled his cloak and struck the water of the Jordan (2:8a). During the heavy monsoon season, the river overflowed, and there were no ferry boat services in those days. But the power of God divided the water, and Elijah and Elisha walked across the river on dry ground (2:8b). This event parallels the dividing of the Red Sea for the Israelites under the leadership of Moses (Exod 14:26–30) and the crossing of the river Jordan under the leadership of Joshua (Josh 3:14–17).

As the time had come for Elijah to bid farewell, he asked his faithful disciple what he could do for him (2:9a). In the Indian tradition, a guru does something to honor a faithful disciple who stands with him till the end. The guru may give the disciple his scepter, *trishul* (a spear with three prongs at the top), or shawl as a farewell gift, symbolically transferring the guru's authority to the disciple who will succeed him. Elisha answered, "Let me inherit a double portion of your spirit" (2:9b). This request surprised Elijah, and he said, "You have asked a difficult thing" (2:10a). The phrase "double portion" was used in legal language in ancient agrarian society as the right of the eldest son to get a double share in the land and produce (Deut 21:15–17). In return, he had to take responsibility for the family and the cultivation of the land. Since Elisha had come from an agricultural background, he used this formula but with a different connotation. He was not asking for a double share of Elijah's property; he was asking for a double portion of Elijah's spirit. The term "spirit" in this context is understood as a spirit-filled ministry. Elisha was asking for the power, strength, and courage to do effective ministry like Elijah, who had faced the principalities and powers of Ahab and Jezebel and stood faithfully for following Yahweh alone. Elisha wanted to receive the gift of being able to perform miracles in his ministry, just as Elijah had done. But, Elijah could not send his spirit into Elisha since it was God's prerogative. So he said, "You have asked a difficult thing" (2:10a).

Nevertheless, Elijah said that the spirit God had given to him could be transferred if Elisha saw Elijah taken up by God (2:10b). God had granted Elisha's request so that he could faithfully continue the prophetic ministry of the Lord to counter the worldly power and idolatry of that period. This scene resurfaces on the day of Pentecost, when the Holy Spirit filled the disciples with power so they could witness for Jesus Christ within the powerful Roman empire (Acts 1:8). As Elijah and Elisha were walking along, a chariot of fire and horses of fire suddenly appeared and separated them (2:11a). Elijah was taken up to heaven in a whirlwind (2:11b). Elisha saw his master taken up into heaven and cried, "My father! My father! The chariots and horsemen of Israel!" (2:12a). Calling Elijah "father" reveals how much Elisha loved his master, who was a spiritual mentor rather than a biological father. Describing Elijah as chariots and horsemen of Israel testifies to Elijah's ministry and achievements. Chariots and horsemen are symbols of the military, who defend the country and protect the nation. This image reminds us that the army of Yahweh in heaven brings about victory in any war. Yahweh's army is more powerful than any military with its chariots and horses. Elisha knew that

Yahweh's army had helped Elijah to fight against the power and authority of the kings. Elisha is using this metaphor for Elijah because he defended the faith of Yahweh on Mount Carmel when Jezebel was killing the prophets of Yahweh. He protected the people from following Baal and protected many prophets from abandoning the true and living God of Israel. Elijah played a key role when Israel was threatened by its enemies, guided the kings in times of war, and championed the cause of poor peasants against injustice. Losing Elijah meant losing a great and powerful defender of the faith and nation. After Elijah disappeared into the sky, Elisha tore his garment into two pieces as a symbolic action to express his sorrow and grief (2:12b).

2:13–25 BEGINNING OF ELISHA'S MINISTRY

Elisha picked up the cloak that had fallen from Elijah as he was ascending to heaven and went to the Jordan bank (2:13). Elisha struck the Jordan River with the cloak and asked, "Where now is the LORD, the God of Elijah?" (2:14a). His faith is expressed through his claim that the miracle will happen in the name of the God of his master, and then the power of the Lord divided the waters for him to cross over (2:14b). For the first time, Elisha experienced the power of the Lord in his ministry.

The fifty prophets were still waiting on the other side of the Jordan. They watched Elisha hit the water with Elijah's cloak and saw the spirit part the waters. They acknowledged that Elisha had inherited the spirit of Elijah and bowed to the ground before him in respect (2:15). Since they had not seen Elijah taken up in the whirlwind, they offered to serve Elisha by going to search for his master (2:16). They thought the Lord God had taken Elijah somewhere and hidden him, as this had happened earlier in his ministry (1 Kgs 18:11–12). Elisha reluctantly allowed them to search, though he knew that they would not find him. The men who volunteered searched all the places in the country, but they returned with great disappointment. Their failure to find Elijah confirmed his ascension into heaven (2:17–18).

The news about how Elisha had inherited the spirit of Elijah and crossed the river spread to the people in that region. They came to Elisha, addressed him as "lord," and complained about the water, which was bad and not useful for agriculture (2:19). Elisha asked the people to bring him a new bowl of the water, and he put salt in it (2:20). The new bowl implies cleanliness and purity, and salt was used as a preservative. Then Elisha went to the spring and threw the salt into it, saying, "This is what the LORD says: 'I have healed this water. Never again will it cause death or make the land unproductive'" (2:21).

Throwing a small quantity of salt from a bowl could not perform a miracle. God healed the water of the spring.

Earlier, Joshua crossed the Jordan and destroyed the city of Jericho. Since then the water of the spring had been bad and useless. But after Elisha crossed the Jordan and returned to Jericho, the water became good and useful. The people humbly acknowledged Elisha as a servant of God and asked him to do a miracle for their city. Their faith in the Lord made their water clean and good once more (2:22).

After doing the miracle in Jericho, Elisha continued to retrace the way he had journeyed with Elijah. As he was on his way to Bethel, a large group of youths came down the road and started to insult him, calling him "baldy!" and telling him to leave (2:23). These youths of Bethel were insulting Yahweh by mocking his servant Elisha, teasing his physical appearance and driving him out of the city. During the reign of Jeroboam, Bethel was converted into a cultic center for the worship of a golden calf (1 Kgs 12:28–29). These youths probably did not want a true prophet of Yahweh to criticize them for following the ways of Jeroboam. Elisha could not tolerate this jeering mob. In his zealousness for the Lord, he cursed the youths, who were against Yahweh and his servants (2:24a). After Elisha cursed the youths, two bears came from the forest and attacked them, tearing forty-two of them into pieces (2:24b). Elisha continued his journey to Mount Carmel, where Elijah had proven that Yahweh alone was the true God (2:25a). From there, Elisha returned to Samaria (2:25b).

This incident of Elisha cursing the youths who were insulting him raises an ethical issue for us today. Can we use the name of God to curse those who insult us or work against our progress? As Christians, we cannot follow Elisha's model and curse our opponents. We cannot misinterpret the words of Jesus when he says that people can ask anything in his name and it will be added unto them. The teachings of the Sermon on the Mount instruct us to tolerate insults from our enemies and not to return evil for evil. Rather, as Christians, we must repay evil with good (Matt 5:11–12, 38–42). Our zealousness for the Lord Jesus Christ cannot lead us to curse others, for we must bless others, whether they are good or bad (Matt 7:12). This is difficult to practice, but it is not impossible. Paul makes a concession for Christians who cannot put up with those who insult them or who work against them continuously. Rather than cursing them or quarreling with them and losing peace of mind, it is better for Christians to keep their distance from such people without holding hatred for them in their hearts (2 Tim 2:14–16).

2 KINGS 3:1–27
ALLIANCE TO DEFEAT MOAB

In ancient Israel, tensions continued between the political authorities who held the power of governance in the country and the religious authority of the prophets who represented the power of Yahweh. After Ahab's death and Elijah's departure, a new chapter of history began with Joram, the son of Ahab and the king of northern Israel, and Elisha, the prophet. Both were new to their positions and had to learn how to relate with each other.

After taking over the ministry from Elijah, Elisha started facing challenges. His involvement in politics began at the invitation of Joram, who faced a threat from Moab. This chapter has four sections: a summary evaluation of Joram's reign over Israel (3:1–3); the alliance between Judah, Israel, and Edom to defeat Moab (3:4–12); Elisha's involvement (3:13–19); and the defeat of Moab (3:20–27). These scenes are narrated using the literary form of dialogue between the king and prophet and the pronouncement of God's prophecy using an oath and messenger formula.

3:1–3 JORAM, KING OF ISRAEL

Joram is an abbreviated name for Jehoram (meaning "Yahweh is exalted"). He was a son of Ahab and Jezebel. He became king of Israel after his brother, Ahaziah, died without a son to succeed him (see 1:17). Joram was in Samaria, and the duration of his reign over the northern kingdom was twelve years (3:1). He started his reign during the eighteenth year of Jehoshaphat king of Judah. Joram took some good actions to remove the sacred pillars of Baal, which his ancestors erected for idol worship, but he also fell into the trap of Jeroboam's sin (3:2). The phrase, "clung to the sins of Jeroboam," states an overall evaluation of his rule, which was that he did not do good in the eyes of the Lord (3:3).

3:4–12 ALLIANCE TO DEFEAT MOAB

The territory of Moab was situated between the Arnon River in the north and Zered Brook in the south. This region was congenial for Mesha king of Moab to raise sheep. He paid the king of Israel, Ahab, a payment of 100,000 lambs and the wool of 100,000 rams each year to continue grazing his sheep in this land (3:4). But after the death of Ahab, the king of Moab rebelled against Israel by not paying the agreed payment to Joram (3:5). Joram had to act against the king of Moab to stop his rebellion. He gathered his troops and formed an alliance with Jehoshaphat king of Judah to fight Moab (3:6–7).

Jehoshaphat asked which route they would follow to launch the attack (3:8a). Joram replied that he planned to go through Edom, which was still a vassal of Israel, and therefore was expected to join the alliance against Moab (3:8b). All three nations marched towards Moab, mobilizing their forces. After seven days of marching, they faced the crisis of a lack of water for the men and horses (3:9). Joram started blaming the God of Israel for the scarcity of water and the danger of being delivered into the hands of Moab's army (3:10). He was suspecting that Yahweh had created this situation so that he would be killed in the war. Noticing Joram's anxiety, Jehoshaphat suggested that they consult a prophet of the Lord to ask why they were facing this crisis (3:11a). Earlier, he had persuaded Ahab to consult a prophet of the Lord before the war against Aram (1 Kgs 22:7). Once again, Jehoshaphat wanted to be sure of the will of the Lord in this war.

One of Joram's officials suggested the prophet Elisha. The official used the idiomatic expression that meant, "pouring water for ablutions," in the sense of washing one's body, which was Elisha's personal service to Elijah (3:11b).[1] In the Indian context, a disciple who pours water on the hands of his guru could refer to cleaning the guru's hands before or after he uses them for eating. When a guru and his disciple travel together, the disciple raises the jar of water and pours it into the hands of his guru so he can drink. It is interesting that the official uses the word "water" here, since the kings were facing the crisis of a water shortage for their armed forces and animals. The official may have heard about Elisha's miracle of purifying the water of the well at Jericho, and he may have been implying that Elisha could either bring about a miracle of water or tell them where water was available, just as Elijah had brought rain after three years of drought and famine.

Jehoshaphat knew about the ministry of Elisha, for he regarded Elisha as a true prophet who had the word of the Lord (3:12a). Instead of calling Elisha to come to them, all three kings went down to meet Elisha to inquire the word of the Lord (3:12b).

---

1. Wiseman, *1 and 2 Kings*, 213.

3:13–19 ELISHA'S INVOLVEMENT

Elisha was hesistant to help. He asked Joram, "Why do you want to involve me?" (3:13a). He knew that Joram usually sought guidance from the prophets of his father and mother, referring to the prophets of Baal, and so he instructed him to go to them. Elisha is indirectly criticizing Joram for not seeking his help before going to war against Moab. But, when he faced the water crisis, he was willing to seek Elisha's help.

Joram pretended that he had consulted Yahweh, who had called the three kings together to go to war against Moab and then abandoned them to face defeat by the king of Moab (3:13b). Elisha replied that he was willing to discern the word of the Lord for the sake of Jehoshaphat, but not Joram (3:14). Elisha respected the king of Judah since he had insisted that they seek a word from a true prophet. Elisha was courageously telling Joram that the king could not treat the true prophets of Yahweh as secondary and only seek their help when his plans went wrong.

After affirming Jehoshaphat's faith, Elisha asked Joram to bring him a harpist (3:14). When the harpist played, "the hand of the LORD came on Elisha," meaning the prophet was touched by the spirit of the Lord, and he was able to receive and speak the words of the Lord (3:15).

Using the messenger formula, "This is what the LORD says," Elisha prophesied that the Lord would fill the ditches and trenches in the valley with water (3:16). Naturally, valleys have ponds and ditches of different depths and brooks that channel water to flow to the low areas. God was going to fill these ponds and ditches with water in a miraculous way, without rain falling from above, so that the animals and soldiers would have water to drink (3:17). Rain is helpful when one needs water, but it can also be a hindrance for armies, who have to live in the field without proper shelters. Elisha assured them that such a miracle was not difficult for the Lord (3:18). And after giving them water, the Lord would deliver the Moabites into the hands of the allied forces and the armies of Israel, Judah, and Edom would destroy every fortified city and major town in Moab (3:19). Elisha said that the Israelites would even cut down all the good trees in Moab, stop up the springs of water, and ruin every good field with heaps of stones, thereby destroying Moab's agriculture.

3:20–27 DEFEAT OF MOAB

Elisha's prophesy was fulfilled on the next morning when water started flowing from Edom and filled the pools and ditches in the valley (3:20). Once again, this narrative reminds us that Yahweh, not Baal, has the authority over nature to bring rain. Yet the miracle did not stop with the arrival of water for the soldiers and animals, for the water began to shine in the light of the rising sun, and to the eyes of the Moabite army, it looked like blood was covering the entire valley (3:21–22). The Moabites likely knew the natural phenomenon of water shining red at sunrise, but God made the water appear to the Moabites as blood. This scene prompted the Moabite army to assume that there had been an internal war among the kings and soldiers of the allied forces, causing great bloodshed and death (3:23). The Moabite soldiers entered the Israelite camp, eager to plunder their spoils, but the allied armies were hiding and struck down the Moabites (3:24). The surprise attack drove the Moabite army to retreat to their country, but the allied forces pursued and slaughtered many soldiers and then invaded Moab, destroying the towns and fields and cutting down the trees, just as Elisha had predicted (3:25a). The capital city of Kir Hareseth was not destroyed because the people surrounding the city protected it (3:25).

When Mesha, the king of Moab, saw that he could not fight against the allied armies, he planned an attack against the king of Edom, breaking the battle line with seven hundred soldiers, but he could not defeat him (3:26). In order to pacify or seek the favor of his national god, Chemosh, to stop the attack of the allies against Moab, Mesha sacrificed his first-born son, who was to succeed him as king, as a burnt offering on the wall of the city, where people, particularly the alliance, would see (3:27a).[2] The allied forces withdrew to their own land (3:27b).

---

[2]. The *Mesha Inscription* says, "for Chemosh was angry with his land," giving the reason as the defeat of Moab. House, *1, 2 Kings: An Exegetical and Theological Exposition of Holy Scripture*, 264.

2 KINGS 4:1–44

ELISHA'S MINISTRIES

Elisha continued his ministry, serving the people and becoming involved in both the social and political affairs of the nation while also strengthening their faith in Yahweh (4:1–8:15). The compilation of stories about Elisha in chapter 4 describes four miracles that he did for needy people in Israel: multiplying oil for the widow (4:1–7), restoring the life of the Shunammite's son (4:8–37), removing poison from stew and serving it to a group of prophets (4:38–41), and multiplying bread to feed the hungry (4:42–44). The people in these stories are socially outcasts and yet significant for God: a widow, a barren woman, the needy, the hungry, and the powerless. The incidents are not located in time, except to say, "one day" (4:8, 11, 18), which was a customary way of introducing stories. These miracles display literary unity in the way that each opens with a problem and then reaches a resolution by God's miraculous intervention through Elisha. Yahweh is powerful and can provide his people with children, bread, and oil, in contrast to Baal, the fertility god, who cannot provide children or food.

4:1–7 THE MIRACLE OF MULTIPLYING OIL

The story of multiplying oil begins with a widow announcing her poverty and debt. She says to Elisha, "Your servant my husband is dead, and you know he revered the LORD" (4:1). By the phrases, "your servant" and "revered the LORD," she is indirectly telling Elisha that he has an obligation to help her family because her husband feared and served the Lord. Her husband may have belonged to a prophetic group and so may have ministered in a cultic center and was an assistant to Elisha. He passed away before he could clear the debt. Often, people gave something to the prophets when they went to find the will of God (1 Sam 9:3–21). Some of the prophets in cultic centers did not receive enough offerings to meet their needs. This widow's husband apparently had to borrow money to make ends meet at his home. After his death, the moneylenders came to enslave the deceased prophet's sons to make up for the money he had failed to repay (4:1). Moneylenders ignored the law that forbade charging taxes (Exod 22:25) and enslaving fellow Israelites (25:39–40). Enslaving children or youths is a common practice of moneylenders in villages in India. These moneylenders sometimes abuse the wives and daughters of the borrower, even though it is against the law and human rights.

As a widow, this woman does not want to lose her children to the creditors and become even more vulnerable in the society. The widow appeals to Elisha for help, expressing her desperate situation and expecting him to help her. Elisha asked her if she had any resources in her house to help repay at least some of the loan (4:2). The widow responded honestly to Elisha's question, saying that she had nothing in her house except a little olive oil (4:2).

Elisha helped her to clear her debt by using what she already had on hand, giving her clear instructions to follow (4:5–6). First, she should collect as many empty jars as possible from her neighbors. Second, she and her sons should shut the door and pour the oil to fill all the jars. As each jar was filled, they should put it aside. The miracle happened as she poured the little bit of oil still left in her house, which kept flowing until it filled all the empty jars. This incident reminds us of how God poured out manna from above so that the Israelites who were wandering in the wilderness could have enough to eat, day by day (Exod 16:31–35). Once all the jars were filled, the widow came to Elisha and reported that she had followed his instructions. Elisha told her to go and sell the oil and repay the moneylender to save her sons from slavery (4:7). Elisha performed this miracle because he was "the man of God," an instrument in God's hands (4:7).

By following Elisha's instructions, the widow demonstrated her faith in the Lord. God cares for the poor and needy. And his will is against child labor and slavery.[1] This concern is also expressed in the Deuteronomic law, which instructs a master to release a slave after he has served for a certain term and with plenty to sustain so that he will not have to seek out another master and become a slave again (Deut 15:1–18). By multiplying what this widow and her sons already had in their house, Elisha empowered them to stand on their own two feet and not fall prey to the exploitation of the moneylenders. This event challenges us today to ensure that our missions do not stop with liberation, but empower the liberated poor to make use of what they already have so that they can build a sustainable life for themselves.

4:8–37 RESTORING THE LIFE OF A SON

The story of Elisha's second miracle demonstrates God's love for a barren woman, his concern for a bereaved family, and his affirmation of Elisha's

---

1. Jeyaraj, "Biblical Perspectives on Children and their Protection," *Children at Risk*, 18–19.

prophetic and healing ministry. The story does not identify exactly when this event happened, but it was on some day during Elisha's visit to the town of Shunem (modern name "Solem"), which is located about eleven kilometers south of Mount Tabor, eight kilometers from Jezreel, and thirty-two kilometers from Mount Carmel.[2]

A wealthy woman who lived with her husband in Shunem approached Elisha and invited him to visit her home and have a meal with them (4:8). Elisha accepted her hospitality whenever he came to Shunem. But this rich woman wanted to do more than giving a meal to Elisha, and so she asked her husband to make a small guest room on the top floor of her house and furnish it with a cot, table, lamp, and chair so that the prophet could stay with them whenever he came to Shunem (4:9).

One time, while staying in the Shunammite woman's house, Elisha asked his servant, Gehazi, to ask her what favor Elisha could do for her in exchange for her hospitality, love, and respect she showed for him (4:11). Elisha offered to speak on her behalf to the king or commander of the army in Israel (4:13). This offer shows that Elisha had a good influence on the king and officials of the northern kingdom. Her reply about owning a house among her people may have been an expression to convey that she lacked nothing because she already had property and respect among her people. Gehazi, however, noticed her need for a child (4:14). Because her husband was old, it would be difficult for her to conceive a child. While her economic status was high, she had the social stigma of being a barren woman. So Gehazi suggested this need to Elisha, who called the woman and assured her that she would have a child the following year by that time (4:15). She was standing at her doorway when Elisha blessed her and promised her a child. This parallels the way that Sarah was standing at the doorpost of her tent and laughed when she heard the messenger of the Lord assuring Abraham that she would have a child in her old age (Gen 18:9–15). Elisha's reference to holding a child in her arms indicates that the words of his blessing would surely be fulfilled. Her response, "No, my lord!" expresses her hesitancy or fear because she did not want to hope for a child and then face disappointment if the blessing was not fulfilled (4:16). Yet the power of God can cross all barriers to make what seems impossible a possible reality, as this woman in Shunem discovered, for she conceived and gave birth to a child, just as Elisha had told her (4:17).

---

2. Wiseman, *1 and 2 Kings*, 216.

The story then leaps ahead and says that "one day" the child went out with his father to see the harvesting of the field (4:18). While in the field, he has a severe headache and is able to cry out, "My head, my head" (4:19). The severe pain may have been caused by the sunlight or some health problem that developed suddenly when the child was exposed to the intense heat. The father asked the servants to take him back to his mother for relief, but the child died on her lap that afternoon (4:20). She realized that she needed help from the prophet who had blessed her with this child. After placing the body of the child on the prophet's bed in the upper room (4:21), she asked her husband, who was still working with the reapers in the field, to send a donkey and a servant to her so she could go and see the man of God, but she did not tell him what had happened to their child (4:22).

Her husband wanted to know the reason for her trip to see Elisha (4:23). According to custom, people visited a cultic center to worship, offer sacrifices, and consult the prophets on New Moon or Sabbath days, which were the preferred days for festivals and community gatherings. A Sabbath indicates once every seven days, and a New Moon indicates once every four weeks, based on lunar calendar. Saying, "That's all right," she saddled a donkey and asked a servant to lead her to Mount Carmel, where Elisha was staying (4:23b–25). The distance they had to travel from Shunem to Carmel was about thirty-two kilometers.

Elisha saw the woman coming at a distance and called his servant, Gehazi (4:25b). He sensed that the Shunammite was facing a problem because she had traveled such a long distance to meet him. He instructed Gehazi to find out the well-being of the woman, her husband, and her child (4:26). His words express his concern for this family, who had helped him with hospitality. But the woman did not want to tell her problem to Gehazi, and so she went straight to Elisha and took hold of his feet, a symbolic action of begging for help (4:27a). This custom is still practiced in South Asia whenever people meet their leaders, gurus, and Babas. When Gehazi came to remove her, Elisha stopped him, although he was mystified because the Lord had hidden the misfortune from him (4:27b).

Holding on to Elisha's feet, the woman poured out her heart with great distress, saying that her hopes for having a child were shattered because her son had died (4:28). Reminding him of their discussion earlier (4:16), she made Elisha responsible for restoring the life of this child, who had come as a gift of his blessing, without her ever asking for it. Her words and actions demonstrate her faith that through Elisha, the Lord can make the boy live again.

Elisha asked Gehazi to take his staff and run to the house of the Shunammite and lay Elisha's staff on the boy's face to heal him (4:29). He was to run, not greet or talk to anyone on the way. Gurus always give conditions to their disciples when they send them on a mission because the disciple is not going on his own authority or capacity but is representing the guru and carrying out his mission. Elisha's staff is an extension of his personality, so it is as if the prophet himself is going there.[3] As the woman listened to Elisha's instructions to Gehazi, she was not satisfied and insisted that the prophet himself should come and restore the life of her child (4:30). The woman knew that Elisha was a man of God, and so he had the power to do miracles. As they were on the road back to Shunem, they met Gehazi, who had not been able to perform the miracle, and so Elisha continued to follow the woman back to her house (4:31). God had planned to work through Elisha to resurrect the child so that there would be a parallel event with Elijah's resurrection of the widow's child (1 Kgs 17:17–24), confirming that Elisha had inherited a double share of Elijah's power. Moreover, Yahweh's restoration of this child's life was also a challenge to the power of Baal, the supposed fertility god.

When they reached the woman's house, Elisha found the boy lying dead on his cot in the upper room (4:32). He shut the door and prayed to the Lord for the boy (4:33). Then he lay on the boy, mouth to mouth, eyes to eyes, hands to hands (4:34). As he stretched himself on the boy, his dead body received warmth from the prophet. Elisha repeated the same action after walking up and down the room and praying for the miracle (4:35a). At last, the boy sneezed seven times and opened his eyes (4:35b). Some who do not believe in God's miracles assume that the prophet simply established body contact and warmed up the boy, who was lying unconscious. But, from the mother's words and Gehazi's report the readers are assured that the boy was dead. Elisha then asked Gehazi to call the Shunammite and when she came in, he gave the boy to her (4:36). The mother of the boy was so happy to see her son alive that she fell down at Elisha's feet and bowed to the ground to express her respect and gratitude to the prophet (4:37a). Then the mother and son departed Elisha's room (4:37b). This miracle proved once again that the God of Elijah was also the God of Elisha.

---

3. For the concept of "Extended Personality," see Robinson, *Corporate Personality in Ancient Israel*, 25–37.

4:38–41 REDEEMING POISONOUS STEW

After restoring the life of the Shunammite woman's son, Elisha returned to Gilgal (4:38). It was an important city in the history of Israel, where Joshua had built an altar with the twelve stones taken from the river Jordan as a memorial sign for God, enabling the Israelites to cross the river and enter the land of Canaan (Josh 4:19–24). Gilgal is also known for the activities of its prophetic groups, with whom Elijah and Elisha had connections (1 Sam 7:15; 2 Kgs 2:1–2).[4]

Elisha discovered that drought and famine had affected Gilgal and its surrounding area. Seeing the situation in Gilgal and wanting to spend time with the prophets, Elisha ordered his servant to cook a stew for the entire group (4:38). Someone in the group went to the field to gather some herbs to be cooked along with the stew, perhaps to make it taste better or to increase the volume, just as some Indian women add coriander or curry leaves or tomatoes and onions to a soup (4:39). Unfortunately, the person mistakenly collected some gourds from a wild vine, possibly wild cucumber, sour melon, or the bitter fruit of a wild plant. The servant added these wild gourds to the stew without knowing they would make the stew poisonous, perhaps causing vomiting or even death. Fortunately, the prophets who tasted a bit of the stew discerned the bitter taste of poison and alerted Elisha, addressing him as "man of God" (4:40). They were ready to pour out the stew as waste, but Elisha calmed them, added flour to the pot, and made the stew good for eating (4:41). This reminds us of his earlier miracle of adding salt to the bad water in the spring at Jericho in order to make it safe for drinking and agriculture (2 Kgs 2:19–22). Adding an agent such as salt or flour is a symbolic action for making something bad become pure and good.[5] Elisha wanted to be helpful to these prophets of Gilgal, who were hungry, and by performing this miracle in front of them, he revealed once again the power of God that he had inherited to use for people in need.

4:42–44 THE MIRACLE OF MULTIPLYING BREAD

The narrative says that a man brought twenty loaves of bread to Elisha as an offering of the first fruits of the barley harvest. He may have heard about the famine and the need for food in Gilgal, and he wanted to express his

---

[4]. Some scholars may suggest that Gilgal in 2 Kings 4:38 is another town southwest of Shiloh. We identify it as the same Gilgal near Jericho. See Kenneth Kitchen, "Gilgal," in *NBD*, 413.
[5]. See the discussion on using an agent to heal the poisonous water in 2 Kings 2:19–22.

appreciation for the prophet by bringing him bread made out of newly harvested barley along with heads of new grain (4:42). The grains of barley are roasted to make flour for further use after the loaves of bread are eaten. The harvest took place in the man's town, Baal Shalishah, which was situated in the plains of Sharon (1 Kgs 17:1–3).

The man has a "servant" with the unusual Hebrew word, *mesharet*, rather than the usual word, *ebed* (4:43). This unusual word is used to identify Joshua as a "special assistant" to Moses (Exod 24:13). So this man may be a leader in his town or a leader of the prophetic group in Baal Shalishah. Nevertheless, he brought the offering of the first fruits to Elisha rather than giving it to a priest. After receiving the bread, Elisha asked his servant to distribute the loaves to all the other prophets (4:42b). A good leader sacrifices his personal needs and interest for those who are suffering. But this servant was surprised and told Elisha that there were not enough loaves to feed a hundred men. The servant wanted to give the bread to Elisha and care for him, but this concern was challenged when Elisha wanted to share it with the other prophets.

The phrase "hundred men" could be a cultural expression to convey that a good number of people were with Elisha. By asking the servant to share the loaves with the other men, Elisha was teaching him that all the servants of God need to receive care. Elisha expressed God's will to share the resources he received with the needy in the phrase, "Give it to the people to eat. For this is what the LORD says" (4:43). The miracle of multiplying the loaves happened as the servant distributed the twenty loaves and then discovered, when everyone had finished eating, that there was still some leftover bread. This miracle happened according to the word of the Lord spoken to Elisha (4:44). Once again, we notice the power of God's word multiplying the resources for the sake of the needy. This incident reminds us of how Jesus multiplied five loaves and two fishes to feed more than five thousand hungry people, with the balance of food that was left over filling twelve baskets (Matt 14:13–21).

We can draw insights for our faith, life, and service today from Elisha's ministry. His leadership took place during a critical period in the history of northern Israel, when the religious and social order were deteriorating. Kings didn't rule the nation according to the law; instead, they were misusing their powers and misleading the people to worship Baal. But the prophets, including Elisha, were constantly drawing the people back to the Lord, often through miracles. We cannot ignore the purpose, goal, and method of the prophets' ministry. Their ministry was to obey God's call and to fulfill the ministry by the word of God to glorify Yahweh. The goal of their ministry was twofold:

to prove Yahweh was the only true God for the Israelites and teach the people to follow Yahweh alone. The primary method of the prophets' ministry was to involve the people as partners in their effort. These prophets were not merely "doers," but "enablers." They invited their servants to fulfill their orders, asked the widows to cooperate in helping to bring about the miracles, and enabled people to bear witness to the power of God and enjoy the fruits of their involvement. Their ministry of enabling and empowering widows, wives, children at risk, servants, and poor peasants can challenge us. Rather than seeing people as passive recipients who depend on our help, we can invite them to cooperate with the mission of God by becoming actively involved in the work of transformation.

All the stories in this chapter illustrate that Elisha inherited double blessing from Elijah and excelled him in his ministry. At the same time, they also demonstrate God's care for the poor and needy. Miracles were meant to help people and not bring self pride and exaltation.

A COMPARISON OF THE MIRACLES IN 1 & 2 KINGS

The writer of 1 and 2 Kings included three miracle stories involving women. Comparing and contrasting these stories can inspire us to promote advocacy for women, widows, and children who are at risk in our communities.

Two of these women were widows, helpless, and poor: the woman of Zarephath (1 Kgs 17:8–16) and the wife of a prophet (2 Kgs 4:1–7). Their circumstances of suffering were different: the widow of Zarephath was affected by severe famine and was counting the last days of her life and her son's life, preparing to eat their last meal with the little flour and oil she had remaining and then to die (1 Kgs 17:8–16). The widow of the prophet was affected by debt and was in danger of losing her sons to become child laborers to moneylenders. The third woman, the Shunammite, was rich, but she was barren (2 Kgs 4:8–36). Although these women belonged to different social classes, all three were socially stigmatized as widows or as barren.

These three women also knew the value of losing one's child. The widow of Zarephath was preparing the final meal for her only son and then facing imminent death. As a victim of social evil, the widow of the prophet lost all hope of repaying her husband's debts and had to face the heartache and shame of having her children sold into slavery. Although the Shunammite woman received the gift of a precious son after experiencing the pain of barrenness, she had to face her son's sudden death. In ancient Israel, debts, poverty, and death affected women more intensively than men.

While carrying these intense pains, all three women leveled accusations at the men of God. The widow of Zarephath accused Elijah of saving her and her son from starvation, but then putting her son to death (1 Kgs 17:18). The widow of the prophet challenged Elisha to help her, because her husband had served the prophetic order and feared the Lord (2 Kgs 4:1). The Shunammite woman rebuked Elisha for raising her hopes and then letting them be dashed by the death of her son (2 Kgs 4:28). These accusations were not meant to anger the prophets but to challenge them to help the women in their desperate situations.

In all these stories, both Elijah and Elisha performed miraculous actions by the word of the Lord and the power of God – not to make money or fame for themselves, but to help the needy. Moreover, the prophets made it clear that they were performing these miracles for the glory of God, so that the women would not idolize them or make them heroes. Elijah multiplied flour and oil to provide sustenance to the widow and son in Zarephath. Elisha multiplied oil to clear the widow's debt so that her sons would not be sold as slaves. Although the Shunammite woman was rich, she was desperate for her son's life to be restored, and so Elisha resurrected him. In each story, the prophets performed the miracles from a source that they found right in front of them rather than out of nothing. Moreover, the prophets involved the women and empowered them to work as agents of cooperation. Elijah saved the widow from Zarephath and her son from starvation by first inviting her to share the flour and oil she already had in her house with him and then multiplying it to feed them all (1 Kgs 17:13–14). Elisha saved the children of the prophet's widow from slavery by multiplying the oil she already had in her house (2 Kgs 4:2, 7). Elisha resurrected the Shunammite's son after she took it upon herself to pursue him, present her case to him, and refuse to leave him until he responded (2 Kgs 4:22, 24, 27, 30).

These stories all communicate the nature and power of Yahweh against Baal, and they encourage us to have a high esteem of God's active presence in our lives. The stories also challenge us to be concerned about the afflicted women and children in our society. Because God cares for them, so should we.

2 KINGS 5:1–27

HEALING OF NAAMAN

The name and fame of the work of the God of Israel through his prophets extended beyond the borders of Israel. The people in Sidon (1 Kgs 17:7–24) and Syria (2 Kgs 5:1–18) came to know that the God of Israel extended his grace to all people. The ministries of the prophets were to declare that truth (2 Kgs 5:8, 15).

Although the story is narrated in length, all the units of the narration are knitted together, showing the unity and logical progression of the narrative. The main characters in the story include Naaman, his servant girl, the king of Aram, the king of Israel, Elisha, and Gehazi. The servant motif runs throughout the story; whereas the servants of Naaman play a positive role, the servant of Elisha becomes a victim of greed. The story begins with Naaman needing healing and reaches its climax when Naaman is healed and confesses that the God of Israel is great. The power of Yahweh is superior to any other gods of Syria.

At the same time, the story plunges into an anti-climax when Gehazi behaves greedily, deceives Naaman and Elisha, and is revealed as a corrupt servant although he worked with Elisha for many years. This leaves the readers with a warning to guard themselves against greed that can corrupt them in an instant and make a person an idolater (Col 3:5).

5:1–3 SERVANT GIRL GUIDING HER MASTER

The name "Naaman" means gracious. He was a valiant soldier who rose to be the commander of the army of Aram (5:1a). Scholars identify the king of Aram as either Ben-Hadad I, who ruled Syria during the period of Johram (2 Kgs 6:24; 8:7), or Ben-Hadad III who made a truce with Israel.[1] The king regarded Naaman as a great man because he brought victories in war for his king. These victories were attributed to the Lord God of Israel (5:1b). This raises a question about Yahweh supporting the king of Aram in the war against Israel or any other nation. In the history of the nation of Israel, the prophetic tradition interpreted wars, victories, and defeats as revelations of God's action, either for punishment or salvation. Naaman, the valiant soldier, wasn't exempt from suffering; he had leprosy.

---

1. Arguments for Ben-Hadad I, see T. R. Hobbs, *2 Kings*, WBC, vol. 13 (Waco, Texas: Word Books, 1985), 62; for Ben-Hadad III, see Wiseman, *1 and 2 Kings*, 219.

His deliverance comes from an unnamed, young, Israelite girl who was captured during a raid by the army of Aram on the land of Israel. The soldiers brought her to Damascus to serve in the house of Naaman (5:2). As a slave girl serving Naaman's wife, she has lost her dignity, been uprooted from her hometown, and alienated from her family and relatives. As a dependent without freedom and rights, she is very vulnerable.[2] Yet, she was concerned for her master who was afflicted with leprosy. The Hebrew word *tzara'at* means an infectious skin disease. From the phrase, "as white as snow" (5:27), the leprosy could have been similar to *lucademia* that makes the skin look white without paralyzing the muscles. Medical science suggests that this kind of leprosy can develop in one's skin at a later stage of life due to some deficiency or physical conditions.[3] In other kinds of leprosy, lepers gradually lose muscle movement, can lose fingers or noses, and can transfer their bacteria to another person through skin contact. In ancient Israel, such leprosy was considered abominable and incurable, and so the lepers were ordered to live outside the city, isolated from others to avoid transferring the bacteria (Lev 13:1–17). Since Naaman had achieved a high position in the army and accompanied the king, we can infer that his leprosy (*lucademia*) did not cause muscle deterioration or loss of sensation and was not infectious.

The Israelite slave girl's care for Naaman's family went beyond her duties as she was concerned to see her master receive complete healing. Without hesitation, she suggested to her mistress that if Naaman went to the prophet in Samaria he would be healed (5:3). She could have kept silent and mourned for her situation as a slave in another land, but as a genuine worshiper of Yahweh, who knew the power of the God of Israel, she came forward and told her mistress that the prophet Elisha could heal her husband. Her persuasion shows her inner faith that Yahweh can heal her master, her courage in proclaiming this information to her mistress, and her strong hope that her master will be completely healed. We should not forget that God can use young children to help adults.[4] They are important agents of God who can challenge the opinion, tradition, customs, and authority of adults. We can also learn from Naaman and his wife, who listened to the guidance of a servant girl. As a great man and master, he could have ignored her or scolded her and told her to mind

---

2. Jeyaraj, "Biblical Perspectives on Children and their Protection," *Children at Risk*, 8–9.
3. Hens-Piazza, *1–2 Kings*, 259.
4. Children as voices of God is seen in Psalm 8:2 and Matthew 21:9–11. Jeyaraj, "Biblical Perspectives on Children and their Protection," *Children at Risk*, 9.

her own business, but he accepted her advice. This is a role reversal. Naaman challenges those in power to develop humility and respect for those under them. Even the seemingly least and smallest can be of great help in our lives.

5:4–7 MISREADING THE LETTER

From the ancient period to the modern day, leaders have had to communicate across cultural and geopolitical boundaries. In the ancient period, letters were written by one king with his official seal and sent through a reliable messenger to another king to make an alliance, declare war, or demand taxes and tributes after a defeat. Such letters were also written to negotiate trade, exchange timber, horses, food, or to seek medical treatment. There seems to have been a truce between Aram and Israel during this period of their history.[5] This peaceful situation helped Naaman's journey to Israel to seek medical assistance.

Naaman asked the king of Aram to give him permission to travel to Israel for medical treatment to cure his leprosy, as per the advice of his girl servant (5:4). The king agreed and offered to write a letter to the king of Israel (5:5a). This may have been customary when a military official of one country wanted to cross the border of another country to meet someone without being suspected of spying. Taking with him ten talents (roughly 340 kilograms) of silver, six thousand shekels (roughly 69 kilograms) of gold and ten sets of clothing for gifts, Naaman left Aram for Israel (5:5b).[6] He assumed that charges for the medical treatment would be costly, and he was willing to give large amounts of gold, silver, and clothing to the prophet if his leprosy could be healed. The king of Aram, instead of mentioning that Naaman would be seeing a healer in Israel, wrote, "You may cure him of his leprosy" (5:6). The king of Israel read the letter and reacted angrily and tore his robes saying, "Am I God? . . . Why does this fellow send someone to me to be cured of his leprosy?" (5:7). He suspected that the king of Aram was sending his military commander to spy on Israel or to pick a quarrel.

5:8–10 ELISHA'S INTERFERENCE

When Elisha heard about the king's reaction, he sent a message to the king, instructing him to send Naaman to meet the prophet so that "he will know that there is a prophet in Israel" (5:8). Elisha is not glorifying himself here

---

5. Hobbs, *2 Kings*, 62.
6. One talent is equal to 34 kilograms. One shekel is equal to 11.5 grams. See *NIV Life Application Study Bible*, 2175.

but saying that a prophet in Israel is an agent and instrument of the power of Yahweh, who is greater than all the gods of Aram. Through Naaman's healing, the God of Israel will be known and glorified beyond the borders of Israel. The king of Israel listened to Elisha and sent Naaman to the prophet's house (5:9).

Elisha, without entertaining Naaman in his house, sent a message saying, "Go, wash yourself seven times in the Jordan, and your flesh will be restored and you will be cleansed" (5:10). Elisha wanted Naaman to believe that the prophet was a man of God and that his words were from God. Thus Naaman had to demonstrate his faith in the God of Israel as well as Elisha, his agent. A commander who gives orders to hundreds of soldiers is asked to obey a simple man of God. In this way, the role of Naaman, a commander in the army, is reversed to that of a servant, who must listen to and obey Elisha, a servant of the Lord. Naaman should have rejoiced in his heart that he has been assured healing; instead, he was upset at the instructions.

5:11–14 MIRACLE OF HEALING LEPROSY

Many Hindus go to temples and ashrams (monasteries), seeking the help of priests, prophetesses, gurus, and babas (Hindu religious leaders), believing that if these intermediaries place their hands on the sick, they will be healed of their diseases. Similarly, Naaman expected the prophet to receive him in person, call on the name of the Lord God, place his hands on him, and heal him (5:11). To his disappointment, nothing like that happened; instead, the prophet asked him to wash himself in the Jordan, one among many rivers. In his anger and frustration, he compared the waters of the rivers of Damascus with the Jordan. Abana and Pharphar, the rivers of Syria, flowed from the mountains of Amanus and Hermon, respectively. He knew that the water from these rivers was used for cleansing, and he could have bathed in those rivers in Damascus. Elisha knew that the water of the Jordan was not medicinal water with any herbal effect that could cure the leprosy. But, he used the river Jordan as an instrument to check Naaman's obedience and prove the power of the God of Israel so that Naaman would believe in Yahweh above all other gods. Naaman lacked this faith, became proud, and planned to go home (5:12).

The servants who accompanied him challenged him to reconsider his plan of returning home in anger. While Naaman compared the waters of Damascus and Israel, these servants compared any hard work or exercises that the prophet could have demanded with the easy work of bathing and getting cleansed (5:13). This is the second time Naaman receives wise counsel from his servants. People in authority need to listen to the servants who work for them. Naaman took the counsel of his servants and obeyed the words of Elisha by immersing himself in the water of the Jordan River seven times (5:14a). As he did, he was completely healed, and his flesh was transformed, just as the prophet had told him (5:14b). All the servants who watched this miraculous healing would have born witness to the great benefit of acting in obedience and faith.

5:15–19A NAAMAN'S CONFESSION AND GIFTS

After the miraculous healing of leprosy, Naaman and his servants returned to meet Elisha in person to acknowledge God's superiority and offer gifts to Elisha. This reminds us of the story about the one leper out of ten who came to thank Jesus for his healing (Luke 17:11–19). The dialogue between Naaman and Elisha reveals the Aramean's faith and conversion to the God of Israel. His words, "Now I know that there is no God in all the world except in Israel" (5:15), is a great confession from a military commander who had worshiped another deity in Aram. He proclaimed his faith because of his experience of healing, not because of some information he had received. The phrase "I know" does not refer to intellectual wisdom but knowing through personal experience. He also affirmed that the God of Israel alone had power and worked in the lives of human beings, not the gods and goddesses in other nations. He wanted to confirm his confession by giving gifts to the prophet. In offering these gifts, he addressed himself as "your servant." The servant motif reappears and this time it is Naaman who offers himself as Elisha's servant. His willingness to humble himself before Elisha shows a reversal in his earlier attitude (5:11–12).

Elisha refused to accept the gifts, declaring an oath, "As surely as the LORD lives" (5:16). The servant motif returns again; this time, Elisha is God's servant. He was serving the Lord without accepting any reward. Regardless of how much Naaman insisted, Elisha refused to accept his gifts.

So, the commander made two requests (5:17–18). First, he wanted Elisha to allow him to carry enough sand from Israel to his country so that he could build an altar for the Lord to offer sacrifices and burnt offerings only to him and no other gods (5:17). Once he disdained the waters of Israel in comparison with the waters of his country. But now, he values the sand from the land of Israel. This notion is seen among Hindus and Buddhists as well as many Christians. Many Hindu priests in South India go on a pilgrimage to Varanasi, a temple city situated at the banks of the Ganges River in northern India, and collect sand and water, which they use to build altars in their local towns. Some Christians in India go on a pilgrimage to the Holy Land and bring back the waters of the Jordan River, sand from Jerusalem, and olive oil from Israel, which they keep in their houses as an extension of God's presence and blessing. Buddhists in northeast India collect water or sand from the cities and mountains where the holy shrines of Buddha are located and bring it back to their houses.

Second, he needed Elisha to forgive him for entering the temple of Rimmon along with his master, something required of his job (5:18). The word "Rimmon" means "thunderer," which was a title used for the storm god, Hadad, in Damascus. "Ben-Hadad" means son of the storm god, Hadad. In the ancient period, kings used the name of their national deity as a title to impress the people that the king was the son of the national god.[7] Worshiping the national deity demonstrated loyalty both to the king and the country. The phrase "leaning on the arms" of Naaman does not suggest that the king has any physical disability, but is a customary expression for being the "right-hand man" of the king. Naaman's genuine conviction is to worship and follow Yahweh alone, but his job requires him to bow down before the god of Syria, which creates tension in him. Having understood Naaman's dilemma and the genuineness of his conversion, Elisha pronounced a benediction, "go in peace" (5:19a). "Go in Shalom" is a common way for priests to send worshipers in Israel. "Shalom" means more than peace, as it is a comprehensive word for experiencing well-being in all aspects of one's life. Naaman not only received relief from leprosy, but he also received an affirmation that he could return to his work in peace, without feeling any conflicts or guilt in his mind.

A survey conducted in South India among people of other faiths points out that many Hindu women have experienced miracles in their lives after coming to prayer meetings and gave oral testimonies to the power of Jesus Christ. These "secret Christians" are unable to come out openly to be baptized and attend worship services in churches because of the control and restrictions of their families. Their prayers are similar to Naaman's prayer, which is that the Lord would forgive them when they go to the temples to worship with their husbands and in-laws.

5:19B–27 GREED AND CORRUPTION OF GEHAZI

While Naaman enjoys the blessing of the God of Israel, Gehazi receives God's punishment. Gehazi was not happy with Elisha being generous and letting

---

[7]. There is a saying in the South Indian tradition that promotes the concept of kings as sons of God: "When people see the king in royal robes and vestments sitting on the throne, they are seeing the god *Vishnu*."

Naaman go back to his country without any payment (5:20). Gehazi called Naaman an "Aramean," implying that a foreigner coming with lots of gifts should pay for the healing he received. Although Gehazi was a servant of Elisha, he failed to understand the values the prophet cherished and practiced. He wanted to receive some gifts from Naaman, even if his master did not. He, too, made a vow saying, "as surely as the LORD lives." So he hurried after Naaman. Seeing him, Naaman got down from his chariot to find out why someone was running towards him (5:21).

Gehazi took advantage of Naaman's humility and willingness to pay silver and gold for the healing he had received. He told Naaman a lie – his master had sent him urgently to collect a talent of silver and two sets of clothing because two young prophets had just arrived from the company of prophets in the hill country of Ephraim (5:22). Believing these words, Naaman gave Gehazi two talents of silver (approximately equivalent to 68 kilograms)[8] in two bags and two sets of clothing (5:23). In the ancient period, silver was melted down into pieces, which were weighed into shekels or talents and kept in bags. A talent of silver was heavy, and so Naaman instructed his own servants to carry them. Gehazi cunningly hid the gifts he had collected from Naaman in his own house and sent the servants away (5:24). He also cleverly sent the servants back to Naaman before Elisha saw them and found out why they were coming with Gehazi (2 Kgs 5:24).

When it was time for him to stand before his master, Elisha asked him where he had been (5:25a). Gehazi lied and said, "Your servant didn't go anywhere" (5:25b). Elisha, the man of God, knew what Gehazi had been doing, for God had revealed Gehazi's greed and deception. After listening to Gehazi's lie, the prophet asked, "Was not my spirit with you?" (5:26a). The word "spirit" is used in various ways in the biblical text to refer to breath, life, and the spirit of God. Here, we can understand that it refers to Elisha's prophetic spirit, which had revealed all of Gehazi's actions to Elisha. Elisha's next question relates to Gehazi's interest in money, clothes, and property (5:26b). Although Gehazi knew all of his master's teachings, he sold his conscience for money. So, Elisha asked him if it was the time to take money or accept clothes or olive groves and vineyards or flocks and herds or male and female slaves. In the critical moment of healing a leper, the "time" was for proving Yahweh as the only true God. Elisha proved this by healing Naaman without taking any money. But Gehazi violated the purpose of the prophetic ministry.

---

8. One talent is 34 kilograms. See *NIV Life Application Study Bible*, 2175.

Elisha took a firm stand against Gehazi for his dishonesty and deception. He told Gehazi that Naaman's leprosy that left him will cling to Gehazi and his descendants forever (5:27a). Just as he said, Gehazi's skin became white as snow, and he left Elisha's presence (5:27b). Gehazi appears again later when the king wants to ask him some questions about Elisha – and Elisha is not with him (8:4–5). Whereas Elisha inherited the spirit of Elijah, Gehazi inherited the leprosy of Naaman. What a sad ending for a servant who had served his master for several years!

SECRET CHRISTIANS

Elisha gives permission to Naaman to enter the temple of Rimmon and bow down before him, along with his king. This story raises an important theological question: what should religious converts to Christ do when they still need to continue in their religious and social networks with their clans and tribes? In South Asian society, many converts to Christianity are afraid of persecution if they openly declare their faith and get baptized. Should we criticize these converts as "secret Christians," or should we encourage them to continue secretly in their new faith until the whole family comes to know the Lord? This problem is even more severe in Islamic states, where converts to Christianity are killed for the crime of blasphemy.

Another prophet, Elisha, understood the precarious situation of his military commander, Naaman. His encouraging benediction, "go in peace," can instruct us about how to bless "secret Christians." We see a parallel situation when Darius declared Yahweh's greatness after Daniel was saved from the den of lions, but we have no evidence about how many of his people accepted Yahweh (Dan 6:25–27). In another parallel incident, Jonah's preaching caused the people of Nineveh to repent, but the story does not say whether or not they converted to Yahweh. From all these narratives, we learn that we are not the judge of so-called "secret Christians." Nevertheless, we cannot ignore the teaching of NT texts that encourage those who hear the Gospel to get baptized and join the Body of Christ (e.g. see Matt 28:19–20; Acts 2:37–42; 8:34–38). God, who is compassionate, will judge all, including converts who are living in difficult situations.

2 KINGS 6:1–7:20
RESCUING ISRAEL FROM WAR AND FAMINE

Elisha's powerful ministry continued as he helped individuals, prophetic groups, and the nation of Israel. After healing Naaman, an Aramean, Elisha continued to help the people in his region. There are two major sections in these chapters: the event of the floating axe head (6:1–7) and the ongoing war with the Aram (6:8–7:24). The theme of Elisha helping those in need unites these episodes.

6:1–7 FLOATING AXE HEAD

One day, the company of prophets told Elisha that their place of gathering was too small and crowded and that they needed to build a larger place beside the Jordan, and Elisha agreed (6:1–2). The phrase "company of the prophets" tells us that there were other prophets besides Elisha serving the God of Israel. These prophets worked as a group in worshiping centers and lived with their own families rather than in a monastery or ashram. They lived in Bethel, Jericho and Gilgal (2:3, 5; 4:38). They helped those who came to them discern the will of God. They looked to a powerful leader, such as Elijah and Elisha, to guide them. Their periodic meetings with a prophetic leader strengthened their shared fellowship. To this end, the prophets met with Elisha and expressed their plan to build a bigger place to hold these meetings since their current place was not sufficient (6:2). The river Jordan offered them water for drinking, bathing, and rituals. They planned to cut down trees and make beams to construct a tent or shed. Elisha liked their corporate plan and agreed to accompany them (6:3).

As one of the prophets was cutting down a tree, the iron axe head he was using fell into the water (6:4). Some of us may have had a similar experience when the head of a hammer comes out of the wooden handle and falls onto the ground. The prophet was upset because he had borrowed the axe and needed to return it to the owner (6:5). Some stretches of the Jordan River are quite deep, and during the monsoon season, the current can be very swift. Since iron was a rare material and costly to melt and mold in those days, iron goods were expensive then. Elisha heard the cry of the prophet and came forward to help this servant by asking him where the axe head had fallen into the water. Picking up a stick, Elisha threw it into the water where the axe head had fallen, and the axe head floated to the surface (6:6). Then he asked his fellow prophet to reach out his hand and lift the axe head from the water (6:7).

Usually, when we throw a stick into the water, it floats down the current of the water and drifts away. How could a weightless stick make a heavy iron object float? This was a miracle of God that went against the natural law of gravity. After the prophet picked up the iron axe head, he could fix it to the handle so that it could be returned to its owner. Elisha performed the miracle with God's power so that he could prevent this poor servant from falling into debt. This story also demonstrates Yahweh's power over water and iron, which floated contrary to nature.

6:8–7:20 ONGOING WAR WITH ARAM

Whenever a change in the political leadership of Aram happened, the new king came up against Israel with his army. Earlier, the king of Aram came against Asa, the king of Judah, ca. 914–874 BC (1 Kgs 15:18–20). Similarly, Ben-Hadad came up against Ahab, the king of Israel, ca. 876–854 BC (1 Kgs 20:1–12). The narrator outlines two more conflicts in these two chapters (2 Kgs 6:8–23; 6:24–7:20). Aram's ongoing political threat caused Israel to live in constant fear and to spend great resources in strengthening their cities near the border of Syria.

6:8–23 First Conflict

The king of Aram wanted to defeat the king of Israel (6:8a). So, he set up his military camps to launch a secret attack against Israel (6:8b). This incident may have happened during the reign of Joram over the northern kingdom (853–842 BC).[1] The military camps were near the border of Israel so they could attack from different directions. The phrase "man of God" refers to Elisha, who informed the king of Israel about the king of Aram's plans to set up these secret camps and prepare for war (6:9). The king of Israel listened to Elisha

---

1. Hobbs, *2 Kings*, 76. Jehoram, son of King Jehoshaphat of Judah is a different king ruling during the period of 850–843 BC (2 Kgs 8:17). He was a contemporary of Joram, king of Israel in the year 853–842 BC. In 2 Kings 3:1, 2 the same Joram, son of Ahab of Israel is mentioned as Jehoram. The reader need not be confused because in one text the name Jehoram is used and later Joram is used for the same person. To avoid this confusion the reader should see the identity of these kings by the name of their fathers and the territories they were ruling.

and watched over his movements. This happened again and again, frustrating the king of Aram (6:10). Throughout the history of Israel, the prophets functioned in this political role of helping the kings plan their attacks to save the nation from their enemies.

The king of Aram was angry that the king of Israel continued to frustrate the attacks from Aram's military (6:11a). He suspected that one of his officials was passing on information to the king of Israel, and so he ordered his officials to find out the culprit in his military or court (6:11b). One of the officials replied that it was Elisha, the prophet, who was giving the king of Israel revelations from God about the movement of Aram's military (6:12a). In fact, even the words that the king spoke in his bedroom were known to the prophet (6:12b). In this way, the God of Israel was guarding his people through his prophet. Hearing this, the king of Aram ordered his officials to find out where Elisha was staying and capture him to kill him (6:13a). They reported that he was staying in Dothan (6:13b).

Hearing that, the king of Aram sent horses, chariots, and a strong troop to capture Elisha in Dothan, which is fourteen kilometers north of Samaria, near the valley of Jezreel (6:14). The army surrounded the city in the night so that Elisha could not escape. Early the next morning, Elisha's attendant saw the chariots and soldiers surrounding the city and informed Elisha about the danger of being captured and killed (6:15). "Oh no, my lord! What shall we do?" is an expression of fear and panic. "Don't be afraid," Elisha said to his servant, because he had already seen a vision from the Lord, which revealed that those who were defending Israel were greater than the Aramean army (6:16). But to assure the servant, Elisha prayed that the Lord would open the eyes of his servant so that he could see the vision of many horses and chariots of fire surrounding Elisha, and the Lord answered (6:17a). The servant saw "the hills full of horses and chariots of fire all around Elisha" (6:17b), and was comforted.

Aram's forces didn't see God's army and advanced towards Elisha, and so he prayed to the Lord to blind the eyes of Aram's forces (6:18a).[2] The Lord answered Elisha's prayer and they lost their sight temporarily to recognize Elisha or understand the direction they were going (6:18b). While the army was in this confused state, Elisha asked them to follow him, and then he led them to the city of Samaria (6:19). Once the army was trapped inside the city,

---

[2]. The army was in a dazed condition, dazzled by the light (Gen 19:11). See Lissa M. Wray Beal, *1 & 2 Kings*. Apollo Old Testament Commentary (Downers Grove: InterVarsity, 2014), 344.

Elisha prayed again for the Lord to open their eyes so that they could see that they were trapped (6:20).

When the king of Israel saw them, he asked Elisha if he should kill them (6:21).[3] The king recognized Elisha's leadership and did not want to take vengeance on his own. Top political authorities who consult men of God must follow important principles, even when taking prisoners, to avoid negative consequences and build good relationships with their enemies. Elisha wanted the captives to be treated well so that they would return to their own country (6:22). Taking advantage of someone's plight is not good in the sight of God. Elisha stopped the king from taking advantage of the prophet's trap for the Aramean army, which would have made the prophet a murderer in a peaceful context, for there was no actual war, and it would be wrong to kill the soldiers off the battlefield. The small force that had surrounded Dothan to capture Elisha was not trying to start a battle. If the trapped captives were killed, it could aggravate enmity and instigate a new war. The prophet wanted to establish a peaceful situation that could continue for years. To this end, Elisha suggested that the king of Israel give the enemies food and drink and then send them safely back to their king. His plan worked; because of this feast, the Aramean bands stopped raiding Israel's territory, and thus the people of Israel could live in peace (6:23).

6:24–7:2 Second Conflict

The peaceful situation did not last long. Greed for territorial expansion so often pushed kings to take offensive action against poorer nations, who had to defend themselves. This time, Ben-Hadad, the king of Aram, wanted to capture Samaria and bring Israel under his control (6:24). Already, Samaria was suffering from a great famine, and so the siege of the army of Aram made the situation even worse for the king of Israel. The siege lasted so long that a donkey's head sold for the exorbitant price of eight shekels of silver (approximately 92 grams) and a quarter of a cab of seed pods sold for five shekels of silver (approximately 57.5 grams) (6:25).[4] The law prohibited the Israelites from eating donkey meat (Lev 11:3). They were so starving that they were willing to eat even food prohibited by the law and for exorbitant prices. Yet, they couldn't find any food.

---

3. For a discussion on the conduct of war, see Roland de Vaux, *Ancient Israel*, 250–257.
4. We can calculate the value of silver in grams according to the market rate today, but we do not know the exchange rate for silver in those days.

Earlier, at Elisha's command, the king of Israel gave a feast and released his enemies, the men from Aram (6:23–24). But now, the enemies besiege the people of Israel, making them starve inside their own city. Often, modern-day governments do the same by imposing economic sanctions and blockades against countries involved in terrorism or preparing to use nuclear weapons to annihilate other nations. People justify such actions as a necessary evil. Whether a war is offensive, defensive, or "just," the violence of any war affects thousands of people. While human rights violations need to be addressed, it is not right to make an entire population starve without food or medical help because of the actions of its leaders.

Within Samaria, people started dying because of the food shortage. The dire situation drove two women to do drastic actions for their own survival. In Israel, killing a human being without a reason is regarded as murder and is forbidden (Exod 20:13). Eating human flesh is equivalent to cannibalism and provides evidence of Yahweh's curse on a nation because of their disobedience (Deut 28:53–57). When the king of Israel was passing by on the wall of Samaria, one of the two women cried out for help and then told him how she had been cheated by another (6:26–27). They had made a pact, against the law. The other woman had said to her, "Give up your son so we may eat him today, and tomorrow we will eat my son" (6:28). Believing these words, the woman killed her son, cooked the meat, and shared it with her friend, who had agreed to kill her son on the following day (6:29a). But on the following day, her friend refused to kill her child and hid him instead (6:29b). These women were so desperate that they violated the law in Israel that prohibited murder. This story resembles the two women who came to King Solomon for advice (1 Kgs 3:16–28). What kind of justice did this woman expect from the king? Did she want the king to order the other woman to kill her child and share the meat, as they had previously agreed? We don't know. The purpose of this story is to show how desperate the people have become because of the siege and starvation.

After hearing this woman's cry, the king tore his robe in despair (6:30a). He was grieved by seeing what was happening to his people. As he tore his outer garment, the people saw that he wore a sackcloth under his robe as a symbol of his mourning (6:30b). Unable to bear the ongoing siege and famine, his patience turned to anger against Elisha. Blaming the prophet for the siege of Samaria, which was being carried out by the same Aramean soldiers to whom he had shown mercy, the king swore to kill Elisha (6:31).

When Elisha realized that the king was angry and had sent messengers to his house to cut off his head, he referred to the king as a "murderer." Elisha asked the elders to shut the door as soon as the messenger arrived (6:32), but the king followed the messenger and shouted, "This disaster is from the LORD. Why should I wait for the LORD any longer?" (6:33). The king was blaming God for the famine and Elisha for the siege and food shortage. He had lost hope that the Lord would rescue his nation from famine and siege.

The Lord heard the king's anger and communicated through Elisha his plan to help the starving people (7:1). The phrase "about this time tomorrow" refers to roughly twenty-four hours after the king accused Elisha. At that time the next day, the price of commodities would drop so that a *seah* of the finest flour would sell for a shekel and two *seahs* of barley would sell for a shekel at the city gate where food products were brought for sale (7:1). A *seah* could be around 5.6 kilograms. By the morning, God would provide for the people everything that they needed and they could escape starvation.

The commanding officer, on whom the king was leaning (as Naaman before), questioned the message of the Lord. Instead of believing and rejoicing, he said, "Look, even if the LORD should open the floodgates of the heavens, could this happen?" (7:2a). He was looking at it scientifically and agriculturally; harvest takes time. But the Lord had other plans. Elisha, frustrated with the commanding officer's criticism said, "You will see it with your own eye, but you will not eat any of it!" (7:2b).

7:3–20 Fulfilled Prophecy and Deliverance

Lepers in Israel were not allowed to live with their families inside the city but had to live as outcasts outside the walls of the city. In this miracle, God not only used a prophet but also lepers as his agents to inform the king of Israel what God had done to bring relief to his people.

Four men with leprosy, who were living outside the gate, could no longer bear the starvation and knew that death was approaching them soon (7:4). They reasoned they would surrender to the Aramean army. If the Arameans showed them mercy and gave them food, they would live; if the Arameans killed them, they would die (7:4). Since death was certain inside and outside the city, they chose to surrender to Aram in the hope of receiving mercy.

The four lepers went to the Aramean camp at sunset. All the tents were empty; no one was there (7:5). The lepers did not know that their enemies had deserted the camp and returned to Aram because the Lord had caused them to hear the sound of chariots, horses, and a great army coming against them (7:6). Fearing that the king of Israel was coming with an alliance of the Hittite and Egyptian armies, the Arameans fled in panic, abandoning their tents, horses, donkeys, and food (7:7). God could perform any miracle to help his people and keep them from dying of starvation. God's intervention amidst the threat of war or attack is a recurring theme in the history of Israel's kings (1 Kgs 20:13–21; 2 Kgs 3:16–19; 19:35–36).

The lepers who risked their lives to enter the enemy camp were surprised and enjoyed the food and drink they took from the tents (7:8a). They also took silver, gold, and clothes from another tent, which they hid for their future need (7:8b). Then they suddenly realized their selfish mistake and remembered the suffering of their people inside the city (7:9a). They were also afraid that they would be punished for not informing the king of Israel, who would discover the flight of the Arameans on the following morning (7:9b). They wanted to make it a day of good news for their people, and so they went and reported the news to the gatekeeper so he could inform the king (7:10–11).

At first, the king did not believe the news from the lepers. He suspected the Aramean army of withdrawing to hide in the country as a military tactic to make the Israelites come out of the city and then trap them outside the gate (7:12). He questioned the information from the lepers and wanted to make sure that the army had returned to Aram. One of his officials suggested that he send a team of men with horses to check the situation (7:13). If they were caught and killed, it was not safe to go out for food. So the king sent two chariots with men and horses to trace the Aramean army (7:14). They journeyed as far as the Jordan River and only found the things that the Arameans had thrown out to reduce the weight they were carrying amidst their flight (7:15). Then the king opened the gate so that the people of Israel could plunder the spoil in the camps of their enemies (7:16). The food stock was so plentiful that the prices dropped, just as Elisha had predicted.

The word of God was fulfilled in the sight of the king and his officials. Though the sarcastic officer who had questioned Elisha lived to see the prophecy fulfilled, he did not eat the food, as he was trampled to death at the gate when the people were rushing to loot the camps (7:17–20). Once again, Elisha became involved in the political situation of his nation by helping to rescue the king and the people from siege and starvation.

2 KINGS 8:1–29
ELISHA AND THE KINGS OF ARAM AND JUDAH

Although the primary purpose of 1 and 2 Kings is to narrate the life and work of the kings, the narrator took the last several chapters to narrate the lives and ministries of two significant prophets: Elijah and Elisha. Several previous chapters narrated the tireless work of Elisha as he helped people and kings or challenged them with the vision of God for the nation of Israel. As the narrative about Elisha draws near its end, the writer describes how Elisha helped the Shunammite woman survive the famine in Israel (8:1–6) and his encounter with Hazael, an officer of Ben-Hadad, the king of Aram (8:7–15) before continuing the evaluation of the kings of Judah and their rule (8:16–29).

The activities of Elisha took place when Joram ruled over Israel in the north and Jehoshaphat, Jehoram, and Ahaziah ruled over Judah in the south. Although the extended narrative about Elijah and Elisha gives the impression that their stories stand aloof from the history of the kings, their activities were clearly connected with the politics of the kings.

2 Kings 8 has three major sections: Elisha's continued ministry (8:1–15), the rise of Jehoram, king of Judah (8:16–24), and the rise of Ahaziah, king of Judah (8:25–29).

8:1–15 ELISHA'S MINISTRIES

Two stories appear in this section. The first is the safety of the Shunammite from famine and the restoration of her lost land and property, both because of her friendship with Elisha (8:1–6). The second in Elisha's vision concerning Hazael, the assistant to Ben-Hadad, king of Aram (8:7–15).

8:1–6 The Shunammite Woman and Elisha

The narrator returns to the story of the Shunammite woman to assure the readers that she wasn't affected by the famine before Elisha's cautionary note to her to depart the land. In addition, after the famine ended and she returned, the king showed her mercy because Elisha restored her son's life. In both these actions, Elisha's friendship with the Shunammite woman helps her.

Elisha could not forget the Shunammite woman; she had shown hospitality to him and challenged him to save her precious son. So to help her avoid the forthcoming famine, he instructed her to leave Israel for seven years until the famine was over (8:1). He made it clear that the Lord called for this famine. She listened to him and went to the land of the Philistines for seven years (8:2). This seven-year famine happened when the king of Aram besieged Samaria (6:24–7:20).[1]

At the end of the seven years, the Shunammite woman returned to her homeland (8:3a). While she was gone, others confiscated her land and house. So, she approached the ruling king and asked him to restore her property to her family (8:3b). In many societies, people can occupy an abandoned house or land unless someone is appointed as a caretaker. The woman's claim reminds us of the Israelite law of inheritance, where the land belongs to a family and no one can purchase or mortgage it (Lev 25:23–25). Any time the property is held by someone outside the family, it must be returned when the original family makes a claim.

The woman's appeal came to the court while the king was talking to Gehazi, the servant of Elisha, asking for a report about Elisha's powerful ministry (8:4). Elisha did not appear for this case, but his servant helped the Shunammite woman. Gehazi's reappearance in this story leads us to think that it may have taken place after Gehazi was punished and left Elisha (5:27).

Just as Gehazi was telling the king about Elisha's miracle of restoring life to the son of the Shunammite woman, she entered the court with her appeal. Through God's timing, Gehazi's account of the woman helped her gain favor in the sight of the king (8:5). After the king verified the miracle with her, he ordered his officials to restore the woman's land and house, along with compensation from the income that had been earned from her land over the previous years by the person who had been using it (8:6). This provision ensured that she would have the necessary resources to restart her agriculture until reaping the harvest at the end of the season. Thus the king ensured justice for the Shunammite woman.

8:7–15 Elisha and Hazael

In the ancient period, prophets rarely crossed the boundaries of their country unless there was a valid reason. Elisha went to Damascus, probably to determine the political situation of Syria in order to help Israel from the attack of

---

1. The date of the famine could have been between 853–842 BC.

the Arameans (8:7). While he was there, Ben-Hadad king of Aram became ill. The news of Elisha staying in Damascus reached the king, who knew very well about the prophet's powerful ministry of doing miracles, including healing his own military commander and releasing his trapped army back to his own country. So, he said to Hazael, "Take a gift with you and go to meet the man of God. Consult the Lord through him; ask him, 'Will I recover from this illness?'" (8:8). Assyrian records identify Hazael as the "son of nobody," meaning he did not have a royal background, but was a commoner.[2] Somehow, he became the chief official of Ben-Hadad. Those who wanted to receive an oracle often took gifts to seers and prophets. So, Hazael went to meet Elisha with "forty camel loads" of gifts, signifying the vastness of gifts (8:9a). Although Ben-Hadad worshiped another god, he believed that Elisha could get the truth from Yahweh about his recovery or death. Kings of other religions often consulted the prophets of Yahweh in desperate situations of sickness, threat of war, or natural calamities because they were syncretistic, and their religion allowed them to do so. Seeing Elisha, Hazael asked the question Ben-Hadad had sent him to ask: "Will I recover from this illness?" (8:9b). Hazael used the phrase, "your son Ben-Hadad," as a polite expression, drawing Elisha to show favor to his king. The Hebrew word for "live" (*hayah*, "living thing"), when translated as "recover," dilutes the seriousness of the illness. The correct translation should be, "Will I live from this illness," indicating that his sickness may cause his death or make him bedridden forever.

Elisha replied in a puzzle: "You will certainly recover . . . [yet] he will in fact die" (8:10). Over the course of the events, the readers will know that the king will survive his illness but die in the hands of an assassin. Saying that, Elisha fixed his gaze upon Hazael, which made Hazael uncomfortable (8:11a). Then, Elisha started to weep (8:11b). There are two reasons for his weeping. First, he knew that the situation for Israel would change when Ben-Hadad died and that it would not be favorable to Israel, which worried him. Second, he knew that Hazael would use this prophecy to justify killing the king and taking over the throne and that Hazael would subsequently do great harm to Israel. A true prophet communicates the message of God with both his heart and mind. Because Elisha understood the consequences of his prophecy to Hazael, he felt the pain that Israel would feel after the change of kingship in Aram. In Elisha's prophecy, he narrated four cruelties that Hazael would bring upon the Israelites after he came to power. First, he would attack Israel, set fire

---

2. Wiseman, *1 and 2 Kings*, 226–278.

to the fortified cities, and destroy them. Second, he would kill young people with swords so that they could not rebel against him. Third, he would dash their little children to the ground (in the sense of crushing their heads). Fourth, he would rip open the wombs of pregnant women so that there wouldn't be a future population to retaliate against the rule of Hazael (8:12). Amos speaks of all these cruelties in his prophecy against the house of Hazael (Amos 1:3–5).

At first, Hazael responded by saying that he was like a servant or mere dog, who did not have the power to take such actions against Israel (8:13a). Hazael described himself as a dog in a metaphorical sense, to convey that he was like a dog, humbling himself without any power to go against the Israelites. Elisha responded by affirming that Hazael would become the king of Aram (8:13b). Although Elisha delivered the prophecy, he did not anoint Hazael.

After hearing Elisha's words, Hazael returned to the king and told him Elisha's reply that he would recover (8:14). Then Hazael began to scheme about how to work out the death of the king and take over the throne. The next day, Hazael soaked a thick blanket with water and then covered the king's face and suffocated him (8:15a). In this way, Elisha's prophecy that Ben-Hadad would not live and Hazael would become the king was fulfilled (8:15b).

In our modern times, we need to learn how to differentiate between a "predictive prophecy" of the OT, which was in fulfillment of God's commands, and an "edification prophecy" in the NT. Speaking in tongues and prophesying to edify people in the church can be helpful, but pastors, elders, and other leaders first need to receive a lot of training. Those who have received this gift need to be taught how to discern which prophecies to speak openly in a meeting, which prophecies to speak directly to an individual, and which prophecies to keep to themselves while praying and waiting for further guidance so that listeners cannot misuse or distort them.

8:16–24 JEHORAM, KING OF JUDAH

The narrator now resumes recollecting the history of the kings of Judah. He picks up where it left off in 1 Kings 22:50. The narrative uses the formula for introducing a king with a brief biodata, mentioning that Jehoram, the son of Jehoshaphat, came to the throne at the age of thirty-two and ruled Judah for eight years (8:16–17). Next, the narrative gives an evaluation of the king, noting how he followed the sinful actions of the kings of Israel by promoting the worship of Baal in Jerusalem because of the influence of his wife, who was a daughter of Ahab (8:18). The narrator also uses a formula for the kings of Judah, which is that Yahweh was gracious towards these kings "for the sake of his servant David" and because of his promise to maintain "a lamp for David and his descendants forever" (8:19).[3]

Jehoram faced a difficult moment during his rule because Edom rebelled against Judah (8:20). So Jehoram went with his army to defeat Edom at Zair, but he could not win the battle; Edomites surrounded his army, and Jehoram and his army fled back to Judah (8:21). Along with Edom, Libnah, a frontier town in Philistia, revolted at the same time, taking advantage of Jehoram's weak situation (8:22). Their rebellion and independence would have cut back on Judah's revenue through the loss of tributes, taxes, and a blockade of trade routes into the southern kingdom of Israel. The narrative concludes with the usual formula about the rest of Jehoram's activities being recorded in the annals of the kings, his death, and how his son, Ahaziah, succeeded him as king (8:23–24).

8:25–29 AHAZIAH, KING OF JUDAH

Before resuming the narration about the rule in northern Israel in chapter 9, there is a brief description of the reign of Ahaziah, the son of Jehoram (8:25). Ahaziah was twenty-two years old when he became king, and he only ruled Judah for one year (8:26). His contemporary in northern Israel was Joram, the son of Ahab. Ahaziah's mother was Athaliah, a granddaughter of Omri, who was a previous king of Israel. This links Ahaziah with Ahab, the former king of Israel, through marriage (8:27). This relationship led Ahaziah to follow the ways of Ahab by promoting the worship of Baal in Judah.

While this marital connection helped the kings of Israel and Judah avoid a civil war, it also led Ahaziah to join Joram in an alliance for war against the king of Aram at Ramoth-Gilead (8:28). The Arameans in the north were a constant threat to Israel. Hazael, who grabbed the throne by killing Ben-Hadad of Aram, defeated this alliance and severely wounded Joram. Ahaziah and Joram fled to their respective kingdoms (8:29a). Later, Ahaziah made a courtesy visit to northern Israel to console and encourage Joram son of Ahab (8:29b). Ahaziah's story doesn't have the standard conclusion of how long he lived and where he was buried. Instead, the writer moves on to talk about Jehu, the king in the northern kingdom of Israel in the following chapter. Nevertheless, this section is important for the alliance the kings of the north and south made in their fight against the Arameans and also to mention that they continued on in their wickedness of worshiping the gods of other nations.

---

3. See my commentary on 1 Kings 8:25; 11:36; 15:4.

2 KINGS 9:1–10:36
JEHU'S KINGSHIP IN ISRAEL

The story of Jehu's kingship in Israel is narrated in two chapters. His reign is connected with God's mission to implement the prophecies of Elijah and Elisha against the rulers of Israel and Judah who did not follow the ways of the Lord. These chapters recount his anointing as the king of Israel (9:1–13), his assassinations of Joram, Ahaziah, and Jezebel (9:14–37), his killing of royal families (10:1–17), and the servants of Baal (10:18–28), and an evaluation of his rule (10:29–36). Though the bloodshed is horrible to read, it is justified as a fulfillment of the prophecies delivered against these rulers for promoting Baal worship and murdering the prophets of Yahweh, along with innocent people.

9:1–13 ANOINTING OF JEHU AS KING

Jehu means "Yahweh is He," and a reference to Yahweh as the one true God. The name reflects Jehu's zeal for the worship of Yahweh and the actions he took to remove Baal and those who promoted the sin of Jeroboam.

As a chief commander of the army of Israel, he was in the battlefield with his officers and soldiers in Ramoth-Gilead, trying to defeat the army of Syria. In this context of tension between Israel and Syria, Elisha's role of confirming Jehu as king of Israel is narrated as a thrilling story, stage by stage, in three sections: Elisha giving instructions to a young prophet (9:1–3), the young prophet anointing Jehu (9:4–10), and the public declaration of Jehu as king of Israel (9:11–13).

9:1–3 Elisha's Instructions to a Young Prophet

Elisha summoned a young prophet from the company of prophets to send him on a mission (9:1). He told the young man to tuck his cloak into his belt, meaning he should arrange his dress so that he could hurry to the military camp. This instruction conveys a sense of time pressure for the journey. He also told the young prophet to take a flask of oil on his mission. The young prophet would have known the importance of this command as oil was used to anoint someone as a priest or king in Israel. The flask would have been small and suitable for carrying on the journey. In light of the secret nature of his mission, the flask may have been small enough to hide inside his cloak so that others in the camp could not see it. Elisha told the messenger to carry the flask of oil to the battlefield at Ramoth-Gilead, where he should boldly enter the camp (9:1).

There, the young prophet should look for Jehu and then instruct him to follow the messenger to an inner room. Rather than describing Jehu's physical appearance, Elisha identified his family. He was the son of Jehoshaphat, who was the son of Nimshi, which was a clan in northern Israel (9:2). Jehu was not from a royal family but was raised up from his military service to rule over the nation. After identifying Jehu and taking him into a secret room, the young prophet was to pour the oil from the flask on Jehu's head as a sign of anointing him as king over Israel (9:3). Then, he was to declare what Elisha had told him, making it clear that the Lord had anointed him to be king over Israel. As soon as he declared the message, he was to run away from the camp without any delay, just in case there was violence in the camp.

9:4–10 The Young Prophet Anoints Jehu

Just as instructed by Elisha, the young prophet went to Ramoth-Gilead looking for Jehu (9:4). When the young prophet arrived at the camp, he noticed the officers sitting together as a council (9:5). He told them that he had a message for the commander. Jehu, the chief commander, asked the prophet to tell him the name of the person who was to receive the message. When the messenger informed him that the message was for Jehu, the chief commander left the rest of the officers and went with the messenger into the inner chamber of a house (9:6a). To Jehu's surprise, the prophet took out the flask and poured the oil on Jehu's head and declared the purpose of anointing him (9:6b). The prophet used the messenger formula, "This is what the Lord, the God of Israel, says," to inform Jehu that the message was from the Lord, not Elisha or him. Then the prophet explained the content of Jehu's mission.

Jehu's mission was to destroy the house of Ahab (9:7–10). The word "house" (*bayit*) refers to everyone who belonged to the family of Ahab. Jehu must strike down all the members in the family of Ahab, who was his master. The verb "strike down" in this verse means that he is to kill them by sword to avenge the blood of the prophets of Yahweh, who were killed by Ahab and his wife, Jezebel (1 Kgs 18:13). In the Mount Carmel incident, Elijah killed all the prophets of Baal who had assembled there, but he spared the family of Ahab (1 Kgs 18:40). Now, the time had come to root out all the male descendants of Ahab, including his servants and slaves so that none would survive (9:8).

The sin of Ahab and Jezebel was similar to the sin of Jeroboam and Baasha (9:9). If those people were punished, then Ahab's family deserved the same punishment. The prophecy of the destruction of Ahab's house in 1 Kings 21:21–22 would now be fulfilled.

Ahab's family deserved more severe punishment because Jezebel had supported the prophets of Baal and killed hundreds of prophets of Yahweh in Israel (1 Kgs 18:4). Moreover, she had also misused her power and authority by signing a letter on behalf of the king to set false witnesses against Naboth, plot to kill him, and take his vineyard (1 Kgs 21:9–10). The prophet informed Jehu that dogs would devour her body on the plot of ground in the district of Jezreel (9:10). Jezebel would not have a proper burial because dogs would eat up her body. This kind of death has social implication in the South Asian context, communicating a lack of respect for the deceased. Jezebel would now be regarded as a cursed person. After communicating these details, the young prophet opened the door and ran away.

9:11–13 Jehu Declared King of Israel

When Jehu returned to sit with his fellow officers, one asked Jehu about the reason for the prophet's visit. A messenger could bring good or bad news to a commander in camp. The officer described the prophet as a "maniac," a negative description for the way prophets go into trances and predict the future (9:11). Accepting the officer's description of the prophet, Jehu tried to evade his question by saying, "You know the man and the sort of things he says" (9:11). His intention was to downplay the prophet's visit as nothing important for the battle at hand, yet the officer insisted that Jehu reveal the prophet's message (9:12). Jehu briefly communicated the message, saying that the messenger had said that the Lord had chosen and anointed Jehu as king of Israel. Jehu did not reveal all the details of the message because he wanted to wait for the other officers' reactions.

All the officers accepted the message of the Lord and quickly acted to respect him. The phrase, "took their cloaks and spread them under him," is a symbolic action of recognizing and submitting to Jehu as the king (9:13; Matt 21:8). This gesture communicated that they were transferring their loyalty to Jehu from Joram. Then they blew the trumpet and shouted, "Jehu is king" (9:13). This acclamation was customarily used to publicly confirm a new king.

9:14–37 JEHU'S KILLINGS

Without any further delay, Jehu began his mission of killing Ahab's family. First, he assassinated Joram, the ruling king in Israel (9:14–26); second, he killed Ahaziah, the king of Judah (9:27–29); third, he acted against Jezebel (2 Kgs 9:30–37).

9:14–26 Assassination of Joram

When Jehu was anointed as king, Joram was not in the military camp; instead, he was in Ramoth-Gilead defending it against Hazael king of Aram (9:14). At that war, Joram was wounded and he went to Jezreel to recover (9:15a). As such, he was not with Jehu. He asked his fellow military leaders' help to keep his trip to Jezreel a surprise (9:15b). If someone slipped away and informed Joram that Jehu had been anointed as king of Israel, Joram would be able to attack Jehu or escape from his hands. His conspiracy had to be carried out secretly so that he could kill Joram.

Jehu left with his troops and headed south to Jezreel, where Joram was recovering, and Ahaziah was visiting him (9:16). The soldier on the watchtower of the fort noticed an army coming towards Jezreel and informed the king (9:17a). Joram asked his official to send a horseman to meet with a message of peace before the army reached the fort (9:17b). The Hebrew word for "horseman" (*rakkav*) denotes a diplomatic messenger rather than an ordinary horseman from the cavalry. The diplomatic phrase, "Do you come in peace?" indicates the need for negotiation. But Jehu rejected the diplomat's question and asked him to join his army, which he did (9:18). The report went back to the king that the diplomat had not returned but had joined the army of Jehu. So the king sent another diplomat with the same question, and again Jehu asked him to follow him instead, and once again, the diplomat did not return (9:19). The watchman in the watchtower sent a report to the king that the driver of the chariot was driving like Jehu, who drove "like a maniac," meaning aggressively and not for peaceful negotiation or compromise (9:20).

Then Joram and Ahaziah decided to go and meet Jehu, each in his own chariot (9:21a). Jehu was waiting for them on the plot of Naboth, the Jezreelite (9:21b). When Joram offered a peace treaty, Jehu refused to negotiate with him because of Joram's mother Jezebel's idolatry and witchcraft (9:22). Securing peace in the land was dependent on worshiping Yahweh alone and not Baal. A peaceful life was closely connected with the fulfillment of the covenantal responsibility. Jehu made it clear that a peace treaty with Joram was not possible.

Joram understood the seriousness of Jehu's words, turned, and fled while shouting to Ahaziah, "Treachery, Ahaziah!" (9:23). But Jehu drew his bow and shot Joram between the shoulders. The arrow pierced his heart, and Joram fell into the chariot (9:24). Jehu instructed his chariot driver, Bidkar, to chase Joram, pick up his body and throw it into the plot of land where Naboth had been killed (9:25a). Joram's body had to be thrown onto Naboth's land to reverse what Ahab and Jezebel had done to Naboth (9:25b–26). This fulfilled the prophecy spoken against them for killing an innocent man (1 Kgs 21:21–22). Once again, the recurring theme of prophecy and fulfillment in 1 and 2 Kings appears in this event.

9:27–29 Assassination of Ahaziah

When Ahaziah saw what happened to Joram, he fled to Beth Haggan (9:27). Beth Haggan refers to the "garden house" of the royal family in Jezreel (1 Kgs 21:1).[1] Jehu chased Ahaziah and ordered his army to kill him (9:27). Jehu's men shot and wounded Ahaziah in his chest as he was heading to Gur near Ibleam, but he escaped to Meggido, where he died from his wounds (9:27). His body was carried to Jerusalem in a chariot and buried there along with his ancestors in his tomb in the City of David (9:28). Unlike Joram, he received a reverential burial because he was David's descendant. A historical note concludes this paragraph: Ahaziah became the king of Judah during the eleventh year of Joram's reign in northern Israel (9:29).

9:30–37 Slaying of Jezebel

Jehu's next target was Jezebel. When Jezebel heard that Jehu was coming to Jezreel, she painted her eyes and arranged her hair (9:30). In some cultures today, women who paint their eyes with black coloring and arrange their hair in a particular fashion are connected with the sex trade. Jezebel was not decorating herself to attract Jehu but rather to negotiate with him. As Jehu entered her gate, she asked, "Have you come in peace, you Zimri, you murderer of your master?" (9:31). Jezebel was clever and experienced in politics, and so her intention was not to antagonize Jehu by calling him a "murderer." Rather, she was comparing Jehu with Zimri, who had killed all the members of the house of Baasha, according to the prophecy of Elijah (1 Kgs 16:9–13). Her implied question was, "Are you going to kill all the members of the house of

---

1. Wiseman mentions that the road could be En-gannim, which is eleven kilometers south of Jezreel. Wiseman, *1 and 2 Kings*, 236.

Joram belonging to the family of Ahab just as Zimri did? Her dialogue with Jehu links the judgment against Baasha that was carried out by Zimri with the action that Jehu is going to take against the house of Ahab, as predicted by Elijah (1 Kgs 21:23) and proclaimed by the young prophet (2 Kgs 9:9).

Jehu ignored her question and called out, "Who is on my side? Who?" (9:32a). Two or three eunuchs looked down at him (9:32b). Jehu ordered them to throw Jezebel down from the tower. They obeyed his order (9:33a). As she fell, some of her blood spattered on the wall and the horses as they trampled her under their feet (9:33b).

After witnessing her death, Jehu went inside the palace and ate a meal. Then he pitied her and said, "Take care of that cursed woman and bury her, for she was a king's daughter" (9:34). He wanted her to have a proper burial worthy of a princess. But, when his men went to prepare her body for burial, they found only her skull, legs, and hands, as everything else had been eaten by dogs (9:35).

When they reported it to Jehu, he remembered the prophecy of Elijah (1 Kgs 21:23–24) and confirmed Jezebel's death as the fulfillment of the word of Lord (2 Kgs 9:36). Where Jezebel ruled and shed the blood of Naboth, there she died and the dogs devoured her flesh. This place has also become the place where her blood was shed. No one could identify her body as Jezebel because most of her body had been eaten up by dogs; what was leftover was like "dung" (9:37).

Killing those who did injustice to fulfill a prophecy of judgment was a special case in ancient Israel. They were under the covenant and law. If kings and commanders killed others to grab a position or enact punishment on their own, then such violence was regarded as sin. Although the OT differentiates between killing to fulfill God's plan and killing to achieve personal ambition, the NT regards all violence as sin. Both the OT and NT make it clear that one human being or a group of people is not allowed to take the law into their own hands to kill others (Exod 20:13; Num 35:16–18; Matt 5:21–26; Luke 18:1–7).

10:1–17 KILLING THE ROYAL FAMILIES

2 Kings 10 continues the story of Jehu's kingship, highlighting his zeal for which he was made a king. Before he could sit on the throne and start ruling northern Israel, he had to eliminate the members and close associates of the families of Ahab as well as the prophets of Baal. The gruesome bloodshed that began in the previous chapter concludes in chapter 10.

The first part of the story narrates how Jehu killed all the members of the families of Ahab as well as the relatives of Ahaziah through clear planning that followed a geographical progression from Jezreel to Samaria (10:1–17). The second part of the story recounts his shrewd plan for killing the prophets of Baal (10:18–27). The concluding note follows the usual pattern with an evaluation of Jehu's rule, his death, and his successor (10:29–36).

10:1–11 God's Judgment Against Ahab's House

To fulfill God's judgment against the entire family of Ahab, Jehu targeted Ahab's seventy sons, who were living in Samaria (10:1a). This number could be literal or figurative. In the OT, "seventy" is often used in a symbolic sense to mean a large number, as with the descendants of Jacob (Gen 46:27), the elders (Num 11:16), and the family of Gideon (Judg 9:5). As a first step, Jehu wrote a letter to the officials of Jezreel, the elders, and the guardians of Ahab's children (10:1a). Jehu wanted to bring these officials, elders, and guardians to his side before killing all the sons of Ahab, and so invited the officials to select the best son of Ahab and make him the king and then fight against Jehu with their army, weapons, chariots, and fortified city for avenging the family of their deceased master (10:2–3). The officials and elders who read his letter were terrified of Jehu's power in light of his military service in the war and his brutal killing of Joram and Ahaziah (10:4). The palace administrator (the chief officer in charge of the affairs of the royal family), the governor of the city of Samaria (the representative of the king), and the elders and guardians sent a reply of surrender to Jehu. In the letter, they addressed themselves as "servants," pledging their loyalty to Jehu (10:5).

Jehu sent a reply and asked them to obey his commands by cutting off the heads of Ahab's sons and bringing them to him in Jezreel (10:6). This was a cruel demand to put upon the officials and guardians of the children of their deceased master. They had to harden their hearts to obey, but they knew the consequences if they failed to do so. So they slaughtered the seventy princes, put their heads in a basket, and sent them to Jehu in Jezreel (10:7). When the heads arrived, Jehu ordered the messengers to heap up the heads in two piles at the entrance of the city gate and to leave them there until the morning (10:8). This was for the people to notice and be terrified.

The following morning, he addressed the people who had gathered in front of the city gate and explained why he had killed all of Ahab's sons (10:9–11). He made it clear that no one among them had done this massacre; they were innocent of the murder of the sons of their master (10:9a). He took the blame for killing King Joram and King Ahaziah upon himself (10:9b). He did not tell the people who had killed the royal princes, nor did he reveal his order to the officials in Samaria. Instead, he asked a rhetorical question, "But who killed all these?" (10:9b). Jehu knew that his audience would have guessed he was responsible for it. The public did not need to feel guilty about the massacre because it had happened according to the prophecy of Elijah (10:8; see 1 Kgs 21:21–22). Saying this, Jehu killed all the chief men, close friends, and priests of Ahab who were living or hiding in Jezreel (10:11). He did not spare anyone who had a connection with the royal family because if they were spared, they could stage a coup against him and claim the throne. The phrase "leaving him no survivor" with the family of Ahab conveys how Jehu ensured that he would have a free hand without any resistance once he sat upon the throne.

10:12–14 Killing the Relatives of Ahaziah

After clearing resistance and drawing support from the people in Jezreel, Jehu headed south to Samaria and met some relatives of Ahaziah at Beth Eked (10:12–13). Since Ahaziah was related to the family of Omri through his mother (8:26), and a cordial relationship existed between Ahaziah and Joram, they had probably come as a courtesy to visit the royal family. These relatives did not seem to be aware of the events that were happening in Israel, and so they had not heard about Jehu's killing of the kings, Jezebel, and the royal princes (10:13). Because Ahaziah had partnered with Joram in the confrontation with Jehu in Jezreel, Jehu ordered his men to kill the forty-two relatives of Ahaziah, leaving none to escape (10:14).

10:15–17 Jehu Displays his Zeal for the Lord

As he left Beth Eked, Jehu met Jehonadab, son of Rekab (10:15). Jehonadab had come to meet Jehu, probably because he had heard about Jehu's actions. Jehonadab was part of the Rechabite community,[2] who vowed to remain a puritan group for the Lord. Their vow included abstaining from wine and leading a simple, nomadic life. The prophet Jeremiah identifies Jehonadab as a leader of the Rechabites (Jer 35:6–16). Jehonadab's reason for coming to meet Jehu is not clear in the text. Jehu invited Jehonadab to ride with him in his chariot and to join him on his journey to Samaria so that Jehonadab could see his zeal for the Lord (10:16). The Hebrew word for "seeing" (*ra'ah*) here means having a personal experience as an eye witness. The word "zeal" (Heb.

---

2. Hobbs, *2 Kings*, 128.

qin'ah) refers to Jehu's enthusiasm, spirit of dedication, and commitment to purge the worship of Baal from northern Israel and to allow the worship of Yahweh alone. When Jehu arrived in Samaria, he killed the remaining members of Ahab's family and justified his massacre as a fulfillment of the word of God spoken to Elijah (10:17).

In his "zeal" for God, he often transgressed such as killing Ahaziah's relatives even when he had no word from God to do so. The prophet Hosea condemned Jehu's violence against the relatives of Ahaziah, who had come to visit the king of Israel (Hos 1:4). Violence against religious communities in the name of one's zeal for gods and goddesses can be a serious issue within the secular and pluralistic context of some Asian countries. Early Hindu reformers, such as Raja Ram Mohan Roy and later Dr. Radhakrishnan, criticized the zeal of Christian evangelists who preached in public meetings against the idols of Hinduism and their temples during the early period. In recent years, this scenario has changed for the better in India.

10:18–28 KILLING THE SERVANTS OF BAAL

The fourth section in the life of Jehu deals with his actions to exterminate all the prophets and servants of Baal in northern Israel. By this time, the news about his extermination of Ahab's family would have reached all over Israel. The people knew about his zeal for the Lord, and so they were waiting for his action to promote the worship of Yahweh. But Jehu surprised them by calling for a grand festival with sacrifices for Baal, and he invited the prophets and servants of Baal to help him (10:18–19a). This was Jehu's deceptive plan to bring all the prophets and servants of Baal into one place and to kill them. To make his claim strong, he said, "Anyone who fails to come will no longer live" (10:19b), leaving them no choice. In the context of fulfilling the prophecy, Jehu's deceptive plan was justified, but it cannot be applied to our modern times.

As Jehu ordered, his command was proclaimed throughout the land (10:20). All of Baal's servants and priests came; the temple of Baal in Samaria was full "from one end to the other" (10:21). Jehu did not want the people to suspect his call for everyone to gather to worship Baal, and so he asked the person in charge of the wardrobe to give a robe to the servants of Baal (10:22). Then, Jehu and Jehonadab went inside the temple of Baal and assured those who served Baal that they alone were there (10:23) and proceeded to make sacrifices and burnt offerings (10:24a). In the meantime, Jehu posted eighty men outside the temple and ordered them not to allow any of the prophets, priests, or servants of Baal escape (10:24b). Jehu himself made a burnt offering in the eyes of all who had gathered inside the temple so as to convince them that he too was truly worshiping Baal (10:25a). Then, he ordered his men, who were standing outside the temple, to go inside and kill the prophets, priests, and servants inside (10:25b). The guards and officers of Jehu killed all the prophets, priests, and servants and threw their bodies outside the temple. Then they destroyed the sacred poles and altars inside the inner chamber of the temple.[3] They destroyed not only the men belonging to the cult of Baal, but also the temple itself. They brought the sacred stone of Baal out of the temple and burned it (10:26). They tore down the temple and the people began to use it as a toilet and remained a toilet for many years (10:27). In summary, "Jehu destroyed Baal worship in Israel" (10:28).

In Kings, Yahweh alone is powerful, not Baal and Ashtaroth. These nature deities could not overpower Yahweh, the creator of the universe. The key reasons to remove these cults in Israel were that they promoted the worship of idols that were created by man, practiced sexual perversions, the sacrificing children, and the use of sorcery. These elements promoted wrong values in the society, and so Yahweh asked the leaders of Israel and Judah to destroy the idols of Baal and Ashtaroth so that the people would worship Yahweh alone.

10:29–36 EVALUATION OF JEHU'S REIGN

Jehu's story concludes with a critical evaluation from the Lord of his reign. On the one hand, Yahweh appreciated Jehu's efforts of destroying the worship of Baal in Israel (10:28). On the other hand, Jehu did not turn away from idol worship: he allowed the worship of the golden calves at Bethel and Dan (10:29). The Lord God appreciated his work; he said to him, "Because you have done well in accomplishing what is right in my eyes and have done to the house of Ahab all I had in mind to do, your descendants will sit on the throne of Israel to the fourth generation" (10:30). On the other hand, Jehu was not careful to keep the Law of the Lord because he allowed the worship of the golden calves representing Yahweh in Bethel and Dan, which had been erected by Jeroboam (10:31). As a result, the Lord began to reduce the size of Israel and Hazael continued to grow in power against the Israelites and captured many tribes' lands (10:32–33).

The narrator abruptly ends the story by asking the standard question, "As for the other events of Jehu's reign, all he did, and all his achievements, are

---

3. "Sacred stones" refer to the explanation in 1 Kings 3:1–3; 14:21–31; 15:9–23.

they not written in the book of the annals of the kings of Israel?" (10:34). As God promised, four generations of Jehu's descendants – Jehoahaz, Jehoash, Jeroboam, and Zechariah – ruled over Israel. Jehu died and was buried in Samaria (10:35a). His son Jehoahaz succeeded him as the next king (10:35b). In all, Jehu reigned over Israel for twenty-eight years, and his capital was in Samaria (10:36).

2 KINGS 11:1–21
JEHOIADA, PRIEST AND KINGMAKER

Sometimes, a political or religious leader arises to contribute in an extraordinary way amidst a critical situation. Jehoiada, a priest, is an excellent example, for he helped bring Joash to power at a time when Judah desperately needed a proper king.[1] 2 Kings 11 explains the life and ministry of Jehoiada, the priest and kingmaker. It has four sections: the revenge of Athaliah (11:1–3); Jehoiada's anointing of Joash as king of Judah (11:4–12); Athaliah's reaction and death (11:13–16); the covenantal ceremony and enthronement (11:17–21).

11:1–3 REVENGE OF ATHALIAH

Athaliah was the mother of Ahaziah, who died after the confrontation with Jehu. After Ahaziah died, the queen mother took control of Judah and then proceeded to destroy the entire royal family (11:1). One possible reason for Athaliah's actions was that she wanted to end dynasty rule in Judah by establishing the descendants of Omri, her grandfather, to rule over Judah as well as the northern kingdom. However, Jehu eliminated all the members of Ahab's family, who were descendants of Omri. The other possible reason was that she wanted to continue ruling over Judah as the queen and did not want to face any resistance or opposition. Whatever the reason, if she had succeeded in killing all the members of the royal family, then there would not have been a descendant from the line of David on the throne of Judah. This would have put the Lord's covenant and promises to David at risk, for the lamp of David would have been extinguished.

To overrule the evil plan of Athaliah, God raised up another woman to act for good. Jehosheba, the daughter of Jehoram and sister of Ahaziah, saw the situation and took away her baby nephew, Joash, the son of Ahaziah, to a hiding place (11:2). The name "Joash" means "Yahweh gave," and because he was a descendant from the royal line of David, his name can be interpreted as a precious gift in the line of David to rule the nation of Judah in the future.

---

[1]. The title "high priest" came to gain more importance in the later period, perhaps during the period of the second Temple (after 515 BC). Although Jehoiada acted like a chief priest, he is not described as the high priest in verse 9, but only the "priest."

From the information in 2 Chronicles 22:11, Jehosheba is identified as the wife of the priest, Jehoiada. She hid the infant and his nurse in a bedroom in the priest's quarters in the precincts of the temple of the Lord for six years so he would be safe (11:3).

11:4–12 JOHOIADA MAKES JOASH KING

During the seventh year of Athaliah's reign, Jehoiada planned to make Joash king of Judah. His actions demonstrate the political role of the priests in Judah. The first section describes Johoiada's plan (11:4–8); the second section describes how he successfully implemented his plan (11:9–12). Because there was no king from the line of David for Judah, Jehoiada planned the public presentation and coronation ceremony for Joash very carefully. He gathered the commanders of the army, the royal bodyguards, and the escorts secretly in the temple of the Lord and had them make an oath that they would protect the boy when he was presented to the public (11:4a). The "Carites" were from the region of Caria in southwest Asia Minor. They were recruited as David's royal bodyguards, as they were known to be good at guarding royal families, and identified as the "Kerethites" in 2 Samuel 20:23.[2] After securing the confidence of the commanders, guards, and escorts, Jehoiada presented Joash to them (11:4b).

Next, Jehoiada commanded this company of commanders and guards, who normally worked on the Sabbath day, to work around the clock to guard the king's house. One third of this company was to guard the royal palace, another third was to guard the Sur Gate or Foundation Gate in the outer court of the temple, and the final third was to guard the gate behind the palace (11:5–6). In addition, the chief priest commanded the priests, who usually did not work on the Sabbath day, to remain on duty so that they could protect the temple (11:7). After stationing all the commanders and bodyguards around the palace and the companies of priests in and around the temple of the Lord, Jehoiada commanded everyone to take up weapons and kill anyone who came to attack the king's son (11:8). Jehoiada instructed all the priests, who were in the service of the temple, to work with the companies of military commanders and bodyguards (11:9). These verses give us some insight into how the priests were divided into groups so that some worked on the Sabbath and others had the Sabbath off from duty. Then Jehoiada brought out the spears and shields belonging to David and gave them to the commanders. The guards also had

---

2. Wiseman, *1 and 2 Kings*, 245.

weapons and were stationed around the king's son, protecting him from the south and north sides of the temple (11:10–11).

As Jehoiada planned the anointing ceremony, he followed a clear procedure. He presented Joash, the king's son, to the commanders and guards and put a crown on Joash's head. He then presented a copy of the covenant to the new king. This act was unique in Israel, and its purpose was to ensure that the king would keep the Sinai covenant and be accountable to the Lord, who had made him king. It bound the king to govern the nation in a responsible way, following Yahweh alone. The priest then anointed Joash with oil to indicate that the Lord chose him to be the king. At this, all the commanders, guards, escorts, and priests clapped their hands and shouted, "Long live the king," to confirm Joash as king (11:12). This enthronement ceremony included all three of the traditional requirements: the divine selection of the king, the anointing by the priest, and the acclamation by the public.

11:13–16 REACTION AND DEATH OF ATHALIAH

The sound of the trumpets and the shouts of the people reached Athaliah (11:13a), who did not expect a son of the king to be anointed as king while she was still on the throne. She came to the temple of the Lord and saw the new king standing between the two pillars near the entrance of the temple, according to the custom of presenting the king to the public after his anointing (11:13b). Upon seeing the king, she cried, "treason." Then Jehoiada ordered the commanders of the army to capture her, take her to the palace grounds, and put her to death by sword (11:15). They followed his command and put her to death (11:16).

11:17–21 COVENANT AND ENTHRONEMENT

Before placing Joash on the throne, Jehoiada conducted a covenantal ceremony, which had two aspects. First, he performed a covenantal ceremony between the Lord and the king, where the king vowed that he would be loyal to his God (11:17a). This may have included an offering of sacrifices in the temple. Second, he made a covenant between the king and the citizens to be mutually responsible and committed to each other (11:17b). The king was to lead the people in the ways of the Lord, and the people were to be loyal to their king. The purpose of making this covenant was to ensure that the people would follow Yahweh and the law of the Lord. This covenantal ceremony was a necessity because every king was required to enter into a covenantal relationship with Yahweh, regardless of his age. God wanted the entire nation, from kings to ordinary citizens, to commit to a covenantal relationship with the Lord and to worship Yahweh alone. The covenantal ceremony obviously impacted the people, as they immediately left the temple of the Lord to destroy the temple of Baal, all the altars and idols, and kill Mattan, the priest of Baal (11:18a).

Leaving some guards to protect the temple (11:18b), Jehoiada led the military commanders, the Carites, the royal guards, the people, and the king to the palace (11:19a). This procession from the temple to the palace may have been intended to announce to the rest of the public that a new king had been chosen and anointed. Once they arrived at the palace, the king was installed on the royal throne (11:19b). All the people rejoiced to see their new king, for he was from the family of David and had been chosen by God and anointed by the priest. The story about how the king had been hidden as a baby, nurtured by the priest, and made a king would have surprised and encouraged the people. The narrator concludes with a report that the land rejoiced because Athaliah had been put to death with a sword at the palace (11:20). Joash was only seven years old when he became king – the youngest ruler in the monarchical history of Judah (11:21).

From a practical perspective, such a young king would have been guided by the elders in the royal court, the commanders of the army, and the priests of the temple until he was old enough to make decisions on his own. Yet Joash rules as a child king. The crisis created by Athaliah, a ruthless woman, was countered by Jehosheba, the wife of Jehoiada. Whereas one wanted to destroy, the other wanted to save and ensure political stability. This crisis was fully resolved by the careful intervention of the priest.

2 KINGS 12:1–21
JOASH OVER JUDAH

The interaction between religion and politics in ancient Israel sheds light on the role of leadership in the development of the nation. In the previous chapter, religion is represented by the priest in the temple, who became involved in the affairs of the state by making a boy the king to save the nation from further political crisis. In 2 Kings 12, the king, who is representing the state, becomes involved in religious affairs to strengthen the worship of Yahweh. Because a cordial relationship existed between the religion and the state, the temple of Yahweh becomes the central focus, paving the way for further religious reforms. There are four main sections in this chapter: a summary evaluation of Joash's rule (12:1–3), the king's effort to repair the temple of the Lord (12:4–16), the attack by King Hazael of Aram (12:17–18), and the death of Joash (12:19–21).

12:1–3 EVALUATION OF JOASH'S RULE

The summary notes of a king usually appear at the end of his rule before introducing the successor. But with Joash, this evaluation is mentioned at the beginning of his rule (12:1–3).[1] The text mentions the identity of his mother, Zibiah from Beersheba, to show that there is a new queen mother in the place of Athaliah (12:1).

This summary evaluation makes two contrasting remarks about the reign of Joash. On the one hand, though Joash was young, he did very well in the sight of God because the priest, Jehoiada, guided him (12:2). On the other hand, he failed to remove the high places, and so the people continued to sacrifice and burn incense in different places all over the country (12:3). It seems that the government had no control over these localized places of worship, and so the worship could not be centralized in the temple in Jerusalem. This made it difficult to destroy idol worship in shrines, as they were scattered in different places throughout the nation.

---

[1]. The Hebrew variant of his name in fuller form is "Jehoash," as it appears in 2 Kings 12:2, 4, 6, and 7, and is used interchangeably in some books and translations of the Bible. The shorter form, Joash, is used more consistently to avoid confusion with Jehoash, the son of Jehoahaz, who was the king of northern Israel. Wiseman, *1 and 2 Kings*, 250.

12:4–16 EFFORT TO REPAIR THE TEMPLE

Although Joash was very young, he wanted to repair the temple of the Lord. Jehoiada and his wife, Jehosheba, may have influenced him to do this. Growing up in the vicinity of the temple, Joash would have witnessed its neglect since the days of Solomon, more than a hundred years earlier. Another possible motivation may have been reading the covenant that had been given to him during his enthronement ceremony. Whatever the reason, the king issued two orders to repair the temple.

12:4–8 First Order of the King

Joash ordered the priests to collect all the money that was brought as a sacred offering to the temple and account it with the treasurers of the temple (12:4a). These included the money collected in the census, the money received from personal vows, and the money brought voluntarily to the temple (12:4b). The money collected during the census refers to the amount that each male Israelite was required to pay as a prescribed ransom for his life (Exod 30:11–14). The list of offerings by individuals was the amount needed to redeem their vows (Lev 27:1–25). The freewill offerings had to be offered according to the rules, and extraordinary care had to be taken to avoid offering unacceptable sacrifices or offerings (Lev 22:18–29; Deut 16:10). Each priest was asked to determine the amount from one of the treasurers and then use it to repair the temple (12:5). Since this income was sacred, it was maintained by priests, who acted as treasurers, rather than political officials.

Unfortunately, the priests did not follow the king's instructions or carry out the repair work on the temple. Twenty-three years passed before King Joash decided to act (12:6). He summoned his old priest, Jehoiada, along with the other priests, to ask why they had not repaired the temple (12:7a). He then instructed them not to take any money for personal use but to set it aside for the repair of the temple (12:7b). The priests agreed that they would not collect any more money from the people to repair the temple, indicating the need for an alternative arrangement involving the king and the government (12:8).

12:9–16 Second Recommendation for the Priest

After listening to the king, Jehoiada introduced another plan to raise money for repairing the temple (12:9–10). He took a special chest and bored a hole in the lid and placed it on the right side of the altar so that the people entering the temple could see it and give their offerings for repairing the temple. The priests guarding the entrance collected the money and put it into the chest as a separate building fund. As the money accumulated in the chest, it was removed and counted by the high priest and the royal secretary in the government (12:10). Rather than going to the treasury, the income was used to purchase timber and dressed stones or paid directly to the carpenters, masons, builders, and stone cutters to repair the temple (12:11–12). This special collection was not used for making silver basins, wick trimmers, sprinkling bowls, trumpets, or the articles of gold for the temple (12:13). The reason for this restriction was to give priority to repairing the temple first (12:14).

The narrator says that the accounting for this special building fund was carried out in honesty (12:15). The joint supervision of the fund by a government official and a religious leader not only promoted accountability but also encouraged the worshipers to give more to the Lord's work because they could be confident that all their gifts were being used for the temple. The money from guilt offerings and sin offerings was not added to the building fund, but given as remuneration to support the priests (12:16).

Joash listened as he read the book of Deuteronomy, which challenged him to give importance to the temple and the worship of Yahweh. Joash could have used his power and authority to repair the temple and reform the religious situation of the country, but he sought a healthy cooperation between religious leaders and government officials to bring the reform. A leader needs to make a deliberate effort to follow the Lord fully. Though we cannot relate Joash's religious reform directly to our present context, we can say that any reforms have to be carried out with right motives and without pride.

12:17–18 ATTACK OF KING HAZAEL

While the repair work of the temple was taking place, the king of Aram went and attacked Gath and captured it (12:17a). After capturing Gath, Hazael prepared to attack Jerusalem (12:17b). Joash, instead of engaging in a battle he might lose, agreed to pay a heavy tribute to the kingdom of Aram. Joash gave to Hazael all the sacred objects that had been dedicated to the temple by his predecessors, along with the gifts that were dedicated to the temple, as well as all the gold in the treasury and palace (12:18). Joash's action provided temporary relief to the kingdom of Judah. While the chapter begins by focusing on the story of raising funds to repair the temple, it ends with an ironic contrast about removing the valuable silver and gold from the temple in order to pay a tribute to Hazael.

12:19–21 ASSASSINATION OF JOASH

The formula in the concluding section refers readers to the annals of the kings (12:19). In this history of the kings, some were killed in battle, others got wounded or died from an incurable sickness, but Joash's end was unexpected because his officials assassinated him at Beth Millo, which was situated on the road to Silla (12:20). The two officials who murdered the king were Jozabad, the son of Shimeath, and Jehozabad, the son of Shomer (12:21a). Joash died and was buried with his ancestors in the City of David. Amaziah, Joash's son, succeeded him as king (12:21b).

The story of Joash begins with Athaliah's ruthless killing of the royal family and ends with him being murdered by his servants. While Joash's life was saved from the sword during his childhood, it came to an end by the sword.

2 KINGS 13:1-25
REIGN OF JEHOAHAZ AND JEHOASH

The silence of Elisha's ministry is broken in 2 Kings 13, which narrates his final prophecy for Israel before his death (13:14–21). But this event is preceded and followed by stories of two other kings of Israel: Jehoahaz and Jehoash. This chapter has two main units: the rule of Jehoahaz (13:1–9) and the rule of Jehoash (13:10–25). But, the account of Jehoash's rule is divided into an evaluation of his rule (13:10–13), the final prophecy of Elisha (13:14–21), and Jehoash's defeat of the king of Aram (13:22–25).

13:1-9 JEHOAHAZ'S RULE

The narrator begins, "In the twenty-third year of Joash son of Ahaziah king of Judah, Jehoahaz son of Jehu became king of Israel in Samaria, and he reigned seventeen years" (13:1). This brief biodata for Jehoahaz includes the identity of his father, Jehu, and locates his rule during the twenty-third year of Joash, the king of Judah. The narrator mentions the name of the contemporary ruler in the neighboring kingdom of Judah, along with the year in which he came to the throne, to focus the history on the entire people of God so that they will not be delinked. The theological implication of this historical statement is that the people living in both Israel and Judah were one people of one God.

But Jehoahaz did evil in the eyes of the Lord by following the sins of Jeroboam in promoting the worship of the golden calf that represented Yahweh (13:2). So the anger of the Lord burned against Israel, and he kept them under the oppressive rule of Hazael, the king of Aram or Syria and Ben-Hadad III (13:3).

The ongoing oppression and suffering under Aram led Jehoahaz to seek the Lord (13:4). Through his prayers, he was asking the Lord to intervene and provide relief for the nation from the hands of their enemies. The Lord understood the situation, heard the king's genuine seeking, and listened to his prayers. He provided a deliverer, who goes unnamed, and the people lived in "their own homes as they had before" (13:5). But the people did not turn away from their sins (13:6a). They continued to worship before the Asherah poles (13:6b). Because they continuously followed the worship of Baal and the Asherah poles, the Lord abandoned them into the hands of the king of

Aram. The army of Aram destroyed the entire army of Jehoahaz, leaving only fifty horsemen, ten chariots, and ten thousand soldiers (13:7).

The other achievements of Jehoahaz were written in the book of the annals of the kings of Israel (13:8). When his time came, Jehoahaz died and was buried at Samaria with his ancestors (13:9a). Jehoash, his son, succeeded him as the next king (13:9b).

13:10–25 JEHOASH'S RULE

Jehoash's rule has the final prophesy of Elisha. His rule is divided into three sections: a summary statement of his rule (13:10–13), a final prophesy of Elisha (13:14–21), and the end of Hazael, king of Aram, in relationship to Jehoash (13:22–25).

13:10–13 Summary Statement of Jehoash's Rule

Jehoash, son of Jehoahaz, became king of Israel in the thirty-seventh year of Joash's rule of Judah (13:10a). He ruled Israel for sixteen years (13:10b). As did the many kings of Israel, Jehoash did evil in the sight of the Lord by following the sins of Jeroboam (13:11). The other events of his reign were written in the annals of the kings of Israel, including his war against Amaziah, the king of Judah (13:12). When the time came, Jehoash died and was buried with the other kings of Israel in Samaria (13:13). Jeroboam II succeeded Jehoash as the king of Israel.

13:14–21 Elisha's Final Prophecy

The narrator refers to a former interaction between Jehoash and Elisha before Elisha's death (13:14–21). Elisha was suffering from an unnamed illness that eventually caused his death (13:14a). While he was suffering, Jehoash went to see the prophet and wept over him (13:14b). The king wept over Elisha's illness, calling him, "My father! my father!" to convey that he was a great leader for the entire nation and a true prophet of the God of Israel. Jehoash addressed Elisha as "the chariots and horseman of Israel," echoing the words that Elisha used to address his mentor, Elijah (2 Kgs 2:12).

The prophet woke up and used a symbolic action to communicate the word of the Lord. He asked the king to take a bow and some arrows, and the king obeyed (13:15). He asked him to take the bow in his hand, and the king obeyed (15:16). Then he asked him to open the window in the eastern direction and shoot an arrow, and the king obeyed (13:17a). Then Elisha said, "The Lord's arrow of victory, the arrow of victory over Aram!" which meant that he would defeat the Arameans completely (13:17b). The king might have wondered if the army of Aram would be destroyed forever, or if they would come again against Israel. So Elisha told the king to take the arrows from his quiver and strike the ground (13:18a). The king struck it three times and stopped (13:18b). Elisha became angry that the king did not strike the ground five or six times because if he had, he would have destroyed the Arameans completely (13:19a). But since he struck only three times, he would defeat them only three times (13:19b). This prophecy nevertheless gave the king hope of defeating Hazael, the king of Aram.

Soon after saying this, Elisha died (13:20). Even during the last stage of his life, the man of God served the nation. Moreover, his powerful ministry continued even beyond his death. When some Israelites were carrying a dead man to be buried, they saw Moabite raiders coming to attack the people and plunder the harvest, something that happened every spring (13:20). Fearing the Moabites, the men threw the dead body into the tomb of Elisha and fled. Tombs in ancient Israel were dug out of rocks, and people also used natural caves to bury the dead (Gen 23:5). When the dead body of this man touched the bones of Elisha in the cave, the man miraculously came to life and stood on his feet (13:21). Yahweh wanted to remind the Israelites that he had the power to raise a man from death, and he gave this power to the prophet Elisha during his lifetime (4:32–37). However, this miracle can be repeated even after Elisha's death. God's power can be manifested through his servants continuously on many different occasions. The great prophets Elijah and Elisha will be remembered forever as protectors and defenders of the nation of Israel, prophets who manifested the power of God.

13:22–25 Jehoash Defeats the Army of Aram

The narrator returns to Jehoash's reign and concludes with positive notes (13:22–25). King Hazael of Aram continued his fight with the Israelites even during the reign of Jehoash, the son of Jehoahaz (13:22). But the Lord was gracious to the Israelites because of his covenant with Abraham, Isaac, and Jacob and was unwilling to banish them from his presence (13:23). So he remained faithful to them.

In the mean time, Hazael, king of Aram, died and Ben-Hadad III succeeded him as king (13:24). The Lord's favor continued to be with Jehoash. After attacking the army of Syria three different times, he successfully recaptured all the towns that had been lost to Hazael during his father's rule (13:25). This outcome indicates the fulfillment of Elisha's prophecy to Jehoash, once again proving the credibility of the genuine ministry of this servant of Yahweh.

2 KINGS 14:1–29

AMAZIAH'S RULE

What was mentioned as a brief note about the war between Jehoash and Amaziah in the previous chapter (13:12) is narrated in detail in chapter 14, explaining the reason for this civil war. This chapter can be divided into three sections: Amaziah's defeat of the Edomites (14:1–7), the civil war with northern Israel (14:8–14), and an account of Amaziah's tragic death (14:17–22). Woven in between Amaziah's story are the death of Jehoash, king of Israel (14:15–16) and the rule of Israel under Jeroboam II (14:23–29).

14:1–7 AMAZIAH'S RULE IN JUDAH

Amaziah, the son of Joash, became king of Judah at the age of twenty-five and ruled the nation for twenty-nine years (14:1–2a). His mother, Jehoaddan (meaning, "Yahweh has given delight"), was a native of Jerusalem and became the queen mother (14:2b). Amaziah followed the Lord and did what was right in the sight of God (14:3a). But, he did not remove the high places, and so the people continued to offer sacrifices to the idols (14:3b–4). In evaluating his actions, the narrator compares Amaziah to David, who set the bar for other kings to follow.

When the kingdom was firmly in his hands, Amaziah took to avenge the blood of his father (12:20–21) and killed those who had conspired against his father, Joash (14:5). Unlike Jehu, Amaziah only murdered the officials who murdered his father, not their children (14:6a). In this, Amaziah followed the law of Moses that says that the parents are not to be put to death for the sins of their children, and the innocent children are not to be put to death for the sins of their parents (14:6b). Each person is responsible for his or her own sins (Deut 24:16). This law protects children because they are powerless, vulnerable, and can be easily abused or killed. Some of the kings and military commanders in many countries have failed to follow this principle and have massacred many children.

After this, Amaziah defeated the Edomites. While the text does not give a specific reason for the conflict, there was constant hostility between Edom and Judah. The Edomites had been attacking Judah ever since David had controlled them (2 Sam 8:13–14). Amaziah's victory helps resolve the long standing conflict between Judah and Edom during the time of Solomon (1 Kgs 11:14–22) and Jehoram (2 Kgs 8:20–22). The place where Amaziah defeated ten thousand Edomites was called the Valley of Salt, which was a perennial battlefield south of the Dead Sea. Amaziah renamed the town of Sela, an important city in Edom, as Joktheel to show his control over Edom (2 Kgs 14:7).

14:8–14 CIVIL WAR IN ISRAEL

Winning a victory over another nation can make a king proud and ambitious for further offensive action to expand his territory. Amaziah sent messengers to Jehoash, the king of Israel, with a challenge: "Come, let us look one another in the face" (14:8). Sensing that Amaziah was trying to intimidate northern Israel because he had recently won a battle against Edom, Jehoash replied to him harshly. Using a parable, he insulted Amaziah's inability to withstand his wrath (14:9). A thistle in Lebanon challenges a cedar in Lebanon by asking the cedar to give his daughter to the son of the thistle. These two plants are in different categories, and such an alliance is not possible. The cedar grows taller and stronger than the thistle, making it particularly useful for timber and construction work. While the wind can trample and beat down the thistle, it cannot shake the cedar. Jehoash was saying that Israel was the cedar, and Judah was the thorny thistle. Thus Judah cannot stand against the might of Israel if the wind of war blows. Jehoash sent this parable as a warning to Amaziah (14:9). Jehoash then makes an assessment about Amaziah's behavior, saying that he has become proud and arrogant after winning the battle against Edom; he should not glorify himself, but be content so that he would not invite trouble and cause the downfall of Judah (14:10). Amaziah was not willing to listen to Jehoash, and so Jehoash attacked Judah at Beth Shemesh, which lies about thirty-two kilometers west of Jerusalem (14:11). Israel defeated Judah, and Jehoash took Amaziah and his men as captives (14:12–13a).

In addition to defeating Judah, Jehoash went up to Jerusalem and destroyed one section of the wall, about the length of four hundred cubits (approximately 180 meters), from Ephraim Gate to the Corner Gate (14:13b). He plundered gold and silver from the temple of the Lord and transported them to Samaria along with all the captives of Judah (14:14).

14:15–16 JEHOASH'S DEATH

The story of Amaziah's rule over Judah is interrupted by a brief account of the death of Jehoash, king of Israel (14:15–16). The usual formula refers to Jehoash's achievements in the annals of the kings, highlighting the civil war against Amaziah (14:15). Jehoash rested with his ancestors and was buried in Samaria, and his son, Jeroboam II, succeeded him as king of Israel (14:16).

14:17–22 AMAZIAH'S DEATH

Amaziah continues to live for fifteen years after the death of Jehoash, most likely as an ordinary person, not a king (14:17). The annals of the kings should have recorded his status and rule after the defeat (14:18). His life in those fifteen years would have been difficult due to his defeat, the loss of gold and silver, and the destruction of the wall of Jerusalem. Furthermore, he lost his reputation and became a target for his enemies (14:19). When some of his officials conspired against him, he fled to Lachish, but they killed him there and brought his body back to Jerusalem to be buried with his ancestors (14:20). Azariah (also known as Uzziah), the son of Amaziah, was made the king of Judah when he was sixteen years old, after the sudden death of his father (14:21). He rebuilt Elath, northwest of the Gulf of Aqaba, and restored it to Judah (14:22).

14:23–29 JEROBOAM'S RULE

To avoid confusing an earlier Jeroboam of Israel, the contemporary of Rehoboam of Judah, with this Jeroboam, successor of Jehoash, commentators refer to him as Jeroboam II. Though he reigned over Israel for forty-one years (793–753 BC),[1] the narrator gives a very brief account of his rule. The familiar formula is used to present an evaluation of his rule (14:23). Amaziah was ruling Judah when Jeroboam II became king; and he did evil in the sight of God, following the sins of his ancestor, Jeroboam I, who is identified in the text as the "son of Nebat" (14:24). This sin caused Israel to continue to worship the idols in the high places.

On the other hand, Jeroboam II restored the boundaries of Israel from Lebo Hamath to the Sea of the Arabah (14:25a). Lebo Hamath marks the ideal northern boundary of Israel with the kingdom of Hamath and the region touching the valley and mountain ranges of Lebanon (Num 13:21; 1 Kgs 8:65). The Sea of Arabah could be the brook or the Valley of Salt in the south. It seems that the king of Judah regained control of the region of the northern border as well as the southern border touching Moab (see Amos 6:13–14). Jeroboam II's success is credited to the fulfillment of the word of God, as prophesied by Jonah, the son of Amittai (14:25b). Jonah was from

---

1. SABC suggests that he ruled for thirty-eight years. *South Asia Bible Commentary*, 476.

Gath Hepher, in the territory of Zebulun (Josh 19:13), which was north of Nazareth. His ministry to Nineveh is known from the book of Jonah.

Jeroboam II was a non-benevolent ruler and as such everyone in Israel, slave or free, suffered and none dared help them. So the Lord God took their case (14:26). Only because of his earlier promise to not blot out the name of David from Israel, he remained faithful to Jeroboam II, even though he was not a good king (14:27). The chapter concludes with the familiar pattern, referencing the annals of the kings for further details about the achievements of Jeroboam II, while highlighting his military achievements in recovering Damascus, which indicates the northern border of Israel, and Hamath, a town in the south (14:28). The region between the northern border to the southern region means that the restoration was useful for both Israel and Judah. After the death and burial of Jeroboam II, his son, Zechariah, succeeded him to the throne (14:29).

2 KINGS 15:1–38

SEVEN KINGS OF ISRAEL AND JUDAH

2 Kings 15 continues to recount the history of the monarchical period in Israel and Judah, giving a brief report about two kings of Judah and five kings of Israel. The stories about the five kings of Israel (Zechariah, Shallum, Menahem, Pekahiah, and Pekah) are embedded between the two stories about the kings of Judah (Azariah and Jotham). The political instability in Israel during this period is revealed through ongoing internal strife and multiple conspiracies and assassinations. The economic and political situations of the nation was further destabilized by attacks from Assyria, whose leaders demanded tributes from the kings of Israel. The northern kingdom was on the verge of collapse, and the southern kingdom was going to fall soon as well. The stories of these kings are presented with the usual formula, including the biodata, a list of key achievements, a reference to annals of the kings, an account of death, and the name of the successor.

15:1–7 AZARIAH'S RULE IN JUDAH

After Amaziah was assassinated, his son, Azariah, was made king of Judah. At this time, Jeroboam II was ruling the northern Israel (15:1). Azariah was only sixteen years old when he began to rule, and he ruled Judah for fifty-two years; his mother, Jekoliah, was from Jerusalem (15:2). The name Azariah means "my help is Yahweh." Azariah's other name, Uzziah ("my strength is Yahweh"), is used frequently in this chapter (2 Kgs 15:13, 30, 32, 34) as well as several prophetic books (Isa 1:1; 6:1; 7:1; Hos 1:1; Amos 1:1; Zech 14:5). Azariah did what was right in the eyes of the Lord, just as his father, Amaziah, had done (15:3). Since he didn't remove the high places, the people continued to offer sacrifices and burn incense there (15:4).

Unfortunately, Azariah was afflicted with leprosy, which forced him to live in a separate house than the palace (15:5a). The narrator of Chronicles says that his leprosy was a punishment from the Lord for unlawfully usurping the priestly function of burning incense on the altar of the temple (2 Chr 26:16–21). So, Azariah's son Jotham was in charge of the palace and governed the people (15:5b).

As with other kings, Azariah's rule and all that he accomplished were written in the annals of the kings of Judah (15:6). He then "rested with his ancestors," meaning he died (15:7). He was buried in the city of David. Jotham succeeded Azariah to the throne after he had already led the nation during the period of his father's leprosy. Throughout this time, he likely received counsel and guidance from his father about how to rule the nation.

15:8–12 ZECHARIAH'S RULE IN ISRAEL

In the meantime, Zechariah, a son of Jeroboam II, became king of Israel (15:8a). He only ruled for six months (15:8b). Like many of his predecessors in Israel, he did evil in the eyes of the Lord and followed the sin of allowing the people to worship idols (15:9). The reference to the "sins of Jeroboam" recalls how Jeroboam I set up images of golden calves in Bethel and Dan and then addressed them as the gods of the Israelites, who had brought them out of Egypt (1 Kgs 12:28–30). This is a formula that is used to indicate the failure of the kings to follow the law of Moses by worshiping Yahweh alone and not any images or idols.

Shallum, the son of Jabesh, conspired against Zechariah, assassinated him in public, and became king (15:10). The text does not mention the political or religious reason for the assassination, but the death of Zechariah marks the end of Jehu's dynasty. Four generations of Jehu's descendants ruled Israel – Jehoahaz, Jehoash (Joash), Jeroboam II, and Zechariah – in accordance with the word of the Lord spoken to Jehu that his descendants would sit on the throne of Israel to the fourth generation (2 Kgs 10:28–31). The rule of Jehu began with the murder of the royal family of Ahab and Jezebel and ended with the violent assassination of Zechariah.

15:13–16 SHALLUM'S RULE IN ISRAEL

Shallum's background is not known, except for the name of his father, Jabesh (15:13a). He could have been a leader of a rebel group inside Zechariah's administration, who turned against Zechariah and assassinated him. He only ruled Israel for one month and reaped the same violence that he sowed (15:13b).

Menahem son of Gadi went from Tirzah, assassinated Shallum, and became king (15:14). The summary of Shallum's reign was recorded in the annals of the kings of Israel (15:15).

2 KINGS 15:1–38

15:17–22 MENAHEM'S RULE IN ISRAEL

Menahem succeeded Shallum. The narrator, however, begins with stating Menahem's violent lifestyle. The phrase "at that time" refers to the period of time when Menahem attacked Samaria (15:16a). On his way from Tirzah to Samaria, he attacked Tiphsah and the inhabitants of that city and the surrounding areas because they refused to open the gates so that he could pass through and take control of the city (15:16b).[1] Menahem attacked this city as a terrorist tactic to suppress the inhabitants' support of Shallum and their opposition to Menahem's ambitions to become the king of Israel. His brutality was unbearable, as the text says that he ripped open all the pregnant women (15:16). Although the Hebrew verbs used for "*opening* the gate" and "*ripping open* the womb" are different, we can infer that their refusal to open the gate of the city resulted in the consequence of his forces ripping open all the pregnant women.[2]

The name of Menahem's father is identified as Gadi (meaning "my luck"), which does not need to be understood as Gad or the tribe of Gad (15:17a). Menahem came to power during the rule of Azariah in Judah and ruled Israel for ten years (15:17b). His sin was following the ways of Jeroboam and doing evil in the sight of Yahweh, including leading Israel to commit idolatry (15:18). As a consequence, he gave up Israel's freedom to the king of Assyria, who attacked northern Israel and took control of it.

Pul, the king of Assyria, was also known as Tiglath-Pileser III (745–727 BC), who became powerful and conducted a series of attacks in the nearby region (15:19). According to the Assyrian policy, he left the countries he conquered in the hands of his army, but he allowed the defeated nations to continue under their own local kings. The defeated kings were required to pay heavy tributes to the king of Assyria. He also appointed Assyrian officials to watch over these nations, and if there were any signs of rebellion against Assyria, then the Assyrian army would invade the country again and destroy it.

Menahem had to pay a thousand talents of silver (approximately thirty-four metric tons) to the Assyrian king to gain his support and continue as

---

1. There is a difference of opinion about the identity and location of the city of Tiphsah. Based on the meaning of the Assyrian word "*tipsah*" (meaning "fording place"), some identify the location of this city at the border of Solomon's kingdom in the northeast (1 Kgs 4:24). But, there was no evidence that Solomon attacked the region in the northeast bordering with Assyria. Some other scholars identify this city as Tappuah on the border of Ephraim (Josh 17:8). For a full discussion, see Wiseman, *1 and 2 Kings*, 269.
2. This brutal violence was influenced by the pagan culture of Aram, as pointed out by Elisha (2 Kgs 8:12). Amos (1:13) and Hosea (13:8) spoke against such violence.

the king of Israel (15:18). To raise this amount, Menahem had to extract money from his people through various ways. Every wealthy person of Israel had to pay fifty shekels of silver (approximately 575 grams) to meet the requirement of the king of Assyria (15:20). Although Pul withdrew from the land of Israel, he squeezed the economy of the nation. By imposing his authority over the nation, he controlled Menahem's power and freedom.

The rising power of Assyria in the region started signaling the slow collapse of the kingdom of Israel. Eventually, it would overpower northern Israel and inflict great harm to southern Judah.

The narrator notes how the annals of the kings recorded the details of the activities of Menahem (15:21). After ruling from Samaria for ten years, Menahem died. His son, Pekahiah, succeeded him to the throne (15:22).

15:23–26 PEKAHIAH'S RULE IN ISRAEL

Pekahiah became the king of Israel when Azariah king of Judah was in his fiftieth year of rule (15:23a). He ruled only for two years (15:23b). Although his name meant, "Yahweh has opened the eyes," he did evil and followed the ways of Jeroboam and led the people to commit idolatry (15:24).

Pekah, one of his chief officers, conspired against the king. With the help of fifty Gileadites, he entered the citadel of the royal palace at Samaria and killed King Pekahiah, Argob, and Arieh (15:25a). "Argob" and "Arieh" may have been other chief officers or king's guards. Some suggest that they were protective statues, such as a lion or eagle, which were positioned at the gate to the castle.[3] After killing the king, he established himself as the new king (15:25b). As usual, the other deeds of Pekahiah's rule were written in the book of the annals of the kings of Israel (15:26).

15:27–31 PEKAH'S RULE IN ISRAEL

Pekah became king of Israel during the last period of Azariah's rule, the fifty-second year of his reign (15:27a). Pekah's father was Remaliah. Pekah ruled Israel for twenty years (15:27b).[4] Pekah also did evil in the eyes of the Lord and caused Israel to sin by following Baal (15:28).

At this time, Tiglath-Pileser, the king of Assyria, attacked Israel once again and captured Ijon, Abel Beth Maakah, Janoah, Kedesh, and Hazor (15:29a). These were strategic locations that enabled Assyria to control all of northern

---

3. Wiseman, *1 and 2 Kings*, 271.
4. Wiseman discusses the problem of the duration of his rule. Wiseman, *1 and 2 Kings*, 273.

Israel. Tiglath-Pileser also took Gilead in the Transjordan region and Galilee in the north as well as the region of Naphtali, thereby surrounding the northern kingdom and deported people from these regions to Assyria (15:29b).

Hoshea, the son of Elah, conspired against Pekah, killed him, and became king of Israel during the twentieth year of Jotham's reign (15:30). Pekah reaped the same violence that he had sown for Pekahiah. The political stability in the northern kingdom was deteriorating because the king and people were sinning against Yahweh. The other deeds of Pekah's reign were written in the annals of the kings of Israel (15:31).

15:32–38 JOTHAM'S RULE IN JUDAH

Jotham, the son of Uzziah (Azariah), began to reign over Judah during the seventeenth year of Pekah's reign in Israel (15:32). He was twenty-five years old when he became king, and he ruled Judah for sixteen years (15:33). Before becoming the king of Judah, he assisted his father after the king was afflicted with leprosy (15:5). Jerusha, his mother (2 Chr 27:1), was a daughter of Zadok, from a priestly family in Jerusalem (15:33). Jotham did what was right in the eyes of the Lord just as his father Uzziah had done (15:34). Unfortunately, he didn't remove the high places of idol worship and the people continued to offer sacrifices and burn incense there (15:35a). Jotham rebuilt the upper gate of the temple of the Lord. The rest of Jotham's achievements were recorded (15:36). While he was ruling, the Lord began to send Rezin king of Aram and Pekah son of Remaliah against Judah, as a warning of their persistent idolatry (15:37).[5] Before he can reform the nation, Jotham died and was buried with his ancestors in the city of David. His son, Ahaz, succeeded him to the throne (15:38).

---

5. Rezin may have been the last king of Aram mentioned in the annals of Assyria (Isa 7:1–8; 8:6; 9:11). Historians call this war against Judah the "Syro-Ephraimite war" (735–732 BC).

2 KINGS 16:1–20
AHAZ, KING OF JUDAH

As the political instability in Israel and Judah continued, the nearby nations noticed the weakening power of these two kingdoms. To the north, Israel was threatened by the power of Aram. Further northeast, the power of Assyria was growing stronger and watching for a chance to attack both Judah and Israel as well as Aram. Continuous assassinations, frequent changes in kingship, and the heavy tributes paid to Aram and Assyria brought both the northern and southern kingdoms to the verge of collapse. The story of Ahaz's rule (735–720 BC) begins with an introduction (16:1–4) and ends with a closing summary (16:19–20). The rest of the chapter narrates the activities in his rule according to the following three parts: the Syro-Ephraimite war and Ahaz's appeal to Assyria for help (16:5–9), his order to construct a new altar in the temple (16:10–16), and the changes he made in the temple structure (16:17–18). The story of Ahaz's rule does not give any hope to the reader that the southern kingdom will revive and become stronger because Ahaz did not follow the Lord. Moreover, he meddled with the worship and began to offer sacrifices himself, taking on the role of a priest.

16:1–4 EVALUATION OF AHAZ'S RULE

Ahaz son of Joram became the king of Judah during the seventeenth year of Pekah's rule (16:1). He was twenty years old when he became king and ruled for sixteen years (16:2a). He did not do well in the eyes of the Lord, as did David his father (16:2b).

Ahaz followed the kings of Israel who did evil and caused the people to commit sin by worshiping other gods; he even sacrificed his own son in the fire, a detestable practice in the eyes of the Lord, a common practice among other nations (16:3). He also offered sacrifices and incense at high places and under every spreading tree – offerings to other gods and goddesses such as Baal and Asthoreth (16:4).

In ancient Israel, the king was supposed to be the guardian of the faith, and Ahaz should have removed the altars in the high places and banned the sexual immorality under the trees. Instead, he offered his own son as a sacrifice, possibly to Molech, who was also known as Milcom in some places in Canaan and the Transjordan region. Molech can be compared to the Indian goddess, Kali, who is a bloodthirsty deity. During the early period in the West Bengal region of India, people sacrificed their children to Kali to receive rain, win a war, please the angry deity, or fulfill their vows.[1] The God of Israel condemned human sacrifices, and the law banned this practice in Israel (Lev 18:21; Deut 12:1). Ahaz practiced these detestable practices during his rule and led the nation to follow after other gods and goddesses.

16:5–9 THE SYRO-EPHRAIMITE WAR

After introducing the reign of Ahaz, the narrator tells us that Rezin, the king of Aram, and Pekah, the king of Israel, joined together to attack Jerusalem and besiege Ahaz (16:5a). This may have taken place between 735–732 BC. The motive may have been to force Ahaz to join their alliance in case Tiglath-Pileser, the king of Assyria, attacked them. In spite of their alliance, Israel and Aram could not overpower Ahaz and take control of Judah (16:5b). When an Israelite king disobeys the law of Yahweh, the Lord raises up powers from outside Israel to pressure the king to repent. Yet in spite of Ahaz's disobedience to the law, the prophet Isaiah tells us that God intervened on behalf of Ahaz and the people of Judah (Isa 7:2), because the God of Israel did not like the evil plan of Aram and Israel coming together to depose Ahaz and make Tabeel the king over Judah (Isa 7:6–7).

Facing defeat from Ahaz, King Rezin focused on recovering Elath for Aram by driving out the people of Judah (16:6). Elath was a city in Edom on the shore of the Red Sea, where Solomon had established shipping connections for trade (1 Kgs 9:26). Later Edomites moved into Elath and stayed until the time of the composition of this book.

Ahaz, in the meantime, sent messengers to Tiglath-Pileser king of Assyria expressing his desire to remain as a servant or vassal king and invited him to help him keep at bay the king of Aram and the king of Israel (16:7). To receive help from the king of Assyria, Ahaz had to pay heavy tributes; he took the silver and gold in the temple of the Lord and the royal palace and sent payments to Tiglath-Pileser (16:8). After receiving these gifts, Assyria attacked Damascus, the capital of Aram, captured it, deported the inhabitants to Kir, and killed

---

1. Under the British rule, Christian missionaries stopped the practice of child sacrifice and *sati*. Elizabeth Giri, "Child Sacrifices in India: A Christian Response," *Children at Risk*, 133–147.

Rezin (16:9). This attack and deportation are fulfillment of the prophecy of the Lord spoken through the prophet Amos (Amos 1:5).

16:10–16 A NEW ALTAR

After capturing Damascus and deporting the people of Aram to Assyria, Ahaz went to Damascus to meet Tiglath-Pileser in person to strengthen his ties with him (16:10a). There, Ahaz was attracted by an altar that the Arameans had built for their worship and sacrifices, and so he sent a sketch of the altar with detailed plans for its construction to Uriah, the priest in Jerusalem (16:10b). For a king who had already been promoting worship in the high places along with the pagan customs of the Canaanites, adding one more altar of another deity in Jerusalem did not seem to be a sin.

Before King Ahaz returned to Jerusalem, Uriah completed the construction of this altar (16:11). The priest should have resisted the king's order and refused to allow any altar connected to idol worship and the values of the kingdom of Aram inside the temple of the Lord. When Ahaz arrived in Jerusalem, he approached the new pagan altar in the temple and presented a burnt offering, a grain offering, and poured out his drink offering for pagan deity (16:12–13a). Moreover, he splashed the blood of his fellowship or communion offering against the altar, implying his due recognition and justification of the new altar (16:13b). By taking on the role of a priest in dedicating the pagan altar and presenting his offerings and sacrifices on it, he demonstrated that he had no regard for the law of God or the temple of the Lord. He had absolutely no fear of Yahweh.

In addition to setting up this new altar in the temple of the Lord, Ahaz changed the location of the original bronze altar that had been built by Solomon (16:14a). He placed it on the north side of the new altar (16:14b). By changing the original position of the bronze altar that had been dedicated during the reign of Solomon, Ahaz gave greater importance to the pagan altar.

Next, the king gave orders to Uriah about how these two altars were to be used. Ahaz ordered the priest to use the new altar to offer three categories of sacrifices: first, the burnt offering in the morning and grain offering in the evening; second, the king's burnt offering and grain offering; third, the people's burnt offering, grain offering, and drink offering (16:15a). Ahaz also ordered the priest to splash the blood of all the burnt offerings and sacrifices against the new altar rather than the old bronze altar in order to give prominence to the worship of pagan gods above the worship of Yahweh (16:15b). By issuing these orders, Ahaz communicated that instead of listening to the instruction of the Lord regarding the temple, worship, and sacrifices, the religion of southern Israel would now be controlled by the political leader of the nation. Rather than objecting to these orders from the king, Uriah obeyed them (2 Kgs 16:16). In this way, Ahaz encouraged the pagan religion to regain prominence in the towns of Judah (2 Chr 28:25). However, he did not throw out the old bronze altar, but used it for getting guidance. Ahaz may have remembered the story about the glory of the Lord abiding in the old altar and how God had promised to keep his presence in the temple. Because Ahaz constructed a pagan altar, relocated the original altar, and promoted new rituals, the Lord became dissatisfied with Ahaz (2 Chr 28:25).

16:17–18 CHANGES IN THE STRUCTURE OF THE TEMPLE

Ahaz then enacted changes in the structure of the temple. Jehoiada, the chief priest under King Joash, had already done some repair work of the temple, but he did not change the basic layout or structure of the temple that Solomon built (2 Kgs 12:1–16). Ahaz, however, cut off the side panels, removed the basins from the moveable stands, removed the sea from the bronze bulls, and set it on a stone base (16:17). He also took away the Sabbath canopy and removed the royal entryway outside the temple of the Lord in deference to the king of Assyria (16:18).[2] This action implies that the king of Assyria was now in control, and Ahaz no longer had power and authority in Judah.

It is ironic to note how Ahaz reduced the importance of worshiping Yahweh and promoted the worship of pagan gods in Judah, while the king of Assyria reduced the importance of Ahaz and promoted his own importance. Because Ahaz failed to follow the law of Deuteronomy, he lost his power and authority over the kingdom of Judah. This story raises an important theological issue for Christian leaders today about the danger of compromising with people of other faiths in religious matters or with the leaders of foreign nations in political matters for the sake of survival. Christian leaders who compromise their faith in the Lord Jesus Christ or who fail to live according to the word of God by obeying the government or an institution or organization to avoid persecution or receive benefits will not please God or people. If good and strong leadership is going to be raised for future generations, we need to develop Christian leaders who believe and obey the Lord Jesus Christ alone.

---

2. Hobbs points out that some of the structures and canopies are moved to another location because of the fear that they would offend the Assyrian king. Hobbs, *2 Kings*, 218.

16:19–20 DEATH OF AHAZ AND SUCCESSOR

According to the familiar pattern, the narrator refers readers to the annals of the kings for the rest of the events during Ahaz's reign (16:19). Like his predecessors, he rested with his ancestors and was buried in the city of David. Hezekiah, his son, succeeded him to the throne, according to the hereditary dynasty system in Judah (16:20).

2 KINGS 17:1–41
COLLAPSE OF ISRAEL

2 Kings 17 outlines the end of the monarchical period of the northern kingdom of Israel. It happened during the reign of Hoshea, the last king of Israel (728–722 BC). The chapter begins with a summary evaluation of Hoshea's rule (17:1–2), which is followed by a narration of Assyria's attack and capture of Samaria (17:3–6), the reason for Israel's collapse and exile (17:7–23), and the resettlement of northern Israel with foreign people of other faiths (17:24–41). The chapter focuses on the people of Israel, recounting their sins and deportation to Assyria. The narrative weaves together the historical tradition of God's promises to his people, the people's covenantal relationship with Yahweh, the exodus, the sending of priests and prophets to teach the people of Israel to obey the law, and the driving out of the Canaanites from their land so that the Israelites could receive the gift of a land of their own. The theme of infidelity binds all the units together.

17:1–2 HOSHEA'S RULE IN ISRAEL

Hoshea means "salvation" in Hebrew. Hoshea the son of Elah became king of Israel in Samaria during the twelfth year of Ahaz king of Judah (17:1a). He ruled as king for nine years (17:2). He did evil in the eyes of the Lord, but when compared with other kings (e.g. Jeroboam I, Ahab), he did less evil (17:2). He came to the throne by conspiring against Pekah and then assassinating him (15:30). He ruled over Israel for only nine years because of the attack from Assyria.

17:3–6 ASSYRIA'S ATTACK AND CAPTURE OF SAMARIA

Soon after Hoshea began his reign, the ruler of Assyria threatened him, and so Hoshea became a vassal of Shalmaneser V, ca. 726–722 BC (17:3). He had succeeded Tiglath-Pileser as the king of Assyria. Shalmaneser discovered that Hoshea was not paying the required tribute and was seeking the help of So king of Egypt; so he treated him as a traitor (17:4). Not paying the required tribute and working out a secret alliance with Egypt were regarded as acts of rebellion against the king of Assyria. Therefore, Shalmaneser attacked Samaria, the capital of Israel, and besieged it for three years (17:5). This long siege placed Hoshea in a tight corner, struggling to survive and save the people of Israel.

Then, in the ninth year of Hoshea's rule (ca. 724 BC), Shalmaneser captured Samaria, took the Israelites as captives, and deported them to Assyria, where he settled them in Halah and Habor on the Gozan River and in the towns of the Medes (17:6).

17:7–23 ISRAEL'S COLLAPSE AND EXILE

The phrase, "all this took place because the Israelites had sinned against the LORD" (17:7), connects this main section with the previous section about Assyria's attack and capture of Samaria. This phrase also makes it clear that all the Israelites are responsible for the northern kingdom's collapse, not just one or two individuals. This section communicates a firm justification for their punishment of losing the land and going into exile.

17:7–13 Sins of the Israelites

Verses 7–13 list the collective sins of Israel, while naming the faithful deeds that God accomplished for them throughout their history as a people. The Lord Yahweh delivered the Israelites from the oppression and bondage of Pharaoh king of Egypt when they cried because of their suffering and oppression (17:7). Ironically, Hoshea sought help from Egypt, who had earlier oppressed the ancestors of Israel (17:4), an act that led to a subsequent period of oppression from Assyria. Moreover, God drove the Canaanites from their land so that the Israelites could have a land of their own to settle and govern. In spite of these faithful actions of Yahweh, the Israelites worshiped other gods and followed the practices of other nations (17:8).

They did not reject the idolatrous practices and worship of foreign gods that the kings introduced. Both the kings and the people were responsible for this sin. They sinned secretly against the Lord, "from the watchtower to fortified city" they built for themselves high places to worship foreign gods, in every town (17:9). Moreover, they set up sacred stones and Asherah poles in every high place and under all the trees (17:10). They burnt incense, just as other nations had done; God had driven them out to stop the Israelites from following their ways (17:11). The Hindus burn incense during their worship in temples or for idols under trees along roadsides and villages to please and venerate the deities.

The people set up idols for themselves (17:12), which was clearly against the law that said, "You shall not do this" (Exod 20:4–7). God had raised up prophets and seers in each generation to warn both the kingdom of Israel and the kingdom of Judah, saying, "Turn from your evil ways" and to observe God's commandments and decrees (17:13), and they ignored those exhortations. Because of these God was handing them over to Assyrians who would take them from the land.

17:14–17 Response of the Israelites

Regardless of all these warnings, they did not listen to the servants of God and proved themselves to be "stiff-necked," referring to their stubborn character. Paradoxically, the stiff-necked Israelites were unwilling to bow to worship and follow Yahweh alone, and yet they bent to worship the powerless idols (17:14). Moreover, they failed to "trust the Lord," meaning that they neither believed nor obeyed him. Instead, they imitated the nations around them, although the Lord had ordered them, "Do not do as they do" (17:15).

To remind them how this had happened, the Lord repeated their specific sins (17:16–17). They made two idols in the shape of calves, an Asherah pole, and bowed down to all the starry hosts, and worshiped Baal (17:16). Jeroboam I reintroduced idol worship during his reign, which had been banned by the Lord (1 Kgs 12:25–33). But the people continued to worship them, and other kings didn't remove them. The Israelites bowed down to all the starry hosts, showing their interest in astrology and astral deities (Amos 5:26). This practice of following astrology and astral deities was forbidden in the law (Deut 4:19; 17:3). The life-controlling force of the universe is God, not planets. In addition, the Israelites sacrificed their sons and daughters to Molech in the fire, practiced divination, and sought omens (17:17a). The Lord God had forbidden all of these (Exod 22:18; Lev 19:26, 31). By doing these evils, they aroused the Lord's anger against them (17:17b).

17:18–23 Result of their Sins

Their persistence in sin resulted in God's just action. He removed the Israelites from his presence except the tribe of Judah (17:18). Yahweh does not merely withdraw his presence from the Israelites; rather, Yahweh casts Israel out from his presence. By "casting" Israel out from his presence, Yahweh is saying that he does not want to relate with his people because they broke the covenantal relationship.

Since the people "would not listen," "were as stiff-necked," "did not trust in the LORD their God," "rejected his decrees and the statues," "followed worthless idols," and "imitated the nations around them" (17:14–15), God too "was very angry," "removed them from his presence," "rejected all the people of Israel," "afflicted them," and "gave them into the hands of the plunderers" (17:18–20). God's punishment matches their rejection of him, the law, and the covenant.

Although God kept the tribe of Judah, they too were guilty of not keeping the commands of God and following Israel's practices (17:19). The people of Judah were no better than Israel, and so the Lord rejected all the people of both kingdoms. This verse alerts the reader that Judah will be destroyed some time after Israel (17:20). However, before thrusting all the people of Israel out from his presence, the Lord afflicted them by sending other nations, such as Aram and Edom, to plunder their cities and harvests so that the people of Israel and Judah might repent. These punishments did not change them from doing evil.

Their wickedness began from the start of the divided monarch: "Jeroboam enticed Israel away from following the Lord and caused them to commit a great sin" (17:21). But the next generations persisted in committing these sins (17:22). They continued this trend "until the LORD removed them from his presence" as he warned them (17:23a). They were taken from their homeland into exile in Assyrian territories (17:23b). Because of the consequences of their collective sins, they lost both their freedom and their land, and so they were forced to become alienated in a faraway country.

The phrase, "they are still there," means that their exile was very long and was still going on when the narrator was reporting this story. Even still, the prophets predicted that the scattered people would return to their land in the future (Hos 11:11; Amos 9:11–15), and the people of the two kingdoms would be reunited (Ezek 37:15–28).

17:24–41 RESETTLEMENT OF ISRAEL

After explaining the sin of idolatry as the cause of their exile, the narrator returns to historical explanations of what happened (17:24–41). The king of Assyria conquered Samaria and brought people from Babylon, Kuthah, Avva, Hamath, and Sepharvaim and settled them in the towns of Samaria to replace the Israelites (17:24). Assyrians now inhabited the Israelites' towns. Kutha, a town located northeast of Babylon, was captured by the Assyrian king, Sargon II.[1] Avva, Hamath, and Sepharvaim were originally towns in the Syrian province, but the Assyrians controlled them during this period.[2] The immigrant population from the colonies continued to worship their deities and practice

---

1. Bright, *A History of Israel*, 274.
2. Wiseman, *1 and 2 Kings*, 286.

their culture in the newly settled land of Israel. Because of that, Yahweh sent lions to kill them (17:25). Earlier, lions were sent to punish the prophets who did not listen to the word of Yahweh (1 Kgs 13:24–30; 1 Kgs 20:35–36). When the news of the lions killing his settlers reached his ears (17:26), the king of Assyria gave orders to send a priest from among the Israelite captives living in Assyria to return to northern Israel and teach the new immigrants to worship Yahweh and practice the law (17:27). The priest came to Bethel and taught the newcomers how to worship the Lord (17:28).

In spite of the teaching from the Israelite priest about the law of Yahweh to worship him alone, the settlers continued to worship their own gods and goddesses (17:29). The names of the gods and goddesses are mentioned to show how each people group brought their own gods and goddesses into Samaria. The people from Babylon worshiped *Sukkoth Benoth* (17:30a), which refers to the goddess *Banitu*, an epithet for the goddess Ishtar. The people from Kuthah made Nergal (17:30b), which is symbolized in the form of a lion, a god of war, pestilence, and death in the shrine at Kuthah (Cutha). The people from Hamath worshiped *Ashima* (17:30c). The reference to *Nibhaz* and *Tartak*, who were worshiped by the people from the city of Avva, is not known in the OT (17:31a). The people of Sepharvites burned their children in the fire as sacrifices to Adrammelek and Anammelek, possibly a husband and wife deity (17:31b). These immigrants didn't solely worship their local deities, they also worshiped the Lord (17:33). They were syncretistic in their worship. Earlier, the Israelites followed this syncretistic trend of worshiping Yahweh for protection and victory in war while also worshiping Baal and Asherah for agricultural fertility. Because of this syncretism in the life of Israel, they lost the land that Yahweh had given to them, and yet the trend continued with the new inhabitants, who brought more gods and goddesses from their foreign nations into the land (17:30–33).

This syncretistic worship continued for a long time. The phrase, "to this day they persist in their former practices" (17:34a), suggests that the situation of worshiping and practicing the customs of foreigners was still happening in Israel as this story was being written. They, just as the Israelites, refused to worship the Lord alone or to follow his decrees and regulations, laws and commands (17:34b).

In the concluding section, the narrator reminds once again why Israel went into exile (17:35–41). When the Lord made a covenant with Israel, the Sinai covenant, he commanded them, "Do not worship any other gods or bow down to them, serve them or sacrifice to them" (17:35). Israel didn't abide by this covenant. They were instructed to only worship "the Lord, who brought you out of Egypt with mighty power and outstretched arm" (17:36). They ignored that and worshiped many gods and goddesses, even starry skies. He told them, "You must always be careful to keep the decrees and regulations, the laws and commands" (17:37), and they ignored this command. He said to them, "Do not forget the covenant I have made with you, and do not worship other gods" (17:38); they blatantly disregarded this. He cautioned them, "Worship the Lord your God; it is he who will deliver you from the hand of all your enemies" (17:39); they forgot it, ignored it, and worshiped Baals and Asheroths. They persisted in their former sins (17:40). They lived as idolaters; with their lips they worshiped the Lord, but they also worshiped other gods and taught their children and grandchildren to do so (17:41). Therefore, the Lord sent them into exile.

This covenant theology is unique to Israel. Their life is tied to the land, and they can enjoy the blessing of God as long as they follow the commandments of Yahweh (Deut 11:13–17). When they fail to obey the law, they lose their land and are dispersed among the nations to live in exile. In the teachings of the OT, God, the people, and the land are interconnected in a triangular relationship.[3]

---

3. Christopher J. H. Wright, *Living as the People of God: The Relevance of Old Testament Ethics* (Leicester: IVP, 1983), 19–64.

2 KINGS 18:1-37
HEZEKIAH'S TRUST IN YAHWEH

After the fall of northern Israel, the history of the people of God focuses on the southern kingdom of Judah and its struggle to stand against ongoing threats from Assyria. Tiglath-Pileser (ca. 745–727 BC), Shalmaneser V (ca. 727–722 BC), Sargon II (ca. 722–705), and Sennacherib (ca. 705–681 BC) were powerful Assyrian kings who attacked the countries along their borders and made them pay heavy tributes. Both good and bad kings of Israel and Judah had to face attacks from Assyria and became vassals to these Assyrian kings. The fall of the northern kingdom made it easier for the Assyrian kings to march towards Jerusalem, the capital of Judah. A series of threats from Sennacherib made the situation even worse for Hezekiah, the reigning king of Judah. The stories in 2 Kings 18–20 depict Hezekiah's struggle to follow the Lord, trust him for deliverance, and resist forming an alliance with Egypt.

2 Kings 18 introduces Hezekiah with a brief biodata and a favorable evaluation of his rule (18:1–8). This summary is followed by a brief report about the fall of Israel during Hoshea's reign (18:9–12), a brief account of Assyria's first threat against Judah (18:13–16), and a long section about Assyria's second threat (18:17–37).

The Hebrew word for "trust" occurs several times in this chapter (18:5, 20, 21, 22, 24, and 30, and 19:10) and is the key theme of Hezekiah's story. Derogatory and arrogant rhetoric fills this chapter as the king of Assyria challenges the power of Yahweh.

18:1-8 HEZEKIAH'S RULE IN JUDAH

Hezekiah son of Ahaz began to reign as the king of Judah in the third year of Hoshea king of Israel (18:1). He was twenty-five years old and reigned in Jerusalem for twenty-nine years (18:2a). His mother was Abijah daughter of Zechariah (18:2b). Hezekiah did what was right in the eyes of the Lord, just as his ancestor, David, had done (18:3). He removed the high places and destroyed the sacred stones and Asherah poles in the land, which none of the other kings of Judah did (18:4a). In addition, he broke into pieces the bronze snake Moses had made, which the people had turned into an object of worship, calling it Nehushtan (18:4b).

Above all, Hezekiah trusted the Lord, the God of Israel (18:5a). This isolated him from all other kings of Judah – "There was no one like him among all the kings of Judah, either before him or after him" (18:5b). He held fast to the Lord and did not cease to follow him, meaning that he kept the commandments of the Lord given through Moses (18:6). Because of Hezekiah's faith in the Lord and his obedience to the law, the Lord was with him and he was successful in whatever tasks he undertook, including rebelling against the king of Assyria (18:7). He utterly defeated the Philistines, with the help of the Lord God, as far as Gaza (18:8).

18:9–12 ISRAEL'S DEFEAT AND EXILE

While the narration explained in detail the destruction of Samaria and the deportation of the people of the northern kingdom in chapter 17, he briefly returns to it in this section as an interlude within the story of Hezekiah's rule (18:9–12). It may be to remind the people of Judah about the failure of the northern kingdom as a warning that they should follow the Lord. What happened to Israel can happen to Judah as well. As we read the rest of the stories in 2 Kings (chs. 19–25), we can notice that the final destruction of Judah (586 BC) was delayed for another hundred and thirty-five years because of Hezekiah's and Josiah's faithfulness to Yahweh.

The defeat and deportation of the northern kingdom of Israel happened in the fourth year of King Hezekiah's rule (18:9a). Shalmaneser king of Assyria marched against Samaria and laid siege of it (18:9b). At the end of three years, Shalmaneser captured Samaria (18:10). Soon, he deported Israel to Assyria and settled the land with other people (18:11). All this happened because the people of Israel "had not obeyed the LORD their God" but violated his commandments and worshiped foreign gods (18:12).

18:13–16 FIRST THREAT FROM ASSYRIA

After briefly narrating how the northern kingdom went into exile, the narrator returns to Hezekiah. During the fourteenth year of King Hezekiah's reign (ca. 701 BC), King Sennacherib attacked the cities of Judah and captured them (8:13). Many cities north of Jerusalem, which had protected the capital city from invasion by foreign forces, had fallen to Sennacherib, and so he put pressure on Hezekiah to surrender. In response, Hezekiah sent a message to Sennacherib, who was at Lachish in Assyria, acknowledging the mistake of not paying a regular tribute to the Assyrian king (18:14a). Hezekiah begged Sennacherib to withdraw from Judah, offering to pay the necessary tribute.

Since Sennacherib had the upper hand over Judah, he demanded three hundred talents of silver (approximately ten metric tons) and thirty talents of gold (approximately one metric ton) (18:14b). Unable to pay this tribute from the royal treasuries alone (18:15), Hezekiah removed the gold that covered the doors and doorposts of the temple and silver from the temple and royal palace (18:16).

18:17–37 SECOND THREAT OF ASSYRIA

After Sennacherib collected the gold and silver from Hezekiah, he was unsatisfied with the tribute and issued his second threat against the king and people of Judah. This threat is narrated as a series of speeches that were meant to provoke the people of Judah so that they would deny their trust in Yahweh and surrender to Assyria.

Sennacherib sent his supreme commander (meaning the commander in chief of the army), his chief officer from the administration, his field commander, who might have been a provincial governor (Heb. *rab-saqe*), along with an army (18:17a). They came from Lachish and entered Jerusalem to address King Hezekiah. They stopped at the aqueduct of the Upper Pool, on the road to the Washerman's Field (18:17b). This was a very strategic place because the water from the spring of Gihon, which was east of Jerusalem, flowed underground through a canal to the lower pool inside the city. If this spring was closed by the enemy, the people of Jerusalem would suffer from a lack of water.

The Assyrian officials called to Hezekiah and asked him to meet them at the aqueduct. Instead of going, Hezekiah sent Eliakim, the palace administrator, Shebna, the secretary, and Joah, the recorder (18:18).

Seeing them, the field commander sent a message to Hezekiah (18:19–25). The message began, "This is what the great king, the king of Assyria, says: On what are you basing this confidence of yours?" (18:19). This was a challenge; how could Hezekiah disobey Sennacherib, the great king? He was the "great king" because he was able to defeat so many countries in that region and was becoming a superpower. Again, he challenged Hezekiah wondering on whom he was depending in his rebelling against Sennacherib (18:20). Then, the field commander raised the suspicion that Hezekiah was forming an alliance with Egypt (18:21a). Then he ridiculed Egypt, comparing it with a splintered or crushed reed, which hurts the hands of anyone who tries to hold it or lean on it. Just as reeds are not strong enough to rely on for support, the nature of the pharaoh of Egypt was unreliable, and so he would inevitably desert Hezekiah in his most critical moment (18:21b). Finally, the field commander challenged Hezekiah's trust in the Lord because he knew that the king of Judah was engaging in religious reform by destroying all the idols, high places, and shrines in the nation (18:22). Moreover, Hezekiah was insisting that the people of Judah should worship only Yahweh, who was present in the temple of Jerusalem. The commander cleverly pointed out that Hezekiah's zeal for and dependence on Yahweh was in vain given Sennacherib's great might. However, the commander did not understand that Hezekiah's religious reform was based on his obedience to Yahweh and the law of Moses.

After challenging the source of Hezekiah's trust, the officer extended an invitation for Hezekiah to abandon his rebellion of Sennacherib and make a bargain with Assyria (18:23). He argued that even if the king of Assyria gave Judah two thousand horses, they could not fight against the horsemen of the Assyrian army. Moreover, even with the support of chariots and horses from Egypt, Hezekiah could not defeat the Assyrian army (18:24). Therefore, it was a waste of time to look for support, and so Hezekiah should make a compromise with Sennacherib. In a desperate act, the commander lied to Hezekiah's officials, saying that Yahweh had sent Assyria to fight and destroy Judah and also claiming that he had come to attack and destroy Judah based on the word of the Lord that he had received (18:25). Using the name of Yahweh to bear false witness was a sin against God, but it was taken for granted by this officer.

After listening to this speech, Hezekiah's representatives asked the Assyrian officer to speak in Aramaic rather than Hebrew (18:26). Aramaic was the diplomatic language of the kingdom of Assyria and its colonies, whereas Hebrew was the local language of the people of Judah. Since the speeches were delivered in a public place, the officials of Hezekiah, who knew Aramaic, wanted the field commander to speak in Aramaic so that the general public would not hear these threatening speeches and feel discouraged or decide to join the king of Assyria and desert the king of Judah.

In response to this request, the field commander delivered an arrogant and abusive reply. He declared that he was speaking purposely in Hebrew so that the public could hear him ordering the king of Judah to surrender to the king of Assyria. His aim was to threaten the people of Israel and dissuade their loyalty to Hezekiah. Moreover, he declared that the listening public would eat their own excrement and drink their own urine if they stood with their king of Judah because there would be a lack of food and water in Jerusalem after Assyria seiged it (18:27).

In spite of the request from Hezekial's officials, the provincial governor continued his speech in the Hebrew language, calling the public to listen to the words of the great Assyrian king (18:28). He used the prohibition, "do not," four times in his speech and told the people not to be deceived by Hezekiah because he could never deliver them from the hands of the Assyrian army (18:29), not to be persuaded by Hezekiah to believe that the Lord would deliver them or Assyria would not destroy Jerusalem (18:30), not to listen to Hezekiah but to surrender to Sennacherib and make peace with him so that they would be able to survive and have an abundance of wine, figs, and fresh water from their own springs and cisterns (18:31), and not to be misled by Hezekiah when he told them that the Lord would deliver them (18:32).

With pride and arrogance, the commander questioned the ability of any gods to protect its people from the might of the Assyrian army (18:33). Then he cited the example of the gods of Hamath, Arpad, Sepharvaim, Hena, and Ivvah, which had not delivered their nations from the hands of Assyria (18:34). Thus the God of the Israelites would also not be able to rescue Jerusalem from the power of Assyria, which had already destroyed northern Israel and deported the Israelites to Assyria (18:35). This comparison of other gods with Yahweh reveals his inability to understand the power of Yahweh and the relationship between Yahweh and the people of Israel and Judah. Yahweh had intervened in the history of these two nations by raising Aram and then Assyria to punish the people of Israel for their failure to worship Yahweh alone. The defeat of northern Israel was the result of their disobedience, not because Yahweh was powerless before the kings of Aram and Assyria. Furthermore, the field commander did not understand the nature of the gods of the nations. He assumed that they had power. They had no power. In contrast, Yahweh, the God of the universe, is powerful, and his sovereignty prevails over all nations.

Just as the commander used "do not," Hezekiah had given a command to the people: "Do not answer him" (18:36). The people of Judah obeyed this instruction from their king and expressed their loyalty by remaining silent. Hezekiah's representatives returned to the palace with their clothes torn as a symbolic act to express their grief and humiliation, and then they reported all the Assyrian governor's words to their king (18:37). In times of threat, fear, and persecution, Christians should not lose faith and hope. We should not argue or fight with neighbors who ridicule God or mock our faith in Jesus Christ. Rather, we should trust that God is powerful and sovereign over all authorities, idols, and evil spirits of the world and believe that our Lord Jesus Christ can be trusted in all circumstances.

2 KINGS 19:1–37

HEZEKIAH'S PRAYER AND ISAIAH'S PROPHECY

When Hezekiah hears the threat from the Assyrians, he prays for his nation. God sends an encouraging word through the prophet Isaiah. The narrator uses several literary forms including a lament, a petition, a report, oracles, symbolic actions, and metaphorical language to convey that Judah will be immediately delivered from the attacks of Assyria. The God of Israel, who is more powerful than any god of the nations, honors the sincere prayers and actions of his devotees.

This chapter can be divided into six sections: Hezekiah's message to Isaiah (19:1–4), Isaiah's message to Hezekiah (19:5–7), Assyria's third threat against Judah (19:8–13), Hezekiah's prayer (19:14–19), Isaiah's prophetic oracle (19:20–34), and deliverance of Jerusalem and the death of Sennacherib (19:35–37).

19:1–4 HEZEKIAH'S MESSAGE TO ISAIAH

The report about the Assyrian field commander's speeches broke Hezekiah's heart and moved him to tear his clothes and wear sackcloth. These symbolic actions express his emotional state as well as his humility before the Lord. Wearing sackcloth, he went to the temple in Jerusalem to pray to the Lord (19:1). Then he sent his overseer, Eliakim, and his scribe, Shebna, along with his leading priests, who were all also wearing sackcloth, to seek help and guidance from the prophet Isaiah, the son of Amoz (19:2). The narrator introduces Isaiah for the first time in this chapter in relation to Hezekiah's rule. Since Hezekiah's efforts to negotiate with the Assyrian officials had failed, he sought the help of the Lord through the prophet.

The content of Hezekiah's message expresses the serious threat from Assyria and his urgent need for help from the Lord. Judah was in big trouble; it was a day of distress and disgrace because the Assyrian official had rebuked the people of Judah with abusive language and questioned their trust in the Lord, their loyalty to the king, and the power of the Lord to deliver them from the Assyrian army (19:3). Hezekiah expressed the situation in metaphorical language, using the image of childbirth. If a mother does not have enough strength when it is time to deliver her child, then both the mother and child might die. Hezekiah wanted the prophet to make sure that the Lord God would remember the ridiculing words that the commander had spoken about the living God, will rebuke him for those words, and deliver the remnant (19:4). The people of Israel in the northern kingdom had already been destroyed, and so the only remaining people (remnant) of God were in Judah, but the Assyrians wanted to destroy them as well.

19:5–7 ISAIAH'S MESSAGE OF HOPE

Isaiah saw Hezekiah's delegation coming in sackcloth, and he listened to their request (19:5). He then prophesied a message of hope for Hezekiah and the people, while also proclaiming disaster for the king of Assyria (19:6–7). The phrase, "this is what the LORD says," is a messenger formula that affirms the authenticity of the prophet's message, confirming that it is coming from the Lord and not Isaiah. He assured the king saying, "Do not be afraid," which is a prophetic form of speech that is often used in salvation oracles to convey the deliverance of the Lord. Whereas the commander threatened the people saying, "Do not listen" (18:29, 31, 32), God through Isaiah comforts Hezekiah and the people, saying, "Do not be afraid." The Lord wants the people of Judah to know that they do not need to be afraid of the threatening speeches from the Assyrians.

The prophet confirmed that the Assyrian field commander's words were blasphemy against Yahweh and that Yahweh had heard their words (19:6). This is an encouraging answer to Hezekiah's complaint about the way the Assyrian officer had ridiculed the living God (19:4). In Hezekiah's complaint, he was not trying to provoke Isaiah to be against the Assyrians, but rather expressing his spiritual concern that people should not ridicule Yahweh. Isaiah told Hezekiah's delegation that the Lord would send a spirit to circulate a report that would force the Assyrians to leave Jerusalem and return to their own country. There, Sennacherib would be killed (19:7). Whereas Sennacherib threatened Hezekiah, in truth, it was he who was in trouble.

19:8–13 ASSYRIA'S THIRD THREAT

While Hezekiah's ambassadors were visiting Isaiah, the field commander of Sennacherib heard that the king of Assyria left Lachish in Judah to fight against Libnah, another city in Judah (19:8). This was the beginning of Isaiah's prophecy coming to fulfillment. Soon Sennacherib received another message:

Tirhakah, the king of Cush, was marching out to fight against Sennacherib (19:9). The kingdom of Cush was the region in the upper Nile in Egypt. So, instead of visiting Hezekiah, Sennacherib sent a third threatening message (19:10–13).

In this third threat, he criticized the king of Judah for being deceived by the God in whom he trusted (19:10). Then he arrogantly recollected his victories (19:11). Once again, Sennacherib listed all the nations whose gods could not deliver them from the power of his ancestors (19:12). The word "ancestors" refers to his predecessors, such as Tiglath-Pileser and Shalmaneser, who ruled Assyria previously and defeated all these nations. If the gods of Gozah, Harran, Rezeph, Eden, Hamath, Arpad, Lair, Sepharvaim, Hena, and Ivvah could not save their nations, then the Lord God of Hezekiah could not save Judah. Sennacherib was measuring victory and success in terms of the power of the gods of the nations, and he arrogantly boasted that he and all the kings of Assyria were more powerful than any of the gods of these nations. This led him to question the nature and power of Yahweh and undermine Hezekiah's trust in the Lord.

19:14–19 HEZEKIAH'S PRAYER

Hezekiah received the letter from the messengers and read it (19:14a). He could not bear the taunts of Sennacherib, so he went to the temple in Jerusalem and prostrated himself before the Lord (19:14b). There he prayed to the Lord God. His prayer includes the elements of lament and petition.

Hezekiah acknowledged the Lord as the God of Israel, implying that there was no other God for the people of Israel because of their covenantal relationship with Yahweh (19:15a). He confessed that the Lord was enthroned between the cherubim and ruled all the kingdoms of the earth, including Assyria (19:15b). He acknowledged him as the Creator of heaven and earth.

Hezekiah then pleaded with the Lord to hear his prayer, open his eyes, and listen to Sennacherib's words that ridiculed the living God (19:16). The words, "hear," "listen," "see," and "open eyes," are often found in the psalms of lament.

Hezekiah acknowledged Assyria's power in successfully destroying the nations mentioned by Sennacherib in his letter (19:17). However, the gods of these nations had been thrown into the fire and destroyed as well because they were mere idols made by humans out of wood and stone. As created images, they did not have any power to defend their nations (19:18).

Having said this, Hezekiah asked the Lord to demonstrate his power and authority over Sennacherib by proving his power and delivering Judah, the kings of all the other nations would then know that the Lord God of Israel alone was the one true and living God (19:19). Hezekiah's prayer not only expresses his lament and petition, but also conveys his strong faith in the Lord as the only true and living God who could save the people of Israel.

19:20–34 PROPHETIC ORACLE OF ISAIAH

The Lord answered Hezekiah's prayer through Isaiah. His message began with the prophetic formula: "This is what the LORD, the God of Israel, says" (19:20a). Then the Lord assured Hezekiah saying, "I have heard your prayer concerning Sennacherib king of Assyria" (19:20b).

With the introduction, the rest of the prophetic message is an oracle against Sennacherib (19:21–34). It has three sections: the destiny of Sennacherib and Assyria (19:21–28), Yahweh's assurance to Hezekiah through a sign (19:29–31), and Yahweh's defense of Judah (19:32–34).

19:21–28 Destiny of Sennacherib and Assyria

In the first section of Isaiah's taunt song, Yahweh addresses the destiny of Sennacherib and Assyria. This section has five smaller units: mocking Sennacherib (v. 21), questioning Sennacherib (v. 22), the boasting of Sennacherib (vv. 23–24), challenging Sennacherib (vv. 25–26), and punishing Sennacherib (vv. 27–28).

19:21 Mocking Sennacherib

In this first verse of the oracle, the word "you" refers to Sennacherib. The phrases, "Virgin Daughter of Zion" or "Daughter Jerusalem," convey the youthfulness of Jerusalem and Judah. The repetitive parallelism in this verse proclaims that Judah will now be able to despise and mock Sennacherib and toss her head as a sign of victory as the army of Assyria flees to their country.

19:22 Questioning Sennacherib

Then Yahweh questions Sennacherib, saying, "Who is it you have ridiculed and blasphemed? Against whom have you raised your voice and lifted your eyes in pride?" The answer is that Sennacherib has ridiculed and blasphemed Yahweh, "the Holy One of Israel!" This strong reprimand from Yahweh is addressed to Sennacherib because he sent his messengers to ridicule the Lord.

19:23–24 Boasting of Sennacherib

Next, in a poetic way, Yahweh points out Sennacherib's pride and arrogance because he boasted about his achievements of defeating Lebanon and Egypt. The poem uses "I," as if Sennacherib himself is speaking, expressing the way he cut down the tallest cedars, the choicest junipers, and the finest forests of Lebanon with his mighty power and how his feet have climbed the heights of the mountains (19:23). His boasts about digging wells in the lands of other nations and drinking the water indicate the control he has exercised over other countries. Even Egypt was not spared from his powerful invasion, for he says that he dried up the streams of Egypt (19:24). Yahweh is mocking him and pointing out his arrogance. There is no limit to Sennacherib's pride, for he ridiculed the Creator of the mountains, forests, water, and streams.

19:25–26 Challenging Sennacherib

Yahweh then challenges Sennacherib's pride and arrogance by declaring that his victories are neither because of his power nor help from his gods. Rather, it was Yahweh's plan to use Sennacherib to turn fortified cities into piles of stone (19:25). By God's foreordained plan, he drained the people of their power, dismayed them, and put them to shame. They had become like the plants in the fields, tender green shoots that have been dried up by the scorching heat of Sennacherib only because the Lord God had allowed those to happen (19:26). Here, Yahweh is challenging Sennacherib's power, saying that only Yahweh has the power to control the destiny of nations. Without Yahweh's plan and permission, the king of Assyria would not have attacked these nations.

19:27–28 Punishing Sennacherib

Sennacherib has no right to be prideful; God knows where he is, when he came against him, and what kind of rage he raised against him (19:27). He heard everything he said against him in his insolence (19:28a). Therefore he would inflict punishment. Yahweh will put his hook in Sennacherib's nose and his bit in his mouth (19:28b). These were metaphors of slavery and oppression. Just as a fish caught on a hook cannot escape, Sennacherib has been caught in the hook set by Yahweh. Just as a bit and bridle control the direction of a horse, Sennacherib cannot run away from the punishment of Yahweh. The Lord will force him to return to his country along the same route that he used to besiege Jerusalem. This prophecy promises certain deliverance for the people of Judah.

19:29–31 Assurance to Hezekiah with a Sign

The second section of Isaiah's oracle is addressed to Hezekiah (19:29–31). In it, Yahweh not only assures Hezekiah of Judah's deliverance but also gives him a sign. Hezekiah can continue to resist Sennacherib and rule Judah with hope and confidence in the Lord, for the siege of Sennacherib will come to an end.

God tells Hezekiah that in the first year after the siege, the people of Judah will eat wild food that grew by itself. During the second year, they will still have to depend on whatever food springs up naturally from the fields. But during the third year, they will be able to cultivate their land and plant vineyards and eat the fruit of their harvest (19:29). Thus the current situation of conflict and distress will be resolved after the third year.

Just as a plant's roots go deeper into the soil as the branches bear fruit above, the remnant of Judah will continue to have life rather than dying and vanishing (19:30). The word "once more" means that God has given them an opportunity to survive and grow in their land again. The word "remnant" refers to the people of Judah who will survive all the threats of attack and destruction from Assyria (19:31a). These survivors within Jerusalem will be like seeds that will bear fruit and multiply again. The zeal of the Lord Almighty will accomplish the withdrawal of Sennacherib's army and the full recovery of agriculture and the food supply in Judah (19:31b). The word "zeal" includes Yahweh's interest and power.

The earlier metaphor that is used to describe the foreign nations as plants that withered and died because of the attacks from the king of Assyria (19:26) is countered by a metaphor that describes the remnant of Judah as plants reviving and bearing fruit because of Yahweh's power (19:30). Just as Yahweh could use Assyria to destroy the foreign nations, Yahweh can deliver Judah from the hands of the king of Assyria. The Lord has caused both events to occur.

19:32–34 Yahweh's Defense of Judah

The third section in Isaiah's oracle describes the end of the attacks from Assyria. The word "therefore" connects the earlier section of the oracle with this concluding section. Because of the zeal of the Lord (19:31), the miraculous deliverance foretold by Isaiah will happen. In addition to this deliverance, the Lord assures Hezekiah that Sennacherib will not return to Jerusalem, will not shoot an arrow in the city, will not carry a shield to it or build a siege ramp against Jerusalem (19:32). By the same way he came, he will return; he will not enter Jerusalem, as the Lord had spoken (19:33). Yahweh himself will defend Jerusalem and save it for the sake of David, his servant, as well as for his own name's sake (19:34). Without doubt, these words would have assured Hezekiah.

19:35–37 DEATH OF SENNACHERIB

The story reaches its climax as the Lord accomplishes the deliverance of Judah immediately after the prophecy of Isaiah. "The angel of the LORD," appears often in biblical stories to carry out God's plans. The night Isaiah prophesied, the angel of the Lord entered the camp of the Assyrians and put to death a hundred and eighty-five thousand Assyrian soldiers (19:35a). The dead bodies were found all over the camp on the next morning (19:35b). This miracle is not how Yahweh put the army to death, but that it happened as a punishment for the pride and arrogance of the king of Assyria. Sennacherib could not bear the loss of his men, and so he withdrew from Judah and returned to Nineveh (19:36).

Later, as Sennacherib was worshiping in the temple of his national god, Nisrok, his sons – Adrammelek and Sharezer – killed him with a sword and escaped to the land of Ararat, a mountainous region (19:37a). Sennacherib was killed just as Isaiah had predicted (19:7). Esarhaddon, another son of Sennacherib, succeeded him to the throne (19:37b).

The theology rising out of this chapter is the faith and prayer of a leader for the people. Hezekiah's genuine lament and prayer of petition were heard by the Lord, who ordered deliverance for Judah from the hands of the Assyrians. We should not boast about our abilities nor take pride in our power, wealth, and achievements. Instead, we should remain humble before both God and people, giving all glory and honor to the Lord.

2 KINGS 20:1-21
HEZEKIAH'S HEALING AND MISTAKE

The story of Hezekiah comes to an end in chapter 20. This chapter explains two significant events in the latter days of Hezekiah: his healing from a mortal illness (20:1–11), and his foolishness in exposing the royal treasuries of Judah to Babylonian envoys (20:12–19). The chapter concludes with the usual formula mentioning his death and successor (20:20–21). Hezekiah's reign attests to his faith and prayer; in the subsequent years, Judah rapidly deteriorated.

20:1-11 HEALING AND SIGN

This first main narrative in chapter 20 has two inner sections: Hezekiah's healing from a grave sickness (20:1–7) and the sign given from the Lord to confirm his complete healing (20:8–11).

20:1–7 Hezekiah's Sickness and Healing

Some time during the course of Hezekiah's life, he became seriously ill and was at the point of death (20:1a). God reveals Hezekiah's hopeless condition to the prophet Isaiah and sends him to deliver a message. The message was: "This is what the LORD says: Put your house in order, because you are going to die; you will not recover" (20:1b). The phrase "put the house in order" is a meaning to arrange the affairs of the family, such as dividing shares of his wealth between his sons, selecting which son will succeed him to the throne, and giving commands to his officials about administrative matters.

Hearing the message, Hezekiah turned toward the wall and prayed to the Lord (20:2). He said, "Remember, LORD, how I walked before you faithfully and with wholehearted devotion and have done what is good in your eyes" (20:3a). Saying this, he wept bitterly, proving his anguish (20:3b). The word "remember" often occurs in laments and it is a demand for an immediate action in a desperate situation. Hezekiah reminded God about the way he had trusted and obeyed the Lord, showed wholehearted devotion, and always kept the commandments and done what was right. This need not be regarded as a self-righteous claim, but an expression of self-analysis as he faced his own death.

In response to Hezekiah's genuine lament and tears, the word of the Lord came to the prophet before he had even left the palace, instructing him to return to the king to inform him that he would be healed and be able to return to the temple in three days (20:4–5). The Lord refers to Hezekiah as "the ruler of my people," attesting to his loyalty to the Lord and God's appreciation for the way Hezekiah ruled the people of Judah. Yahweh is usually identified as the God of the fathers, meaning Abraham, Isaac, and Jacob, but here God identifies himself as the God of "your father David," indicating the long covenantal relationship that began with David is continuing with Hezekiah.

Following this assurance, the Lord promises to add another fifteen years of life to the king and to deliver him and Jerusalem from the hand of the king of Assyria, for the sake of David, the Lord's servant (20:6). Hezekiah does not need to worry hereafter, because the Lord has taken the responsibility on himself to defend and deliver Judah. Hezekiah's prayer stirs God to grant him another fifteen years of life. It also moves God to change the prophecy he gave to Isaiah earlier, implying prophetic predictions are not controlled by a prophet, but by God, who can make changes to any prophecy.

After proclaiming this message from the Lord, Isaiah asked the king to prepare a poultice of figs. When the servants did as the king instructed, Isaiah applied it to the king's boil and Hezekiah recovered (20:7).

20:8–11 A Sign from the Lord

Hezekiah wanted the Lord to give him a sign to prove that he would be healed and be able to go to the temple in three days (20:8). So Isaiah asked the king if he wanted a shadow to move ten steps forward or ten steps backward (20:9). The shadow may have referred to a measuring object such as an ancient sundial. At that moment, the shadow would have been going forward ten steps, and so Hezekiah said, "Have it go back ten steps" (20:10). Isaiah called on the Lord, who made the shadow move back ten steps down on the stairway of Ahaz (20:11). By this sign, Hezekiah knew what Isaiah said was truly from the Lord.

This raises a theological question about whether or not Christians should ask God for a sign to confirm that their prayers have been heard and will be answered. God may take the initiative to show a sign to people through a vision or incident to communicate his purposes and will. In this case, people do not ask for or seek such a sign. A person may ask God to provide a sign as an assurance that his or her prayers have been heard and will be fulfilled. While some Christians today may want to receive a sign from the Lord for their prayers, the New Testament reveals the greatest sign ever given by God, which is that he sent his own son, Jesus Christ, to be with people and to show them the way of salvation. Moreover, Jesus taught us to exercise our faith rather than seeking signs (Mark 8:11; Luke 11:16; John 20:29; Heb 11:6), and so it is better to walk by faith rather than seeking signs and wonders.

20:12–19 FOOLISHNESS OF EXPOSING WEALTH

When Marduk-Baladan, the son of the king of Babylon, heard about Hezekiah's sickness, he sent an envoy with a letter and gifts to the king in Jerusalem (20:12). Marduk was the famous god of Babylon, whose name was often included as part of the title of Babylonian kings. Hezekiah enthusiastically received the envoy and, without thinking, showed the envoy all the treasures of his palace, including gold, silver, spices, fine olive oil, and armory (20:13a). He hid nothing from them (20:13b).

When Isaiah heard that the king had an envoy from a distant land, he visited Hezekiah and asked where the envoy had come from (20:14a). Hezekiah answered that they came from a distant land, Babylon (20:14b). When Isaiah asked what they saw, Hezekiah replied honestly saying that "nothing" had been hidden from them (20:15). After hearing the words of the king, Isaiah delivered the third oracle in this chapter.

He said to Hezekiah that the word of the Lord came to him to say that sometime in the near future everything in his palace and all the possessions of his predecessors will be carried off to Babylon; nothing will be left behind (20:16). The prophet picks up the information from the king that "nothing" was hidden to inform the king that "nothing" will be left in Judah. In addition, some of his male descendants would be carried away as captives to Babylon and made eunuchs in the palace of the king of Babylon (20:18).

Hezekiah responded to this prophecy by saying that it was "good" while wondering if there would be peace and security in his lifetime (20:19). The king accepted the verdict from Yahweh although he knew the immensity of all his wealth and sons being taken away by the Babylonians.

20:20–21 HEZEKIAH'S DEATH

The last two verses of this chapter have the standard concluding formula (20:20–31). All the events of Hezekiah's reign, all his achievement (including the pool and tunnel he made to bring water into the city) were written in the annals of the kings (2 Kgs 20:20). His work of collecting water in a pool outside the city and bringing water through an underground tunnel to the city of Jerusalem helped the people survive during the siege of the city. Hezekiah died and was buried with his ancestors in Jerusalem. His son, Manasseh, succeeded him to the throne (20:21).

2 KINGS 21:1–26
DISINTEGRATION OF JUDAH

2 Kings 21 continues the history of Judah with the reigns of Manasseh and then his son, Amon. They both did evil in the eyes of the Lord. Their rules can be contrasted with the previous king, Hezekiah, who followed the Lord and reformed the religious practices in Judah and also developed the city of Jerusalem. This chapter can be divided into two main sections: the rule of Manasseh (21:1–18) and the rule of Amon (21:19–26).

21:1–18 RULE OF MANASSEH

Manasseh was twelve years old when he became the king of Judah (ca. 692–638 BC) and reigned in Jerusalem for fifty-five years, which was a long period in comparison with the other kings of Judah (21:1a). He was born after Hezekiah was healed from his illness (20:5–6). Manasseh literally meant, "He was made to forget." Manasseh's mother's name was Hephzibah (20:1b), which means "my delight is in her." Manasseh "did evil in the eyes of the LORD, following the detestable practices of the nations the LORD had driven out before the Israelites" (21:2). In the following verse, the narrative will expand on these detestable practices. He rebuilt the high places his father Hezekiah had destroyed, erected altars to Baal, made an Asherah pole as Ahab king of Israel had done, and worshiped starry hosts (21:3). He built altars for other gods in the temple of the Lord in Jerusalem where the Lord promised to put his name (21:4). In addition, he built altars to all the starry hosts in the two courts of the temple of the Lord (2:5). Most horrifically, he sacrificed his own son in the fire (21:6a). Also, he practiced divination, sought omens, and consulted mediums and spiritists (21:6b), all banned by the law of Moses (Exod 22:18; Lev 19:26, 31). Basically, he did every evil under the sun before the eyes of the Lord, arousing his anger.

But that was not all. He took the carved Asherah pole and placed it in the temple (21:7a). It was concerning this temple, the Lord had said to David and Solomon, "In this temple and in Jerusalem, which I have chosen out of all the tribes of Israel, I will put my Name forever" (21:7b). The temple also assured the Israelites of God's continued promises including never again wandering from the land as long as they kept his promises and obeyed the law

Moses gave them (21:8). Without any regard for the Lord and his promises, Manasseh continued to desecrate the temple. His actions led the people into further idolatry, against their promises to the Lord (21:9). These verses accuse Manasseh of leading Judah to worship idols and for placing altars to other gods in the temple. In a way, they "did more evil than the nations the LORD had destroyed before the Israelites" (21:9b). These foreign nations had not known the laws of Yahweh, and so they were ignorant in their sin, but this king of Judah did know the Deuteronomic law, and yet he surpassed other nations in sinning against Yahweh.

Because of these sins, the Lord spoke through the prophets' punishments against Manasseh, king of Judah (21:10–16). Once again, the oracle said that Manasseh did more evil than other nations that lived in the land; he led the people to commit those sins against God (21:11). As such, the Lord will bring disaster on the city of Jerusalem and the entire land of Judah. This news will be continuously tingling in the ears of the people (21:12). The Lord will use the same measuring line that he used against Samaria and the house of Ahab against Manasseh and Jerusalem (21:13a). As one wipes a dish, he will clean out Jerusalem and turn it upside down (21:13b). The Lord will even forsake the remnant that has been left in Judah and give them into the hands of the enemies; they will be looted and plundered by all their enemies (21:14). They have simply followed their ancestors who aroused the anger of the Lord repeatedly by doing evil (21:15).

After pronouncing this judgment, the narrator adds one more sin to the previous long list: Manasseh has shed the blood of many innocent people because of his bad administration (21:16). Manasseh may have killed those who raised their voices against him. In any case, the prophecy against Manasseh ends with a last biting indictment about his rule.

The story of Manasseh's reign concludes with the usual reference to the annals of the kings, where all the other details about his rule are recorded (21:17). Using the familiar formula, the narrator tells us that he rested with his ancestors and was buried in his palace garden, which was also known as the garden of Uzza (21:18). Amon, his son, succeeded him to the throne.

21:19–26 RULE OF AMON

Amon became king at the age of twenty-two and only ruled for two years (21:19a). His mother, Meshullemeth, was the daughter of Haruz and came from Jotbah (21:19b). This was a region in the north of Aqaba (Num 33:33; Deut 10:7). Her name and place of origin suggest that she was probably an

Arab who had merged with the people of Judah. Amon's rule was similar to Manasseh's – he followed all the evil that his ancestors did against the Lord (21:20). He worshiped idols and forsook Yahweh, the "God of his ancestors," and did not walk in obedience to God (21:22).

Amon's officials conspired against him and assassinated the young king while he was in his palace (21:23). The people of the land turned against the officials who assassinated the king and killed them (21:24a). Then, they made Josiah, son of Amon, king (21:24b).

The other events of Amon's reign and what he did were written in the book of the annals of the kings of Judah (21:25). The assassinated king was buried in the garden of Uzza, where his father had been buried (21:26a). Josiah succeeded him as king (21:26b).

2 KINGS 22:1–23:30
JOSIAH KING OF JUDAH

While the kingdom of Judah went through problems under kings, its religious situation was not always gloomy. Religious reforms took place under the leadership of some good kings, including Josiah, whose story is narrated over two chapters in the book of 2 Kings. Chapter 22 focuses on him repairing the temple, reading the book of the law of Moses, and committing to accept and follow it. Chapter 23 continues the story of his reforms, which included renewing the people's covenant with Yahweh, purifying the national worship, and restoring the celebration of Passover. These chapters remind us that when one listens to the law with a genuine mind and penitent heart, it has the power to transform the lives of many people and even an entire nation.

These chapters have several sections: a customary evaluation of Josiah's rule in Judah (22:1–2), repair of the temple (22:3–7), reading the book of the law (22:8–14), prophecy of Huldah (22:15–20), renewal of the covenant (23:1–3), a series of reforms (23:4–20), celebration of Passover (23:21–23), removal of mediums and spirits (23:24–25), confirmation of God's punishment on the nation in the near future (23:26–27), and Josiah's death (23:28–30). Josiah's life teaches us that when the people obey God's word, they can be saved from God's punishment.

22:1–2 JOSIAH'S RULE IN JUDAH

The assassination of Amon, Josiah's father, created an emergency situation: a land without a king (21:23). The people of Judah rectified it by appointing his son, Josiah, as the king at the age of eight (22:1a). Josiah was the second youngest king to rule Judah, as Jehoash was seven years old when he became king (11:21). Josiah reigned in Jerusalem thirty-one years; his mother was Jedidah daughter of Adaiah from Bozkath (22:1b). Jedidah meant "beloved" and Bozkath was between Lachish and Eglon (Josh 15:39). He reigned from 638 to 608 BC.

Josiah did what was right in the eyes of the Lord and followed completely the ways of his father David (22:2). The phrase "not turning aside to the right or to the left" is a figurative way of expressing his complete obedience to the laws of God.

22:3–7 REPAIRING THE TEMPLE OF THE LORD

During the eighteenth year of Josiah's rule, Josiah decided to repair the temple. This was similar to the restoration Joash did nearly two hundred years earlier (12:4–16; 837–798 BC). Josiah sent his secretary, Shaphan son of Azaliah, to the temple of the Lord with his instruction (22:3). Hilkiah, the high priest, was to collect the free-will offerings that the doorkeepers of the temple collected and kept in the chest near the entrance and to entrust that collection to the men who were appointed to supervise the work on the temple instead of bringing it to the treasury (22:4–5a). Those supervisors, in turn, should pay the workers, such as carpenters, masons, builders, and other laborers, directly for their work and also for the purchase of material and dressed stones (22:5b–6). They need not give an account to the state since the king trusted them to be honest in their dealings (22:7).

22:8–14 THE BOOK OF THE LAW

When Shaphan met Hilkiah and conveyed the king's instructions, the high priest reported that he had found the "Book of the Law" in the temple of the Lord and gave it to Shaphan, who in turn read it (22:8). The "Book of the Law" referred to the Deuteronomic law in the Pentateuch (Deut 28:61; 29:21; 30:10; 31:26) that required the Israelites to honor their covenantal relationship with Yahweh by keeping the law. Shaphan returned to the king, gave a report about the payment for the repair work, and mentioned the book that had been given to him by Hilkiah (22:9–10a). As the secretary specialized in writing and reading official records, he read it in front of the king (22:10b).

As soon as the king heard the "Book of the Law," he tore his robes in penitence for failing to keep the law of Moses (22:11). Then he wanted to know more about this book, and so he asked his officials, including Hilkiah (the high priest), Shaphan (his secretary of state), Ahikam Akbor son of Micaiah, and Asaiah (his attendant), to inquire of the Lord for the sake of the king and the people if there was a way to rectify the damages they had done to the covenant by not keeping the words of that book and if they had roused God's anger (22:12–13). Josiah connected the fate of his nation with obedience to the Deuteronomic law, and he linked the welfare of his nation with preserving the covenantal relationship with the Lord. They went to speak to the prophetess Huldah (22:14a). She was the wife of Shallum,[1] the son of Tikvah, the son

---

1. Hens-Piazza, *1–2 Kings*, 385. The identity of another person named "Shallum" is son of Jabesh who ruled over Israel according to 2 Kings 15:13. Wiseman suggests that the word

of Harhas, keeper of the wardrobe. Huldah lived in Jerusalem, in the New Quarter. The couple's professions and residence in Jerusalem indicate their connection with the temple of the Lord.[2]

22:15-20 PROPHECY OF HULDAH

While any high priest could interpret the law in ancient Israel, only a prophet or prophetess can discern the mind of God. So, the king's delegates approached Huldah.

Huldah prophesied saying, "This is what the LORD, the God of Israel, says" (22:15a). That formula confirms that the prophetic word is God's revelation.[3] Huldah's prophecy came in two parts. In the first oracle, she declared God's judgment on the nation (22:16-17). The Lord was going to destroy Jerusalem and the people of Judah because they had abandoned everything written in the book that Josiah read (22:16). Also, he was going to destroy the nation because they had forsaken Yahweh, burnt incense to the idols of other gods, and aroused his anger (22:17a). This oracle confirms that the anger of the Lord would not be quenched (22:17b).

In the second oracle, Huldah delivers a word from the Lord about King Josiah (22:18-20). This oracle was addressed to him because he sent people to inquire the heart of the Lord (22:18). Since his heart was responsive to what he read, since he humbled himself before the Lord when he realized that the people had not kept the laws of God and incurred God's punishment of the land being turned into a wasteland, and since he tore his robes and wept in God's presence, the Lord God will hear his prayers (22:19). These actions moved the Lord not to destroy the nation during Josiah's lifetime, but to assure the king of a peaceful death and burial (22:20a). Some time after the period of Josiah, however, the foretold disaster would come upon Judah. Josiah's eyes, however, will not see any of these disasters that the Lord God will bring on Jerusalem (22:20b). The king's envoy took the message back to the king.

"Jabesh" could be the place of this Shallum or son of a man called Jabesh. Wiseman, *1 and 2 Kings*, 268. This identity is mentioned to differentiate another person named Shallum, son of Tikvah (Tokhath – 2 Chr 34:22) who is connected with the temple (2 Kgs 2:14). The name "Shallum" is common in Israel. Moreover, King Shallum in 2 Kings 15 ruled for one month only and his period could be 753 BC. Shallum in 2 Kings 22:14, husband of Huldah, could have lived during the reign of Josiah's period in 638 BC (see the list of Kings and their periods in SABC). *South Asia Bible Commentary*, 475-478.
2. Hens-Piazza, *1-2 Kings*, 385.
3. H. D. McDonald, "Bible, Authority of," in *Evangelical Dictionary of Theology*, ed. Walter A. Elwell (Grand Rapids: Baker Academic, 2001), 152-155.

23:1–3 COVENANT RENEWAL EVENT

Hearing Huldah's prophecy, King Josiah was motivated to undertake major reforms in the religious practices of the people of Judah. Josiah had actually started enacting reforms during his twelfth year of reign, before he had even heard the high priest read from the book of the law or received the prophetic word from Huldah (22:3–7). After hearing the oracles, his religious reforms became more intensive.

King Josiah called together all the elders of Judah and Jerusalem (23:1). This indicates that each village and town had elders to look after the local affairs of the area and serve as the representatives of the local communities. Then the king went to the temple of the Lord with priests, prophets, elders, and all the people of Judah (23:2a). The phrase, "from the least to the greatest," indicates the inclusive aspect of all the people gathering together, whether rich or poor, powerful or powerless, of low or high status. In the temple, the king read the entirety of the Book of the Covenant that was found in the temple so that all those who had assembled could hear it (23:2b). By reading from the book himself, Josiah signaled to his audience that it was important for the nation to follow what he was reading.

Standing by the pillar, the king renewed the people's covenant with Yahweh in the presence of the Lord (23:3a). The covenant promised that they would "follow the LORD and keep his commands, status and decrees" with all their hearts and souls (23:3b). In this way, the people pledged themselves to the covenant. The benefit of renewing the covenant was not only to remember the people's earlier history as the special people of God and to revive their faith commitment, but also to foster their unity as one people of Yahweh. Coming together as God's people and renewing the covenant helped Josiah gain their support so that he could enact a series of reforms at the national level.

23:4–20 REFORMS BY JOSIAH

Societal reform is not possible without the cooperation of the people. The covenant renewal ceremony paved the way for further religious reform in Judah. The king ordered Hilkiah, the high priest, along with the priests next in rank and the doorkeepers of the temple, to carry out twelve reforms in the people's religious and social life.

The first reform was to cleanse the temple by removing all the articles that had been made to worship Baal, Asherah, and the starry hosts from the temple of the Lord (23:4a). These vessels and other articles were burnt outside

Jerusalem in the fields of the Kidron Valley (23:4b), a place once used for worshiping idols and offering sacrifices to Baal and Asherah.

The second reform was to target the priests that had been appointed by the various kings of Judah to conduct worship for the idols, burn incense to Baal, the sun and moon gods, and the constellations and starry hosts of the sky, which were represented as idols all over the land of Judah (23:5). He did away with their duties as priests.

The third reform was to remove the Asherah poles from the temple of the Lord and carry them to the valley outside Jerusalem, the Kidron Valley, where they burned them and threw away the ashes on the graves of the common people (23:6). This action desecrated the religious icons and objects used to worship foreign gods to convey that the people of Israel despised these gods and those who worshiped these poles and idols.

The fourth reform was to tear down the dwelling places for the shrine prostitutes in the vicinity of the temple of the Lord and the quarters where women weaved for Asherah (23:7). The Hebrew word for these prostitutes (*qedeshim*) in its masculine form could be used to refer to both males and females who had been set apart as cult prostitutes.[4] The king also removed the houses that had been built for women to weave and make decorative articles for Asherah. Josiah removed all the idols from Judah, along with all who were connected to the worship of idols.

For the fifth reform, the king brought all the priests of Judah who were burning incense for gods and goddesses, from the northern border town of Geba to the southern border town of Beersheba, so that they could eat with the true priests of the Lord, but could not serve as priests any longer (23:8a, 9). Because they were priests, Josiah didn't kill them.

Sixth, he broke down the gateway called the "Gate of Joshua," which was built at the entrance of the city and was named after its governor (23:8b). The text does not mention Josiah's reason for breaking down this gate, but he could have been destroying all the idols and shrines that had been erected in public places, such as gateways, to honor the gods of foreign nations when Judah was made to be a vassal of Assyrian kings.

Seventh, Josiah destroyed Topheth, the firepit in the Valley of Ben Hinnom, where children had sacrificed in the fire to Molek (23:10). This place was southwest of Jerusalem and was also known as the "place of Torment."

---

4. See *HALOT* 3:1075.

Eighth, Josiah removed the horses that had been dedicated by the kings of Judah to the sun, which were kept in the temple court of the Lord (23:11a). They were near the room of an official named Nathan-Melek (23:11b). Josiah burned the chariots dedicated to the sun, which those horses pulled.

Ninth, the king pulled down the altars that had been erected by Ahaz on the roof near the upper room of his palace, along with the altars that Manasseh had built in the two courts of the temple of the Lord (23:12a). These altars were smashed and thrown into the Kidron Valley (23:12b).[5]

Tenth, Josiah destroyed all the high places on the east side of Jerusalem on the south of the Hill of Corruption (23:13a; also known as the Mount of Destroyer, 1 Kgs 11:5–11). These were the high places Solomon built for Asherah (the vile goddess of the Sidonians), Chemosh (the vile god of Moab), and Molek (the detestable god of the people of Ammon) (23:13b). Josiah smashed the sacred stones, cut down the Asherah poles, covered the destroyed sites with human bones so that it looked like a cremation yard, making these desecrated places ritually unclean so that people would be afraid to use these sites to rebuild altars for foreign gods (23:14).

Eleventh, Josiah did not spare the altar erected by Jeroboam I, the son of Nebat, at Bethel (23:15a). This altar caused the people to sin by worshiping idols and engaging in detestable practices (23:15b). He destroyed this high place and burned it to powder.

Twelfth, Josiah removed the bones from the tombs on the hillside and burned them on the altar to defile it, in accordance with the Lord's command proclaimed by the man of God (23:16). Some of the priests or prophets of Baal or worshipers of idols may have been buried in these tombs. The king wanted to remove every trace of those who had worshiped idols from the land, even their bones and ashes. The narrator observes that this action is in accordance with the word of God proclaimed by a prophet against Jeroboam I (1 Kgs 13:1–5). While the name of the prophet is not mentioned in the narrative in 1 Kings, Josiah's name was foretold in the prophecy. This is another incident

---

5. Usually valleys are used to build altars for worship of idols in Israel in contrast to the trend in India to keep idols at the top of hills and mountains all over the country and climb up these hills to worship the idols as their *karma* (salvation by work). Kidron is a small brook which begins to the north of Jerusalem and runs through the Temple mount and the Mount of Olives and reaches the Dead Sea. It is filled with water during rainy season but dry in the rest of the seasons. The area along the brook became suitable for building altars for worshiping idols by the Israelites or throwing the destroyed idols from the rest of the land or from the Temple when religious reform was done by the kings (2 Kgs 23:12). G. W. Grogan, "Kidron," in *NBD*, 653–654.

that reflects the literary pattern of prophecy and fulfillment in the history of the kings. In this final reform act, when he saw a tomb of "the man of God" from Judah (23:17), Josiah told the people not to destroy the tomb and disturb the dead prophet's bones (23:18).

Josiah's twelve reforms crossed the old boundary with Israel and reached into Samaria. He did not want the same detestable practices to penetrate into Judah from the north, and so he removed all the shrines at the high places that had been erected by the kings of Israel and had aroused the anger of the Lord to punish the northern kingdom (23:19). He slaughtered all the priests of those high places on the altars and burned their bones on them (23:20a). When Josiah finished this reform in Samaria, he went back to Jerusalem (23:20b).

23:21–23 CELEBRATION OF PASSOVER

Soon after performing all these reforms, Josiah reinstituted the celebration of the Passover festival, as required in the "Book of the Covenant" (23:21). This was one of the three important festivals that the Israelites were supposed to celebrate together in Jerusalem (Deut 12:4–6; 16:1–8). The Passover festival was established to remind the people of God to remember the historical event of the Passover during the time of the exodus (Exod 12:1–14; 23:14–17), and it combined the history of the people's deliverance from bondage with the theology of the liberating power of Yahweh.[6] God gave orders to all the people in Judah to celebrate this festival so that they would remember their history of being delivered from bondage in Egypt. Celebrating Passover, like the covenant renewal festival, helped the nation unite as one people of Yahweh (Exod 12:21–27).

Josiah's Passover feast was so great that the narrator says, "Neither in the days of the judges who led Israel nor in the days of the kings of Israel and the kings of Judah had any such Passover been observed" (23:22). In the eighteenth year of King Josiah, however, the people celebrated to the Lord that glorious Passover in Jerusalem (23:23).

23:24–25 REMOVING MEDIUMS AND SPIRITISTS

In addition to all the previous reforms, Josiah removed the mediums and those who used evil spirits or promoted divination and sorcery from Judah so that he might fulfill the law (23:24a). The people sought spirits to foretell their

---

6. J. B. Jeyaraj, "Festivals, Communication and Development," *Journal of Dharma*, vol. 28, no. 3 (July–September): 340–365.

futures or give guidance rather than seeking the Lord. So Josiah removed the mediums and spiritists. Because some families kept household gods inside their homes and worshiped them, he also removed this practice from the nation so that all the people of Judah would worship the Lord alone. He did all these reforms to fulfill the requirements of the law written in the book that Hilkiah the priest discovered in the temple of the Lord (23:24b). Undertaking all of these religious reforms was a great achievement. The narrator's admiration and appreciation for Josiah reaches its height when he says, "Neither before nor after Josiah was there a king like him who turned to the LORD as he did with all his heart and with all his soul and with all his strength, in accordance with the Law of Moses" (23:25).

We gain great theological insights by comparing the stories of King Hezekiah (720–692 BC) and King Josiah (638–608 BC). The gap between their rules was fifty-four years. Both served the nation for a longer period of time: Hezekiah reigned for twenty-nine years, and Josiah reigned for thirty-one years. Both reigned during a critical period in the history of Judah, when there were threats of war, ongoing attacks from neighboring nations, and a deteriorating political situation within Judah. Hezekiah is remembered for his commitment to trust and follow Yahweh alone and his prayer, which brought deliverance for Judah from its enemies. Josiah is remembered for his childhood pietism and love for Yahweh, which motivated him to begin his reforms at an early age. Whereas Hezekiah was a test case for proving the power of Yahweh, Josiah was a test case for proving the power of God's word.

23:26–27 JUDGMENT RESERVED

Although the Lord's decision to hand Judah into the hands of its enemies was delayed because of Josiah's faithfulness, it was bound to happen, because Manasseh had disobeyed the Lord and promoted all sorts of detestable practices in Judah (23:26). Josiah's reforms could not change Yahweh's decision to reject Jerusalem and the temple in which he had chosen to dwell (23:27). The living God of Israel and the false gods of other nations could not be worshiped in the same temple. The Lord is the Creator of all, who has divine values and acts throughout the history of Israel and Judah. Idols, however, are the creation of human beings.

23:28–30 JOSIAH'S DEATH

The concluding section about Josiah's reign refers readers to the annals of the kings for more information about his achievements (23:28). Unlike what a reader might expect, Josiah's life ended abruptly in the battlefield. The new pharaoh of Egypt, Necho, marched to the Euphrates River to help the weakening nation of Assyria fight against Babylon. Josiah felt that having the pharaoh's army march through Palestine was a threat to his rule and the nation of Judah. So he marched out to meet him in a battle. Necho faced him and killed him at Megiddo (23:29). Josiah's servants brought his body in a chariot from Megiddo to Jerusalem and buried him in his own tomb (23:30a). The people of Judah anointed his son, Jehoahaz, as the king of Judah (23:30b).

2 KINGS 23:31–25:7
FINAL FOUR KINGS

Soon after the glorious days of Josiah ended, the people of Judah returned to their ways. The Lord's promise to send them into exile loomed over their heads. Yet, they lived without honoring him or his laws. God raised up four more kings – Jehoahaz, Jehoakim, Jehoiachin and Zedekiah – before the nation went into exile.

23:31-35 JEHOAHAZ'S RULE

Jehoahaz, whose name meant, "Yahweh has seized," became the king of Judah at the age of twenty-three and reigned in Jerusalem for only three months (23:31a). His mother, Hamutal, was the daughter of Jeremiah and was from Libnah (23:31b). The narrator mentions the name of her place to distinguish her father from the prophet Jeremiah, who was from Anathoth. Jehoahaz did evil in the eyes of the Lord during those three months, similar to the majority of his predecessors (23:32).

Pharaoh Necho arrested Jehoahaz and kept him in chains at Riblah in the land of Hamath so that he might not reign in Jerusalem (23:33a). The pharaoh then imposed a levy of a hundred talents of silver (approximately 3.4 metric tons) and a talent of gold (34 kilograms) on the people of Judah (23:33b). Pharaoh Necho then appointed Eliakim son of Josiah as the king and changed his name to Jehoakim (23:34a). Eliakim meant "God has established" and Jehoiakim meant "raised by Yahweh." Changing the name of a king was a practice to show his status as a vassal king under Pharaoh's authority. As he left Jerusalem, he took Jehoahaz with him to Egypt, where Jehoahaz died (23:34b).

Jehoiakim paid Pharaoh Necho the levied amount of silver and gold (23:35a). To do that, Jehoiakim had to collect taxes, silver, and gold from the people of Judah, according to their assessments (23:35b). Ironically, Egypt was the land where the ancestors of Israel had been slaves and were liberated by Yahweh, and now they had regained control of Israel and were keeping the Israelites captive once again, even though they were inhabiting their own land.

23:36–24:7 JEHOIAKIM'S RULE

Jehoiakim became the king of Judah when he was twenty-five years old, and he reigned in Jerusalem for eleven years (23:36a). His mother's name was Zebidah, and she was the daughter of Pediah from Rumah (23:36b). Just as his predecessors, Jehoiakim did evil in the eyes of the Lord (23:37). While he was ruling, Nebuchadnezzar king of Babylon invaded the land (24:1a). This could have happened around 608–607 BC. Jehoiakim became the vassal of the Babylonian king for three years, but then he rebelled against Nebuchadnezzar's oppressive control and the burden of paying tributes to Babylon (24:1b).

Because the Lord was angry with Judah for their idolatry, he sent Babylonians, Arameans, and Moabites to raid and destroy Judah (24:2). This statement emphasizes the validity of Judah's punishment and collapse, since they had been given a long period to repent. The Lord's anger remained firm against Judah because of Manasseh's sins of building altars and shrines inside the temple, worshiping foreign gods, and shedding innocent blood (24:3; compare 21:3–7, 16). The most heinous of the crimes was the shedding of the innocent blood all throughout Jerusalem, which the Lord was unwilling to forgive (24:4).

The remainder of Jehoiakim's events were recorded in the book of the annals of the kings of Judah (24:5). After his death, his son Jehoachin, succeeded him to the throne (24:6).

In the meantime, the pharaoh of Egypt no longer fought against Judah because the Babylonians had taken control of the territory from the Wadi (brook) of Egypt, which is along the northern border of Egypt, to the Euphrates (24:7). Their defeat and exile will come from Babylon and not from Egypt.

24:8–17 JEHOIACHIN'S RULE

Jehoiachin became the king of Judah at the age of eighteen and reigned in Jerusalem for only three months (24:8a). His mother, Nehushta, was the daughter of Elnathan from Jerusalem (24:8b). Jehoiachin did evil in the eyes of the Lord, just like his father (24:9).

Jehoiachin was not able to rule for long because Nebuchadnezzar's army and his officers marched to Jerusalem and surrounded it (24:10). The seriousness of the besieging is indicated by the presence of Nebuchadnezzar himself with his army (24:11). Unlike Hezekiah, who resisted the Assyrian army when it besieged Jerusalem through his faith and prayers, Jehoiachin surrendered to the Babylonian king, along with his mother, attendants, nobles, and his officials (24:12a). While surrendering enabled him to live, he became a prisoner of Babylon; it was the eighth year of reign of the king of Babylon (24:12b).

2 Kings 24:13–17 details the changes made after Jehoiachin's surrender, which all happened according to the word of the Lord. The Babylonian king removed all the treasures from the temple of the Lord and the royal palace, including the gold articles crafted during Solomon's reign (24:13). Nebuchadnezzar carried away as captives all the officials, fighting men, skilled workers and artisans, a total of ten thousand people; only the poorest people of the land were left behind (24:14). The "poorest" could have included those who were aged, weak, sick, or disabled.

Nebuchadnezzar took Jehoiachin, his mother, his wives, his officials, and other prominent people as captives to Babylon (24:15). In addition, Nebuchadnezzar deported seven thousand fighting men, fit for war, and one thousand skilled workers and artisans (24:16). Finally, Nebuchadnezzar appointed Mattaniah (meaning "Gift of Yahweh"), who was the third son of Josiah (1 Chr 3:15) and the uncle of Jehoiachin, as the king in charge of Judah (24:17a). Nebuchadnezzar changed Mattaniah's name to Zedekiah, meaning "Yahweh is righteous" (24:17b). This was yet a reminder that the people entered exile because they did not treat God as a righteous God and honor him. So he let them go into Exile to purify them.

24:18–25:7 ZEDEKIAH'S RULE

Zedekiah was twenty-one years old when he was appointed to take charge of Judah (597–586 BC), and he reigned in Jerusalem for eleven years under Nebuchadnezzar's control (24:18a). His mother's name was Hamutal, who was the daughter of Jeremiah from Libnah (24:18b; compare 23:31). Like Johoiakim, Zedekiah also did evil in the eyes of the Lord and did not follow the Lord or obey the law (24:19). Jerusalem and Judah were in the predicament they were in because they disobeyed the Lord and his anger flared up against them (24:20a).

25:1–7 Zedekiah's Rule in Judah

Given the power of Nebuchadnezzar, Zedekiah should not have rebelled against him and invited more trouble for the nation of Judah. But he didn't think; he rebelled against the king of Babylon (24:20b). The rebellion forced Nebuchadnezzar to march against Jerusalem on the tenth day of the tenth month of the ninth year of Zedekiah's rule (25:1). The Babylonian king and army besieged Jerusalem until the eleventh year of Zedekiah's rule, blocking the food supply for nearly two years (25:2).

At the same time, a severe famine came in the land. By the ninth day of the fourth month of the famine, there was no food for the people to eat (25:3).

Outside the city, the city wall was broken through (24:4a). Zedekiah and his army, taking advantage of the night time, fled through the gate between the two walls near the king's garden towards Arabah, the Jordan Valley, even though the Babylonians were surrounding the city (24:4b). Seeing them flee, the Babylonian army pursed the king and overtook him in the plains of Jericho (24:5a). The soldiers were separated from him and scattered (24:5b). The soldiers captured Zedekiah and took him to the king of Babylon at Riblah (24:6a). There, a sentence was pronounced on him (24:6b). Zedekiah's sons were executed before him, then his eyes were blinded, and he was bound with bronze shackles and taken as a prisoner to the capital of Babylon (24:7). This reminds us of Ezekiel's prophecy (Ezek 12:13), which said that Zedekiah would be taken to Babylon, but he would not be able to see it, as he would be blind. Zedekiah died later in Babylon, ending Judah's reign in Jerusalem.

2 KINGS 25:8–30

THE FALL OF JERUSALEM

The final chapter describes the destruction of the temple in Jerusalem and the execution of the priests of Yahweh (25:8–21). After this, the narrative reports on the governance of the land of Judah, which was left in the hands of Gedaliah, who had been appointed by Nebuchadnezzar (25:22–26). The last unit closes the history of the monarchy in Judah on a positive note as Jehoiachin is released from prison, which offers a sign of hope for the future (25:27–30). Some of the information about these last kings and the fall of Judah can be supplemented from 1 and 2 Chronicles as well as the prophetic books of Jeremiah and Ezekiel.

25:8–21 DESTRUCTION AND EXECUTION

Judah was unable to recover and regain its power after losing thousands of fighting men and skilled people to Babylon. On the seventh day of the fifth month during the nineteenth year of Nebuchadnezzar's rule, the commander of the imperial guard, Nebuzaradan, came to Jerusalem (25:8). Nebuzaradan destroyed the religious, political, economic, military, and social institutions of Jerusalem.

He set fire to the temple of the Lord, the royal palace, and the houses of Jerusalem (25:9a). He also burned down every important building, possibly the court, administrative offices, and sheds for the chariots and horses (25:9b). The whole Babylonian army worked together and broke down the walls around Jerusalem (25:10). Then, he deported the remaining people as captives to Babylon (25:11). This was the third deportation to exile (586 BC). The first happened during the period of Jehoiakim around 601 BC (24:1), and the second happened during the period of Jehoiachin around 597 BC (24:15–16). Although he deported the vast majority of the people, he left the "poorest" – referring to the old, weak, unskilled, and physically handicapped people – who could not be taken into exile and were left behind to work in the vineyards and fields of Judah (24:12).

The Babylonian army destroyed the temple for religious reasons and also to plunder its treasures. They broke up the bronze pillars, the moveable stands, and the bronze Sea that were in the temple of the Lord and carried them to

Babylon (25:13). They also carried away the bronze vessels and articles that were used during the worship service by the priests including pots, shovels, wick trimmers, and dishes (25:14). The commander of the imperial guard carried away the censers and sprinkling bowls, which were made of pure gold or silver (25:15).

The narrator informs the readers that the weight of the bronze from the two pillars, the Sea, and the movable stands are incalculable (25:16). Each pillar was eighteen cubits (roughly 8:1 meters) high and was decorated with a network and pomegranates of bronze all around (25:17a). Even the two pillars had similar network (25:17b).

In addition, the commander of the guard took important priestly personnel as prisoners, including Seraiah, the chief priest, and Zephaniah, the priest next in rank, and the three doorkeepers of the temple (25:18). From the city, he took captive the officers in charge of the fighting men, five royal advisers in the court, the secretary who was in charge of conscripting the people of the land, and sixty of the conscripts who were found in the city (25:19). He led all the captives to the king of Babylon who was at Riblah in the land of Hamath (25:20). There, the king of Babylon executed them (25:21a). The words, "So Judah went into captivity, away from her land" (25:21b), seals off the end of the monarchy, the glory of the temple, and the life of the people in their Promised Land.

25:22–26 GOVERNANCE OF GEDALIAH

Nebuchadnezzar, the king of Babylon, appointed Gedaliah, the son of Ahikam, the son of Shaphan, as the governor of Judah to take care of the land and all the Israelites who had been left behind (25:22). It is not known how much power was given to Gedaliah, but he had to remain loyal to Nebuchadnezzar, collect the fruits of the vines for the Babylonians, and to govern over the poor.[1] A delegation of soldiers and army officers, including Ishmael son of Nethaniah, Johanan son of Kareah, Seraiah son of Tanhumetha the Natophathite, and Jaazaniah son of the Maakathite came to talk with Gedaliah at Mizpah (25:23). Mizpah was located fourteen kilometers north of Jerusalem and had been an important administrative center before Jerusalem became prominent during the period of David (1 Kgs 15:22). The identity of each army officer is linked to the name of his father to distinguish him from others with the same name. These leaders seemed to have known and trusted Gedaliah. When they arrived,

---

1. Hens-Piazza, *1–2 Kings*, 399.

Gedaliah made an oath to reassure them of a peaceful existence and advised them to "Settle down in the land and serve the king of Babylon" so that the Israelites could live well on the land (25:24).

In the seventh month of Gedaliah's rule, Ishmael son of Nethaniah, the son of Elishama, who was of the nobility, came with ten men and assassinated Gedaliah, along with some men of Judah who were at Mizpah (25:25). Hearing this, all the people, from the least to the greatest, left Judah and fled to Egypt to escape from the backlash of the Babylonians (25:26).

25:27–30 RELEASE OF JEHOIACHIN

In the thirty-seventh year of the exile of Jehoiachin king of Judah, the new king of Babylon released him from prison (25:27). The new king's name was Awel-Marduk meaning "Man of Marduk," the god of Babylon. On the twenty-seventh day of the twelfth month of his reign, he released Jehoiachin. Awel-Marduk spoke kindly to Jehoiachin, perhaps concerning his health, family, and former land, and then he seated him in a seat of honor, higher than those of the other kings who had been taken as captives to Babylon (25:28). So Jehoiachin put aside his prison clothes and ate at the king's table for the rest of his life (25:29). In addition, the king gave him daily allowances as long as he lived (25:30).

The text does not mention Awel-Marduk's reason for releasing Jehoiachin and granting him status, a steady food supply, and allowances, but we can infer that the God of Israel raised Awel-Marduk to have mercy and show favor to the exiles in Babylon. These changes indicate that a favorable situation would come to them in the future. Isaiah predicted that God would raise Cyrus, the king of Persia, to release the Israelites to return and restore their Promised Land (Isa 44:28; 45:13). Although the account in 2 Kings 25 does not extend beyond the release of Jehoiachin, 2 Chronicles 36 narrates the rising of Cyrus and his concern to rebuild the temple and let the Israelite captives return to Jerusalem. This account offers a ray of hope, for Jeremiah predicted that the captives would return from Babylon to Jerusalem (Jer 32:36–41). God's faithfulness never fails! "For his anger lasts only a moment, but his favor lasts a lifetime; weeping may stay for the night, but rejoicing comes in the morning" (Ps 30:5).

SELECTED BIBLIOGRAPHY

Adeyemo, Tokunboh, ed. *Africa Bible Commentary: A One-Volume Commentary*. Grand Rapids: Zondervan, 2006.

Aharoni, Yohanan. *The Land of the Bible: A Historical Geography*. Translated by A. F. Rainey. London: Burns and Oates, 1979.

Beal, Lissa M. Wray. *1 & 2 Kings*. Apollo Old Testament Commentary. Downers Grove: InterVarsity, 2014.

de Vaux, Roland. *Ancient Israel: Its Life and Institutions*. London: Darton, Longman and Todd, 1978.

DeVries, Simon J. *1 Kings*. WBC. Vol. 12. Waco, Texas: Word Books, 1985.

Giri, Elizabeth. "Child Sacrifices in India: A Christian Response." *Children at Risk: Issues and Challenges*. Edited by J. B. Jeyaraj, C. Gnanakan, et al. SPCK: Delhi, 2009.

Goldingay, John. *1 and 2 Kings for Everyone*. Louisville: Westminster John Knox Press, 2011.

Gordon, R. P. "War." In *NBD*. 3rd ed. Edited by J. D. Douglas. Leicester: IVP, 1996.

Gotom, Musa. "1 and 2 Kings." In *ABC*. Edited by Tokunboh Adeyemo. Nairobi: Word Alive Publishers, 2006.

Harrison, R. K. "Cherubim." In *NBD*. 3rd ed. Edited by J. D. Douglas. Leicester: IVP, 1996.

Hens-Piazza, Gina. *1–2 Kings*. AOTC. Nashville: Abingdon Press, 2006.

Hobbs, T. R. *2 Kings*. WBC. Vol. 13. Waco, Texas: Word Books, 1985.

House, Paul R. *1, 2 Kings*: *An Exegetical and Theological Exposition of Holy Scripture NIV Text*. NAC. Vol. 8. Nashville: Broadman & Holman Publishers, 1995.

Jeyaraj, J. B. "Biblical Perspective on Children and their Protection." *Children at Risk: Issues and Challenges*. Edited by J. B. Jeyaraj, C. Gnanakan, et al. SPCK: Delhi, 2009.

———. "Festivals, Communication and Development." In *Journal of Dharma*, vol. 28, no. 3 (July–September), 2003.

———. "Jubilee and Society: Reflections." In *ERT*, vol. 25:4, 2001.

———. "Naming and Renaming as Communication in Ancient Israel." In *AJTR*, vol. 1–2 (January–December), 1992.

———. "Religion and Politics in Ancient Israel: Interactions and Issues." In *Integral Mission: The Way Forward*. Edited by C. V. Mathew. Tiruvalla: Christava Sahitya Samithi, 2006.

———. "Siding with the Landless: Important Mission Ahead." In *AD 2000 and Beyond: A Mission Agenda*. Edited by Vinay Samuel and Chris Sugden. Oxford: Regnum Books, 1991.

Keil, C. F. and F. Delitzsch. *Joshua, Judges, Ruth, 1 and 2 Samuel*. COTOT. Vol. 2. Peabody, MA: Hendrickson, 2006.

Kitchen, Kenneth. "Gilgal." In *NBD*. 3rd ed. Edited by J. D. Douglas. Leicester: IVP, 1996.

McDonald, H. D. "Bible, Authority of." In *Evangelical Dictionary of Theology*. Edited by Walter A. Elwell. Grand Rapids: Baker Academic, 2001.

McKelvery, R. J. "Temple." In *NBD*. 3rd ed. Edited by J. D. Douglas. Leicester: IVP, 1996.

Motyer, J. A. "Idolatry." In *NBD*. 3rd ed. Edited by J. D. Douglas. Leicester: IVP, 1996.

Payne, D. F. "Baal." In *NBD*. 3rd ed. Edited by J. D. Douglas. Leicester: IVP, 1996.

Provan, Iain W. *1 and 2 Kings*. NIBC. Boston: Hendrickson Publishers, 2008.

Robinson, Wheeler H. *Corporate Personality in Ancient Israel*. Philadelphia: Fortress Press, 1980.

Spear, Percival. *A History of India*. Vol. 2. London: Penguin Books, 1970.

Thapar, Romila. *A History of India*. Vol. 1. London: Penguin Books, 1965.

The New Illustrated Everyman's Encyclopaedia. Vol. 1. London: Octopus Books, 1985.

Tyagi, B. P. *Agricultural Economics and Rural Development*. Meerut: JaiPrakash Nath and Company, 1990.

von Rad, Gerhard. *Old Testament Theology: The Theology of Israel's Historical Traditions*. Vol. 1. London: SCM Press, 1977.

Wintle, Brian, ed. *South Asia Bible Commentary: A One-Volume Commentary on the Whole Bible*. Udaipur, Rajasthan: Open Door Publication, 2015.

Wiseman, Donald J. *1 and 2 Kings: An Introduction and Commentary*. TOTC. Nottingham: IVP, 2008.

Wright, Christopher J. H. *Living as the People of God: The Relevance of the Old Testament Ethics*. Leicester: IVP, 1983.

Asia Theological Association
54 Scout Madriñan St. Quezon City 1103, Philippines
Email: ataasia@gmail.com Telefax: (632) 410 0312

OUR MISSION

The Asia Theological Association (ATA) is a body of theological institutions, committed to evangelical faith and scholarship, networking together to serve the Church in equipping the people of God for the mission of the Lord Jesus Christ.

OUR COMMITMENT

The ATA is committed to serving its members in the development of evangelical, biblical theology by strengthening interaction, enhancing scholarship, promoting academic excellence, fostering spiritual and ministerial formation and mobilizing resources to fulfill God's global mission within diverse Asian cultures.

OUR TASK

Affirming our mission and commitment, ATA seeks to:

- **Strengthen** interaction through inter-institutional fellowship and programs, regional and continental activities, faculty and student exchange programs.
- **Enhance** scholarship through consultations, workshops, seminars, publications, and research fellowships.
- **Promote** academic excellence through accreditation standards, faculty and curriculum development.
- **Foster** spiritual and ministerial formation by providing mentor models, encouraging the development of ministerial skills and a Christian ethos.
- **Mobilize** resources through library development, information technology and infra-structural development.

To learn more about ATA, visit www.ataasia.com or facebook.com/AsiaTheologicalAssociation

Langham Literature, along with its publishing work, is a ministry of Langham Partnership.

Langham Partnership is a global fellowship working in pursuit of the vision God entrusted to its founder John Stott –

> *to facilitate the growth of the church in maturity and Christ-likeness through raising the standards of biblical preaching and teaching.*

Our vision is to see churches in the Majority World equipped for mission and growing to maturity in Christ through the ministry of pastors and leaders who believe, teach and live by the word of God.

Our mission is to strengthen the ministry of the word of God through:
- nurturing national movements for biblical preaching
- fostering the creation and distribution of evangelical literature
- enhancing evangelical theological education

especially in countries where churches are under-resourced.

Our ministry

Langham Preaching partners with national leaders to nurture indigenous biblical preaching movements for pastors and lay preachers all around the world. With the support of a team of trainers from many countries, a multi-level programme of seminars provides practical training, and is followed by a programme for training local facilitators. Local preachers' groups and national and regional networks ensure continuity and ongoing development, seeking to build vigorous movements committed to Bible exposition.

Langham Literature provides Majority World preachers, scholars and seminary libraries with evangelical books and electronic resources through publishing and distribution, grants and discounts. The programme also fosters the creation of indigenous evangelical books in many languages, through writer's grants, strengthening local evangelical publishing houses, and investment in major regional literature projects, such as one volume Bible commentaries like the *Africa Bible Commentary* and the *South Asia Bible Commentary*.

Langham Scholars provides financial support for evangelical doctoral students from the Majority World so that, when they return home, they may train pastors and other Christian leaders with sound, biblical and theological teaching. This programme equips those who equip others. Langham Scholars also works in partnership with Majority World seminaries in strengthening evangelical theological education. A growing number of Langham Scholars study in high quality doctoral programmes in the Majority World itself. As well as teaching the next generation of pastors, graduated Langham Scholars exercise significant influence through their writing and leadership.

To learn more about Langham Partnership and the work we do visit **langham.org**

www.ingramcontent.com/pod-product-compliance
Lightning Source LLC
Chambersburg PA
CBHW070335240426
43665CB00045B/2041